AT THE TEA PARTY

O/R

AT THE TEA PARTY

THE WING NUTS, WHACK JOBS AND WHITEY-WHITENESS OF THE NEW REPUBLICAN RIGHT ... AND WHY WE SHOULD TAKE IT SERIOUSLY

Edited by
LAURA FLANDERS

OR BOOKS
NEW YORK

© 2010 Anthology selection © Laura Flanders.

Published by OR Books, New York.

Visit our website at www.orbooks.com

First printing 2010.

Library of Congress Cataloging in Publication Data:
A catalog record for this book is available from the Library of Congress

British Library Cataloging in Publication Data:
A catalog record for this book is available from the British Library

Paperback 978-1-935928-23-2
E-book 978-1-935928-22-5
Paperback + e-book 978-1-935928-21-5

Typeset by Wordstop

Printed by BookMobile, USA

10   9   8   7   6   5   4   3   2   1

To Carl Vollmer, who shows daily by his deeds and care that he is a friend and comrade, regardless of his TV-watching habits.

ACKNOWLEDGMENTS

To Colin Robinson, for the grand idea for this book and its title, as well as to Joana Kelly and all the folks at OR Books for their bold, brilliant, not to mention fun new model for publishing. To Seth Michaels at Media Matters for America for research help and graphics (which I only wish we could have used). And to artist Tom Humberstone for caricatures of Beck, which I dearly hope will appear soon on tea bags in hot water. At this country's independent media toil visionary women and men who keep those outlets humming with the best journalism in the business. Those who helped us by commissioning many of these pieces in the first place (and granting us republishing rights at rock-bottom prices) include Matt Renner at Truthout, Sarah Posner at Religion Dispatches, Matt Rothschild at *The Progressive*, Ben Wyskida and Habiba Alcindor at *The Nation*, Peter Meredith at *Mother Jones*, Becky Grant at *CounterPunch* Dorothy Thomas at EXTRA! and Peter Gamble at *The Black Commentator*. My thanks too, to Adele Stan of AlterNet for staying on this beat even when the spotlight wasn't on it. And extra-special thanks to Suzanne Pharr, who shows the way, and Dan Petegorsky and Kelley Weigel at the precious Western States Center for permission to publish the transcript of their meeting.

The transcripts from GRITtv come courtesy of the terrifically talented, indefatigable, and heart-driven GRITtv team, which has included so far: Jason Abbruzzese, Sam Alcoff, Lisa Guido, Sarah Jaffe, Gina Kim, David Rowley, Suzy Salamy, Diane Shamis, and Tami Woronoff with additional help from Alexa Birdsong, Laura Chipley, Hesu Coue, Jodi Daley, Patricia Foulkrod, Sarah Friedland, Carl Ginsburg, Rich Kim, Sayle Milne, and Tere Mele among others. Thank you for being such a daily pleasure to work with.

Sarah Jaffe made this book possible. Without her research help, sharp eye, wit, and grace under pressure, this book would never have come together—and at least one critical piece would have been left out of the final manuscript by accident. Watch out for her, folks. Especially you straying to the right—she's coming after you, all keyboards blazing.

As always and forever, my deep love and thanks to the incredible flying Elizabeth Streb, my tea-eschewing partner.

CONTENTS

Part Two: Toxic Tea

Part Three: The Pedagogy of Shock (and Lunacy)

INTRODUCTION: BEHOLD THE BECCHANAL!

Laura Flanders

"Hello, America."

The chatty man on the TV grins, and gives his audience a come-on wink. Fox News's Glenn Beck is about to let his audience in on a little secret.

Flourishing a slim bound pack of pages, Beck begins:

> Last week I showed you this, the playbook of the left. It is the manifesto from the Weather Underground.... They hated America, and they would do whatever it took to overthrow America and—their words—"institute communism and a dictator."

Notwithstanding a speckled yellow tie, a jauntily pinstriped shirt, and baby-blue-framed eyeglasses, Beck stares out, severe.

"Two years ago I would have said, This is crazy talk. Two years ago I would have made fun of these people." Breathy pause. "Don't do it..."

Funnily enough, not so long ago, that's what I might have said about Glenn Beck. I might have said—and I heard plenty of people say—that Beck's fans were simply wackos, wing nuts, whitey-white fringe elements from people-scarce states. I might have said that people like that always fret when they lose power or jobs, or get smacked in the face by change, like the first nonwhite president and his family settling into the White House. I might have pointed out that in tough times, frustrated folks are always easy to fire up, and the filthy rich have always been wiling to pay for the match. As Rick Perlstein, historian of the Goldwater era, has remarked, outbreaks of reactionary ranting have a habit of accompanying liberal victories: Consider 1993, 1977, 1971. Liberals don't have to be scared to death.

Except today it's ranting with television ratings and it's not far off, it's close. A contractor friend who for ten years has shared our very large, very metro-sexual Thanksgiving, *our friend Carl Vollmer* is telling me I must watch Beck. He and his twin brother, both eighty years old, watch daily, in Brooklyn. In fact, says Carl, "we only got a TV to watch Glenn Beck."

So what is Glenn Beck saying this hot afternoon in August? As real unemployment stands at over 16 percent and an estimated 29 million Americans are looking for work, Beck's telling his audience that the 1960s Weather Underground planted bombs and blew things up, and now they're wielding power.

"[The Weather Underground] believed back then, and they believe now, the ends justify the means," says Beck. "Most of these radicals were part of Students for a Democratic Society (SDS.) It's code language, goes all the way back to Lenin.... Now they are in positions of power."

Just when I'm thinking that Plato might object to ceding to Lenin the whole "democratic society" concept—and what does any of this have to do with anything right now, in any case?—Beck moves over to his blackboard. He clutches photographs purporting to be the headshots of former SDS members: Andy Stern, former president of the SEIU; Wade Rathke, founder of the poor people's group ACORN; and Jeff Jeffords, now a member of the green jobs outfit called the Apollo Alliance (whose occupation Beck describes as "spending the stimulus").

"They're just kind of behind the scenes, but we know how all this is working.... This radical thought is commonplace with the powers in and around the current administration."

To explain what he means by "radical thought," Beck quotes the mission statement (he calls it the "battle-cry") of a separate group, founded by different people, forty years after SDS. The "New SDS" (founded in January 2006) aims to "take back our schools, our communities, and our nation." Lest anyone think that refrain sounds familiar to a million mild nonprofits and, frankly, to the so-called Tea Party mobilization that Beck helped to launch, our host helps his viewers spot the sinister: "Not only is this the violent rhetoric from the '60s, but it's coming straight from those who actually blew stuff up."

Except it isn't. In fact, the loudest people talking about blowing things up today tend to name Beck as their inspiration (see Eric Boehlert's "Beck's Incendiary Angst Is Dangerously Close to Having a Body Count"). The last "terrorist" to target civilians and claim one life was a suicidal tax resister who crashed his plane into the Austin, Texas, office of the IRS. With health insurance premiums rising, house values falling, and wages and employment remaining stagnant, the at-home-at-5:00-p.m. Americans watching Beck's program have far more immediate threats to their lives than the Weather Underground. Still, Beck continues, in a lowered voice: "2006—that's two years before Barack Obama was elected, but about the time the campaign was starting up." All but scratching his chin, he calls on his viewers to help him connect the dots: "Help me, Watchdogs!"

This is a book for those who'd like some dots connected but may not have millions of willing "watchdogs" to help them (or hours to spend watching Fox). It's a book for those who'd like a better grasp of what's happening around them—the "Carls" in their own lives—and what, if they care to, they might do in response.

Want to know whether to take Beck seriously? There are contributors here, including former CIA officer turned bestselling novelist Barry Eisler and the comedian W. Kamau Bell who'll remind you that

Beck is an entertainer, "more poodle than panther," as Eisler puts it. Beck's a shlock jock, a graduate of many a morning radio "zoo" where a devotion to dollars set in way before any ideological thought, reports Beck biographer Alexander Zaitchik. Full of vitriol, but fully inconsistent, Beck was for the bank bailout, for example, before he was against it. Six months before he started calling it "socialism," Beck called the government's $700 billion bank-out "necessary" and "also not nearly enough."

Before they scoff, however, the contributors here would have liberals and those further to the left pause and reflect. Clown he may be, but Beck has three million viewers. He traffics in conspiracies that for many of his devotees are the only explanation of the world they've got. The Weather Underground takeover, government death panels, a BP oil spill plot to speed an oil-drilling ban, it's wing nuttery, but Beck's laughing all the way to power and influence. Whatever the outcome of the 2010 midterms, the Tea Party movement that Beck has helped to brew has turned the tide on what should have been a progressive moment.

How that happened is the question at the heart of *At the Tea Party*. First, there's the money—the billionaires at Beck's back. And then there are the media—the simple arithmetic of message control through owning many media at once. There's also the bigger picture. For thirty years, a loose amalgam of loonies, libertarians, religious extremists, white supremacists, gun-rightsers, tax resisters, antigovernment zealots, billionaires, and members of the Republican Right have been brewing a backlash. As wages stagnated, jobs disappeared and manufacturing shrank, the Right's voice grew loud while the Left's got drowned out, to the point that even the threat of pressure from the mob was enough to intimidate administrations from both political parties. Successive governments spent more on war, less on human needs and watched, inert as the scapegoating of women the poor, people of color, LGBT people and migrants intensified.

In 2008, two wars of choice and an economy in hock later, 53 percent of American voted for "change." They elected a Democrat, the first black president, and claimed majorities in both houses in Congress. For progressives, that should have been just a start. Instead, as Democrats celebrated the victory of Barack Obama and at least one liberal demographer, Ruy Teixeira, declared "A new progressive America is on the rise," the 47 percent of voting Americans who did *not* vote for Barack Obama, and the even larger number of Americans who were watching their 401(k)s, their homes, and their job prospects crash, witnessed the national political discussion drift off into crazy fights over not very much. (A big bank bailout or an even bigger one? Inadequate stimulus or none at all?) Blame our media, blame our budgets, blame our cowardice, blame their billionaires (there's plenty of blame to pass about)—at the height of the layoffs, in the winter of 2009, from the left came mostly silence, and from Fox News there was Glenn Beck.

Beck wasn't alone stirring the pot in which the Tea Party stewed. Plenty of resistance to all things Obama had been on display during the presidential campaign. Sarah Palin said not a word when "Obama=Hitler" signs showed up at her rallies and shouts of "terrorist," "nigger," and "kill him" rose from the crowd. The Obama=Hitler comparison emerged early in election season. The Rev. James David Manning from Harlem sermonized on the topic back in June 2008 (there's a clip on YouTube). Manning's spew never received the Jeremiah Wright treatment; it got him invited onto right-wing radio instead. Indeed, some right-wing shock-jocks used their mikes to deliver almost daily diatribes questioning Obama's religion and his citizenship throughout 2008. In 2009, money fears got added to the pool of public fears to be stoked.

On January 19, 2009, after a dismal run on CNN Headline News, Glenn Beck took to the air on Fox, on the Dr. Martin Luther King Jr. holiday, with Palin as one of his first guests. By the end of his first full month Glenn Beck netted 2.2 million viewers, more than twice as many as the previous year's show in the slot. By March he was calling

for a multimillion strong "9/12" demonstration "to surround them"—
"them" being the "socialist" (or alternatively, "fascist") elites. As Zaitchik has reported in his biography of Beck, Beck's "9/12 Project" was
largely a ratings-grab to make sure another character on cable didn't
steal his limelight.

In February, on the floor of the New York Stock Exchange, a
Chicago-based CNBC correspondent named Rick Santelli was asked
about a newly announced $75 billion plan to help homeowners fac-
ing foreclosure. Santelli let rip: "The government is promoting bad
behavior.... Why don't you put up a website to have people vote
on [whether] we really want to subsidize the losers' mortgages....
President Obama, are you listening?" The same traders that had applauded an interest-free bailout of a very badly behaved finance industry cheered, and by the end of the day, "Santelli's Rant" had been
posted and praised on conservative media and tweeted through antigovernment social networks. Websites started appearing, claiming
to be inspired by Santelli's outburst. Researchers Mark Ames and
Yasha Levine found on these sites buried links to corporate-funded
think tanks like FreedomWorks and Americans for Prosperity, which
specialize in pseudo-grassroots PR campaigns commonly known as
"astroturf."

April 15 saw the first tax-day protests, organized by the same
groups. The idea was ostensibly to stop wasteful spending and excessive taxation in the spirit of the Boston Tea Party of 1773—a protest
by American colonists against the British government. Beck headed
up Fox's all-day coverage, live from the Alamo in San Antonio, featuring Texas Governor Rick Perry and a bevy of secessionists. Between
tax day and September 12 came the hot summer of health care. Town
hall meetings intended to discuss the Democrats' health-insurance-
reform plan, turned into shouting matches between politicians and
angry people asking about socialism and Obama's birth. In June in
Delaware, a wild-eyed regular talk-radio caller cowed Congressman Mike Castle and an entire roomful of health-care advocates

into reciting the Pledge of Allegiance to prove they were American enough.

One didn't have to attend any of these events: You could watch at home on your computer, or on every network. The same media that shunned the pro-immigration-reform "March for America" (200,000 attending), or the pro-choice "March for Women's Lives" (500,000–1.1 million), and the antiwar march of January 18, 2003 (100,000–200,000) or the March on Washington for Gay and Bi-Equal Rights and Liberation (300,000) showers coverage on Glenn Beck's rallies, the attendance at which CBS News estimated to be around a 87,000 in 2010 and roughly the same in 2009, according to the DC Fire Department.[1]

Arun Gupta writes that the reactionary outburst that is today's Tea Party is not a new movement; it's the latest expression of an old sort. Likewise, Beck, as Fox News's own Eric Burns has put it, "is Huey Long without the political office. He is Father Coughlin without the dour expression. He is John Birch without the Society."

Beck's personal rodeo has been built by big business. First, by Clear Channel (the radio empire) and then News Corp. (The TV, print, and publishing monster owned by Rupert Murdoch). Both are behemoths brought to us by politicians—of both parties—who eviscerated congressional oversight of broadcasting, loosened the limits on media ownership, and were rewarded generously by aspiring media monopolies as a consequence.

Before Beck, the country's most widely heard red- and race-baiter was Bob Grant, who was temporarily chased off the flagship station of the ABC Radio Network in the mid-1990s after African-American groups and the media watch group FAIR raised a ruckus about his racism. (Grant's favorite name for African-Americans was "savages"; for Haitian refugees, "swine" and "subhuman infiltrators.") By the time Beck hit his stride in political talk, the power of a single media company (News Corp.) was so great, and its interest in Beck' s anti-regulatory tirades so strong, that when Beck called President Obama a racist as he did in early 2009, even an organized boycott of his show by Color of Change and more than 200 past and potential advertisers couldn't dislodge him, even if today Beck's prime advertisers are a pet-druggist and a gold peddler (see Stephanie Mencimer's "Beck's Golden Fleece").

There have long been paranoids with pamphlets. Ron Arnold, for example, at the Center for the Defense of Free Enterprise tried to scare the world about the left-wing terrorists long before Beck took up the task. Arnold was testifying in Congress about what he called "the eco-terror threat" when Beck was still boozing and (by his own admission) snorting cocaine. When Beck trashed the Apollo Alliance and began his assault on Van Jones, Arnold gushed: "Fox talk show star goes a little over the top, but seems to have been reading the [CDFE's website]." But whereas Arnold took on activists at the edges, Beck goes after government officials. And whereas in the past politicians with spines might have called out the red-baiting gone bonkers, today it works. In Jones's case, the most powerful man in the world, the president of the United States, took the bait and went along with Jones's resignation as green jobs czar. And after the Jones case, Obama's administration went one worse, forcing the Agriculture Department's Shirley Sherrod to resign when she came under attack, before even checking the facts.

Ideologically minded funders have long paid for influence in Washington. Beck feeds at a familiar food line. As oil was tinting Gulf Coast shellfish black in the summer of 2010, Beck was thanking Charles Koch, on the air, for helping him to pillory Big Oil's critics. The multibillionaires behind Koch Industries (oil, gas, and chemical guys who own the second-largest privately held company in the country) have funded decades of antiregulatory propaganda, from the Cato Institute to *Reason* magazine—and self-respecting journalists have long accepted those "experts" as legitimate, quoting them in articles and planting them on TV shows night after night. Koch et al now have their own network and their own astroturf. Americans for Prosperity and FreedomWorks—and Beck, courtesy of Fox. It's a same-sort media marriage that social conservatives love.

The point is, reactionaries are nothing new; it's the reaction to them that makes today's clutch dangerous. As Perlstein pointed out, fifty years ago, the reactionary revolt that greeted the election of John F. Kennedy (the nation's first Catholic president) and led to the nomination of Barry Goldwater, was met with a certain amount of *tsk*ing disdain by the establishment and their media. "Whenever the ultras arise," *Time* magazine observed in 1961, "they cause domestic acrimony" and should be "wooed back into normal channels of political expression." The same magazine, in 2009, put Glenn Beck on its cover: "the hottest thing in the political-rant racket...tireless, funny, self-deprecating...at once powerful, spellbinding, and uncontrolled...a huge bestseller...has lit up the 5 pm slot in a way never thought possible by industry watchers."[2]

Will Beck and the Tea Partiers claim seats in Congress? It's possible. It's also not, primarily, the point. Congress—and the White House—cower plenty already. (Just ask Van Jones or Shirley Sherrod.) The fact that a housing bubble, a bank collapse, an economic depression, and two disastrous wars are being accompanied by a right-wing revolt rather than a left one, speaks to just how well the reactionaries are ensconced.

Beck, Palin, and the Tea Parties aren't the beginning; they're the bacchanal; ecstatic expressions of the riotous victory of the rule of the irrational.

The rodeo clown is there to distract. The really dangerous bull isn't Beck, it's a whole slew of once "fringe" ways of looking at the world that have become what he calls "common sense." The idea that civil rights are special rights and regulations are theft, that taxes are bad for the economy and the poor are best helped by helping the rich... In the absence of any more persuasive explanation for the situation so many are facing, what Lisa Duggan calls Beck's "pedagogy of shock" works.

This August, Carl turned 81. A proud Korean War veteran, he's still working with his hands in an economy that's driven wages for men like him down for his entire adulthood. Medicare is the first health insurance he says he's ever had. He rents cheaply and devises good business plans that never find investors. While I see deregulation and globalization and the assault on workers and wages as an explanation for his struggle, he sees greedy union bosses, busybody bureaucrats, and people who don't work as hard as he does getting help. When it comes to threats-that-we-face, I see war and the growing schism between America's rich and poor; Carl sees government by pencil-pushers who've never met a payroll, and the seizure of private assets. Just look at the government takeover of GM, he says, or the way they penalized BP!

That Carl could have listened to Air America radio plenty and yet fall for Beck, I take as a personal defeat (even if Air America never had the ad dollars or the production values or the corporate bankrollers Clear Channel has). Similarly, that anyone could be confused about what a Palin presidency might mean for women speaks volumes about how shallowly journalists cover politics, especially women in politics. (See a whole chapter here on that.) The numbers may be overblown by a fetishizing media, but the women working their hearts out for Tea Party candidates speak to how hungry many women still are for gratifying engagement—and how welcomed—or not—they've felt at other "parties."

There's no excuse for Tea Party racism but it is also true that as a nation—and yes, even the left flank—we have yet to disarm our stockpiles of the stuff. That's why the hot buttons remain so toasty. Instead, we keep the weapons of white supremacy sharp, just out of sight, for use in the process of abandoning the state's commitment to affirmative action, or welfare, or waging war on other (other-looking) people. There's profit to be made off the idea that America is special, white, and Christian. Mark Penn suggested as much in a March 2007 memo in which he wrote that he could not "imagine America electing a president during a time of war who is not at his center fundamentally American in his thinking and in his values."[3] Penn's boss, Hillary Clinton, would comment to USA Today soon afterward that her opponent's support was flagging among "hard-working Americans, white Americans."

Suffice it to say that Glenn Beck is not the first to notice that it's easy to get away with questioning the patriotism of minorities in the USA. And Barack Obama's hardly the first person to discover that unless you're white and Christian and straight (and, ideally, male), it takes more than a birth certificate to be accepted as truly "American." Nor, sadly, are the good people at the Tides Foundation the first to feel the chill of being targeted for violence by men calling themselves "patriots." (Just ask immigrants, LGBT people, and abortion providers.)

Alexander Cockburn's contribution here takes a stab at what's happened on the left as the fringe-right went mainstream. While ideologically-driven, membership-based groups were red-baited virtually to death or self-destruction, nonprofit puppet armies rose in their stead, funded and fenced in by foundations and private interests. Chris Hedges hints at what's needed to correct the balance, as do Bill Fletcher Jr. and Rebecca Traister. Sally Kohn, until recently with the Center for Community Change, points out that however much Beck rails at community organizers, he is a pretty nifty organizer.

If the Working Families Party had kept up their bus tours through the leafy suburbs of Connecticut to protest the $165 million in bonuses paid out to AIG executives, after a $180 billion government bailout, would their "Lifestyles of the Rich and Infamous" tours have become the force that pushed Congress and the White House to take a different course? Americans for Prosperity and FreedomWorks, whose first Tea Parties were announced just days after these bus tours, clearly have assets that the Working Families, to put it mildly, do not. But silence is not the answer. The conversations from GRITtv quoted here with a Tea Party leader and a member of a white supremacist group are the kind of conversation I believe we need more of. The best antidote for fake working-class solidarity is the real kind. I'm particularly happy to reproduce for the first time here the transcript of a panel convened by the Western States Center in Portland, featuring longtime organizers, on the ground, on what not-giving-in looks like.

Those on the left can laugh all they like at the absurdity of Beck and his tears and his conspiratorial chalkboard dating maps. But they'd be better off figuring out how Beck's megaphone grew so big while ours shrank so small. I hope this book is just a start.

—August 2010

Notes

1. Alex Sundby, "Glenn Beck Rally Attracts Estimated 87,000," CBSNews.com, August 28, 2010, and Russell Goldman, "Tea Party Protesters March on Washington," ABCNews.go.com, September 12, 2009.

2. David Von Drehle, "Mad Man: Is Glenn Beck Bad for America?" *Time Magazine*, September 17, 2009.

3. Green, Joshua, "The Hillary Clinton Memos," *The Atlantic*, September 2008.

PART ONE: THE MAD PARTY

DROPPING IN ON THE TEA PARTY

Gary Younge

Kentucky

It's hard to imagine how a town like Leitchfield (population: 6,139) in central Kentucky could survive without government. Sitting between Nolin and Rough River Lakes, it's on the way to nowhere in particular, so no private interest would build a road to it. In surrounding Grayson County more than one in five people and one in three children is on food stamps, so no one would feed it. It does not produce enough wealth to sustain itself. Unemployment, long in double figures, stands at 16 percent. One in five lives below the poverty line; the median income is $35,011. Were it not for the redistributive effects of taxation, its residents would literally go nowhere and many would be incredibly hungry when they got there.

But when Republican Senate primary hopeful Rand Paul arrived in town in December to argue that the spread of government represents America's greatest threat, he had an eager audience. Paul, the son of Congressman Ron Paul, who attracted a huge libertarian following during the last presidential election, was the insurgent Tea Party candidate in May's primary. Now he's the front-runner. According to a Rasmussen poll he leads both potential Democratic rivals.

He now wears the glass slipper that is Sarah Palin's endorsement.

Just when you thought the Republican Party could not get more right wing, along came the Tea Party movement—people who fault George W. Bush for not being conservative enough. The temptation of liberals to deride this tendency has, for some, been irresistible. There are mad hatters here, for sure. According to a recent Daily Kos poll of self-identified Republicans, 36 percent believe Barack Obama was not born in the United States, almost a third think he is a racist who hates white people, and almost a third believe contraceptives should be banned.

But for all the derision heaped upon it, the Tea Party movement that began with people in period costume has become a serious electoral force. Rasmussen polls in December revealed that if the Tea Party were an actual party it would beat the Republicans; among voters not affiliated with either major party it was the most popular. As Paul's candidacy shows, these hypotheticals are becoming actuals. A year ago "moderate" Florida Governor Charlie Crist led unknown ultraconservative Marco Rubio 57 to 4. Then Crist embraced Obama and his stimulus package. Now Rubio is leading by 12 points and is favored to trounce his prospective Democratic challenger. A few days before I met Paul, I attended a Tea Party rally in Little Rock, Arkansas: It was 300-strong and standing room only. All the Senate candidates who plan to challenge Democrat Blanche Lincoln attended to kiss the movement's ring.

At this stage the Tea Party's influence can be exaggerated. A group of people brought together by things they don't like can easily splinter. The recent Tea Party Convention sparked as much division as unity, and a large share of its attendees were not participants but reporters. Still, it should not be underestimated.

Blasting bank bailouts and NAFTA, the Tea Partiers espouse a brand of populism that resonates in the absence of coherent analysis of America's economic decline coming from progressives and the administration. These may be people who voted for Bush twice, but they are not turning out for the same reasons as they did before. This time, their agenda is more economic than social. In more than an hour neither Paul nor any of the thirty-five audience members at Leitchfield's town hall meeting mentioned abortion, gay marriage, stem cell research, creationism, or religion in schools. "Remember when one of Clinton's aides said, 'It's the economy, stupid'?" Paul asked me afterward. "It still is the economy.... I'm not running for preacher. I'm running for office."

The movement is almost exclusively white. The fact that its agenda is informed by issues of race and its ranks infected with racism is undeniable, but the driving force behind it is clearly much more complicated. If Condoleezza Rice were president they would probably love her. And if Obama were half as liberal as his base thinks he is, he would spark opposition regardless of his race.

While some have drawn an equivalence between the Tea Partiers and Obama voters, the comparison is more asymmetrical. Obama launched a campaign that aspired to become a movement; the Tea Partiers have created a movement that is trying to gain electoral expression. The former found its focus via a candidate; the latter have no obvious champion. It's not even clear they're looking for one. (Most love Palin, but the movement would survive quite well without her.)

This movement's leadership is in the media. In the absence of Republican leadership it has been stoked by Fox News and talk radio. Every Tuesday at a nonalcoholic Bar None in Lexington, a 9/12 Project group meets. This is Fox presenter Glenn Beck's initiative, aimed at returning America to the values it embraced the day after 9/11—not the outpouring of gratitude toward government workers like firefighters and police but the flag-waving patriotic and religious unity that ostensibly engulfed the nation. Fourteen showed up the night I was there. A straw poll revealed that they blamed the entire establishment, not Obama alone, for leading America in the wrong direction. Half believed Obama is a Muslim, just one thought he's a Christian, and the vast majority thought he was a communist, socialist, and Marxist. None believed he was born in America; most said they did not know.

With words that could have come from a liberal in the run-up to the Iraq War, Abigail Billings chided the media for their incompetence:

They are "not doing any research. They're not asking any questions. They're not reporting any longer. They're now opinionated talk shows. They're no longer offering factual news coverage." Billings watches Fox News. And so does everyone else.

—February 11, 2010

SOMETHING NEW ON THE MALL

Michael Tomasky

We have never seen, at least in the modern history of the United States, a right-wing street-protest movement. Conservatives who oppose *Roe v. Wade* march on Washington every January 22, the anniversary of that 1973 decision; but aside from that single issue and that single day, the American right over recent decades has, until this summer, carried out its organizing in a comparatively quiet fashion, via mimeograph machine and pamphlet and book and e-mail and text message, and left the streets to the left.

So we have something new in our political life—the summer's apoplectic and bordering-on-violent town-hall meetings, and the large 9/12 rally on Washington's National Mall that drew tens of thousands of people to protest America's descent into "socialism" (or "communism," or, occasionally, "Nazism"). How extreme is this movement, and how seriously should we take it?

The September 12 rally, the culminating (for now) event of the Tea Party movement that sprouted to life earlier this year, was organized chiefly by FreedomWorks, a conservative lobbying organization founded in 1984, and supported by nearly thirty conservative organizations, ranging from the well known (Club for Growth, Competitive Enterprise Institute) to the obscure (Ayn Rand Center for Individual Rights). It was also promoted heavily on the Fox News channel, especially by the hard right's new man of the moment, Glenn Beck.

Much of the sentiment on display expressed a genuine fury on the part of citizens who believe in limited government and are opposed to the bank bailout, the auto bailout, health-care reform, the deficit, and other policies of the administration. But another kind of anger, less respectable, was also expressed, and most of it was directed at one person in particular. "Parasite-in-Chief" read one sign, showing Barack Obama standing at the presidential lectern. "TREASON" read another, the "O" rendered in the familiar Obama campaign poster style, with the receding red lines suggesting a horizon. Another maintained that "Obammunism Is Communism."

Many placards reproduced the widely circulated image of Obama as the Joker character played by Heath Ledger in last year's Batman film *The Dark Knight*. On Pennsylvania Avenue, a group of marchers I was walking with spontaneously began chanting "No You Can't!" I did not see any overtly racist signs (although a TV reporter showed a poster of a largely naked African, and the Joker placards have affinities with old Sambo cartoons).

There was also plenty of animus toward Nancy Pelosi, Harry Reid, and Ted Kennedy—I saw several attendees carrying a sign that said "Bury Obamacare with Kennedy," which had been printed by a group called the American Life League, a leading Catholic anti–abortion rights group. Its motto is "From Creation to Natural Death," and its president wrote recently that the fact that the "pro-abort" Kennedy received a Catholic burial was "a total, absolute insult to Christ the Lord" that went "beyond anything I have witnessed in my more than 65 years of life."[1]

There were many signs devoted to the idea of purging Congress, and not a few marchers carrying brooms, symbolizing the desire to sweep clean the halls of the Capitol. Across from the National Archives Building—a nine iron away from the revered documents we read so differently—I ran into (actually, he, and his baby stroller, almost ran into me) Grover Norquist, the influential head of Americans for Tax Reform, the conservative lobbying and advocacy group and one of the cosponsors of the march. I've interviewed the accessible

Norquist several times. I'd never seen him giddy, as he was while describing to me the growth of these protests since a smattering of anti-tax marches last spring. He was like an alumnus just before kickoff at the homecoming game. He reluctantly agreed that health-care reform would probably pass: "They've got the votes to do something," he said. "The question is how damaging it is."

But he quickly regained his optimism—he argued that once there's a final, written-down bill, "you have a bigger target, not a smaller target," and he moved to an assessment of next year's elections: "They've already given us enough votes to lose twenty to forty House seats," he told me.

Midterm election predictions seem absurdly premature. By next fall, the economy could well be growing at a good pace (Alan Greenspan says it will happen this year), unemployment could be decreasing, and Obama could be back near a 60 percent approval rating. What is not hypothetical is that the Tea Party movement has materialized, to those who don't monitor conservative websites and media outlets, seemingly out of nowhere, with an intensity no one would have predicted three months ago (certainly the White House did not). It does not represent a majority of the country, or probably anything close to a majority. Perhaps, based on certain indicators—Sarah Palin's popularity, George W. Bush's at the very end, the percentages in polls that strongly disapprove of Obama's leadership—we can conclude that its followers make up 25 or so percent of the electorate.

But we kid ourselves if we think they are not capable of broader impact. We've seen it already: The degree to which self-identified independent voters flipped on health care over the summer from support to opposition, in part because of the toxic town-hall protests, was astonishing. One oft-quoted poll from mid-August by *USA Today* found that independents said, by 35 to 16 percent, that they had become more sympathetic to the town-hall protesters.

This movement could flame out, and the September 12 march be forgotten. It's worth recalling that the AFL-CIO organized a march on the mall eight months into Ronald Reagan's first term that drew 250,000 people, three or four times the September 12 group's total. That movement had little impact on the course of subsequent events.

This conservative protest movement, though, has three powerful forces supporting it: bottomless amounts of corporate money; an ideologically dedicated press, radio, and cable television apparatus eager to tout its existence; and elected officials who are willing to embrace it publicly and whose votes in support of the movement's positions can be absolutely relied upon. The 1981 marchers and all the left-leaning protest movements with which we've been familiar over the years—and that serve in our minds as the models for street protests and political rallies—have typically had none of this kind of support. For the foreseeable future, what we witnessed on September 12, and over the summer at the town-hall events, is likely to be a permanent feature of the political landscape.

The Tea Party movement started in February, during the debates over the stimulus bill and the bank bailout. The right-wing blogger Michelle Malkin was among the early agitators for protest. But all remained inchoate until February 19, when CNBC correspondent Rick Santelli delivered what has become famous in some circles as the "Santelli rant." Santelli is a former Chicago trader who joined CNBC in 1999. During one of his regular reports from the floor of the Chicago Board of Trade, reacting to an earlier on-air segment about the Obama administration's $75 billion plan to help several million homeowners avoid foreclosure, Santelli—who called himself an "Ayn Rander"—erupted:

> The government is promoting bad behavior…. I'll tell you what, I have an idea.
>
> You know, the new administration's big on computers and technology—how about this, president and new administration? Why don't you put up a website to have people vote on the Internet as a referendum to see if we really want to

subsidize the losers' mortgages; or would we like to at least buy cars and buy houses in foreclosure and give them to people that might have a chance to actually prosper down the road, and reward people that could carry the water instead of drink the water?

As he carried on, the traders who normally serve only as his backdrop began to turn, face him, and cheer. He asked them how many of them "want to pay for your neighbors' mortgage that has an extra bathroom and can't pay their bills?" They booed loudly—not at him, but at the idea. He announced plans for a "Chicago Tea Party" for July (whether he did this spontaneously or not is an interesting question[2]). Thus was born the current grassroots movement, on a stock-trading floor ("This is America!" he roared at one point, gesturing toward the traders around him as if they were representative of average folk) and animated by anger at "the losers" and their mortgages.

Within hours, websites started popping up. FreedomWorks, a conservative lobbying organization founded in 1984 with a current budget of undisclosed millions (its most recent report to the IRS covers 2007), helped support this activity from the start. It is funded in part by Steve Forbes and headed by former Republican Congressman Dick Armey of Texas, who was a featured speaker at the September 12 rally. FreedomWorks has a history of setting up "astroturf" groups, so named because they resemble grassroots organizations but in fact have significant hidden corporate backing, on a range of issues.

While President Bush was trying to promote Social Security privatization, a woman in Iowa who identified herself as a "single mom" won a coveted spot on the stage from which she praised Bush's plan. It was later revealed that she was FreedomWorks's Iowa state director. She had spent the previous two years as spokeswoman for something called For Our Grandchildren, a pro-privatization group that is itself, according to SourceWatch, the nonprofit monitoring website, an offshoot of another group, the American Institute for Full Employment (an outfit advocating reform of welfare that was funded initially by a multimillionaire in Klamath Falls, Oregon, who made his fortune in doors, windows, and millwork).

I mention all this because it suggests how astroturfing works. An existing nonprofit group sets up an ad hoc one devoted to a particular cause or idea. It is given an otherwise good-sounding name, and is presented as having sprung up spontaneously. But always, there is corporate money behind it, donated by rich conservatives who have the sense to see that an image of broad populist anger will be more convincing to the unpersuaded (and to the press) than an image of a corporate titan pursuing a narrow and naked interest.

With respect to the Tea Parties and especially the summer's town-hall meetings, a key corporate titan appears to be Koch Industries of Wichita, Kansas. Fred Koch (pronounced "coke") founded the company in 1940 as an oil business but it has expanded into natural gas, pharmaceuticals, fertilizer, and many other areas. He helped create the John Birch Society in the late 1950s and died in 1967. His two sons who run the business now, David and Charles, have foundations that donate millions to conservative and libertarian causes and groups, including notably the Cato Institute. One Koch-funded group used to be called Citizens for a Sound Economy. It became Americans for Prosperity (AFP) in 2003, a group that has advocated limited government and opposed climate change legislation. Earlier this year, Americans for Prosperity launched a website called Patients United Now, which ran frightening television ads opposing health-care reform (showing, for example, a Canadian woman who supposedly couldn't get treatment for a brain tumor in her native country[3]). According to the liberal website Think Progress, the AFP helped distribute signs and talking points at a town-hall event hosted by Virginia Congressman Tom Perriello.

Think Progress is one of three organizations that did extensive reporting over the summer on how the town halls were organized.

Media Matters for America, the group run by David Brock, set up a comprehensive website, now publicly available, that tracks the complex relationships between donors, nonprofit groups, and the activist organizations to which they funnel money.[4] Campaign for America's Future, the labor-funded advocacy group that's been trying to keep a public option in the final health care bill, produced a helpful flow chart laying out the connections.[5]

The sources of money can be hard to track. These are mainly 501(c)4 groups, which are allowed to lobby and engage in political activity. They are like 501(c)3 groups, which are supposed to be purely educational, in that groups in both categories do not pay federal taxes. However, (c)3 donations are tax-deductible for the donor, while (c)4 gifts are not. The groups have to file annual reports listing major donors, but the fines for late filing are so light that many groups prefer to pay the fines, or file extensions, thus putting off disclosure for months or years.

It isn't just conservative (c)4 groups that backed the town halls. America's Health Insurance Plans, or AHIP, is the enormous lobbying organization for private health insurance companies headed by Karen Ignagni, who makes frequent television appearances discussing health care. According to Think Progress's Lee Fang, AHIP mobilized 50,000 of its employees to attend town-hall meetings and otherwise lobby against the inclusion of a public health insurance option in the reform.[6] AHIP's effort was coordinated by Democracy Data & Communications (DDC), which has helped various corporate clients set up front groups. DDC is headed by B.R. McConnon, who was once an employee of the Koch-funded Citizens for a Sound Economy.

Not everything is hidden under such layers. The website for the September 12 march, for example, lists its sponsors on its home page (first among them: FreedomWorks Foundation). And the high-powered operations of these groups do not mean that none of the opposition to Obama's policies is genuine and spontaneous. Liberal and conservative bloggers have sparred over this question, the former tending to overstate the control that astroturf groups have over people, the latter tending to deny it completely.

The argument over spontaneity versus coordination largely misses the point, which is the way that a loose network of groups sustains and encourages opposition to the administration and gives the movement currency and power it would not otherwise have. Money is the ultimate lubricant of politics, and the potential money supply for Tea Parties and other astroturf contributions is virtually limitless. In this case, though, it may not be the most important force contributing to the rise of this movement.

Many signs at the march were critical of the press. The universal view among these folks is that the country's major media outlets are virtually state-controlled and obedient to Obama's every wish. They have tuned out NBC, CBS, CNN, and others completely. This, too, is a new thing: Millions of Americans who get their "news" only from outlets that will tell them exactly what they want to hear.

Rush Limbaugh and the Fox News channel are by now familiar even to people who never listen to or watch them. But if you don't do so, you have no idea the extent to which they very directly fuel talk of socialism, and twist and sometimes invent information, and create scandals that keep their listeners agitated. To liberals, and to nonideological Americans who might have heard of him, Cass Sunstein is a highly regarded Harvard law professor who might someday be a plausible Supreme Court nominee and who, if anything, is not a lockstep liberal on such matters as civil liberties. To consumers of the right-wing mass media, however, Sunstein is nothing short of a nut, who believes that meat-eating and hunting should be banned, that pets should be able to sue their owners, and that the government should order that organs be ripped fresh from the bodies of people who die in emergency rooms.

These spurious charges are based largely on selective and distorted quotations from his writings and in any case have nothing to do with the White House job to which he was nominated. But the

United States Senate has taken notice of them. Sunstein's nomination by Obama to head the Office of Information and Regulatory Affairs, announced January 8, was held up by Republicans for months. On September 9, he finally—but just barely—survived a cloture vote to allow his confirmation to proceed. He was confirmed the next day by a vote of 57–40, with just five Republican votes.

The charge against Sunstein was led by Fox's Glenn Beck, who now, even more than Limbaugh, is the guru of this new right wing. Beck, famous for saying that Obama is a "racist" with "a deep-seated hatred for white people or white culture," now has (on some nights anyway) more than three million viewers and has surpassed Bill O'Reilly as the leader among cable news hosts.[7] Beck has been crusading against Obama's "czars"—the appointees who don't require Senate confirmation. Obama is hardly the first president to name such officials—the practice dates to the 1940s and presidents of both parties have named them. And many of them are just subcabinet-level appointees whom the press—or Beck himself—happens to have labeled czars. For example, Dennis Blair is the director of national intelligence. But he's also the "intelligence czar," adding to the supposedly terrifying total of unaccountable, unconstitutional radicals infiltrating the government.

The September 12 marchers carried many a placard denouncing the czars, urging Obama to take them back to Russia and so on. "Russia," of course, means "communistic," which the czars, of course, were not. But all that matters is that the conservative base be kept in an excitable state and that Obama suffer political defeats, as he did when Beck was able to claim the scalp of Van Jones, the "green jobs czar" who resigned in September after it was revealed that he'd signed a petition with language suggesting that members of the Bush administration may have known that the September 11 attacks were impending and didn't stop them.

These right-wing outlets—which include "news" websites like Newsmax and World Net Daily, the latter affiliated with Jerome

Corsi, a writer connected with Swift Boat Veterans for Truth—create a world in which their consumers have a reality presented to them that is completely at odds with the reality the rest of us live in. Their coverage of the town halls helped drive the way those meetings were presented in other media. E.J. Dionne reported in the *Washington Post* that North Carolina Democratic Congressman David Price was told by a stringer for a television network: "Your meeting doesn't get covered unless it blows up."[8]

The third source of support for this movement is Republican elected officials. Thanks in part to millions of dollars of donations to Republican senators like Charles Grassley and Mike Enzi, the Tea Party movement can count on virtually every Republican in Congress to vote with it on major bills. Only Maine Senator Olympia Snowe seems not to bother with them much, which is one reason why she might yet vote with the Democrats on health care. (She has made her opposition to the public option clear, but she did on September 17 sign a letter with three Democrats indicating that she might back a bill without one.) This, again, is a situation without precedent. When the labor or anti–Vietnam War or civil rights movements held their marches, they knew they still faced a battle within Congress to win over a broad majority of Democrats. Within today's congressional Republican Party there is little or no such tension.

This is hardly surprising, given the increasing homogeneity of the GOP in recent decades, as most moderates from New England and elsewhere have left the party. But it is striking to see elected of-ficials staying silent in the face of extremism or even egging it on, as are the eleven Republican cosponsors of a House bill that would re-quire future presidential candidates to produce their birth certificates when they file their statements of candidacy, an obvious sop to the so-called "birther" movement whose adherents claim that Obama is not an American citizen. Instead of elected officials acting as a sort of restraining ego to the activists, everyone here shares one big id.

There is, of course, one last trait all these people have in common.

They, or at least 98 percent of those I saw on the Mall on September 12, are white. It's difficult to say what part race plays in their anger. But because they are so overwhelmingly white, everything these folks say about "their" country being taken away from them has an inevitable racial overtone. Would this movement have started if, say, Hillary Clinton or John Edwards were president? I think it probably would have—Lord knows, there are few Hillary Clinton admirers among these groups. And I think it does have ideological rather than racial roots and causes. But it seems unlikely that it would have emerged with quite this ferocity—unlikely, for example, that the presence of a President Edwards would have led to people carrying guns to presidential speeches, as happened when Obama spoke to veterans in Phoenix this summer. And there seemed a racial angle, too, in the anger that exploded last spring about having to pay for "losers'" mortgages.

We can't measure this, and I'm not sure what good it would do us to know even if we could. What we do know is that this movement is backed by corporate millions, powerful media organizations, such as Fox News, and votes in Congress, and that it will be around for quite some time, advancing new fake scandals and lies. The next phase in all this, if health care passes, might well be "nullification" lawsuits or resolutions in states that don't want to have to implement Obama's reform.

There's a name for the followers of this movement, too—the "tenthers," as in the Tenth Amendment, which reserves unenumerated rights to the states. So far this year, thirty-seven states have introduced so-called "sovereignty resolutions," and North Dakota, South Dakota, Idaho, Alaska, Oklahoma, Louisiana, and Tennessee have passed them. South Carolina Senator Jim DeMint, Minnesota Congresswoman Michele Bachmann, and Minnesota Governor Tim Pawlenty have all intimated that if Obama's health care plan is enacted, nullification may be the best course of action. If they choose it, I'm sure there will be another march.

—*September 24, 2009*

Notes

1. The essay, by ALL President Judie Brown, was posted on the website LifeSite-News.com on September 1, 2009.

2. An article on *Playboy*'s website by Mark Ames and Yasha Levine suggested that Santelli's performance was "a carefully planned trigger" for the Tea Parties. CNBC threatened libel, and *Playboy* removed the article from its site. Santelli issued a statement after that piece appeared denying any affiliation with Tea Party movements, swearing that he had no political agenda, and even saying he hoped that Obama would succeed in passing his stimulus bill.

3. Republican Senate leader Mitch McConnell picked up on the story of this woman, Shona Holmes, giving it wide circulation. A Canadian newspaper reported later that while she was indeed told under the Canadian system to wait months for treatment and chose to go to the Mayo Clinic for quicker treatment, she did not in fact have a brain tumor, but something called a Rathke's Cleft Cyst, which is benign. See Julie Mason, "A Reality Check on a Reality Check," *the Ottawa Citizen*, July 29, 2009.

4. See www.mediamattersaction.org/transparency.

5. See Sarah Shive, "Who's Paying to Kill Health Reform?" at CAF's Website, www.ourfuture.org.

6. See Lee Fang, "Health Insurance Lobby's Stealth Astroturf Campaign Revealed!" August 28, 2009, at www.thinkprogress.org.

7. Fox is way ahead of its competitors. It averages around three million nightly viewers; MSNBC, around 1.1 million; CNN, around 900,000. See tvbythenumbers.com.

8. See E.J. Dionne Jr., "The Real Town Hall Story," the *Washington Post*, September 3, 2009.

"ON 9/11, I THINK THEY HIT THE WRONG BUILDING"

Mike Madden

Washington

The gathering in Lafayette Square, in honor both of tax day and of a generalized fury at Barack Obama, his budget, the Federal Reserve and whatever else ails the conservative movement, was going just fine, despite the rain. But there's an old saying in protest organizing: It's all fun and games until someone tea-bags the White House.

And so it went Wednesday for the most geographically prominent Tea Party protest of the hundreds held around the nation. At around 2:30 p.m., a little before the rally was supposed to break up, someone threw a box of tea bags over the fence around the executive mansion, and the Secret Service moved in like, well, like they were cornering a bunch of liberal protesters gathered outside of George W. Bush's White House.

Before you could say, "Who is John Galt?" the party was over. It turns out the Secret Service's devotion to keeping people from throwing things at the president is fairly bipartisan. Unlike the Tea Parties. Organizers said the day drew people out to more than 700 sites nationwide. Fox News was practically a co-sponsor; the network broadcast live from San Antonio, with Glenn Beck; Sacramento, with Neil Cavuto; and Atlanta, with Sean Hannity. There was no official count of total national attendance, but estimates ranged from 4,000 in Lansing, Mich., to a few hundred in Boston, home of the Revolutionary

War–era tea party that inspired the general motif. (The right-wing website Pajamas Media put the national figure at 184,064, as of 8:17 p.m. Eastern.) But whatever the size of the crowds, from Washington to San Francisco the rallies were pretty much a right-wing thing. They drew a mixture of the conservative base, Ron Paul zealots, libertarians and assorted others who are dead certain that Obama's administration is taking the country into socialism—or worse.

To find extreme sentiments in Lafayette Park, it wasn't necessary to look for the people with the most eccentric tea bag–themed costumes. You could just pick a protester at random. "I think Obama's plan is to create a catastrophic failure in our economic system, because then people will get desperate, and then you have the ability for a totalitarian government to move in," said J'Neane Theus, 54, who retired from the Navy and now manages investments. She drove about an hour from Clarksville, Maryland, battling Washington's horrific rush hour traffic, to be an official marshal of the Tea Party (she had a white hat with "marshal" hand-scrawled in red ink to prove it). Her son, a 19-year-old Marine named Galen, stood next to her in a red, white, and blue tie-dyed shirt, holding a sign accusing Barney Frank and other Democrats of treason. "I think that sounds very wacko; Americans don't want to believe that. But we've seen this movie before," the elder Theus said. I asked her where. "How about, well, Fascist Italy, under Mussolini—and look at what happened to him, I would remind Obama of that," she said. "Hitler. Stalin. Socialism has been proven not to work."

Another seemingly sedate protester, Brian Smith, a marketer from Greenville, South Carolina, who was in Washington on business and came by the rally, wandered equally off message. "I love my country and I don't like what's going on," Smith said. "Government—to be honest with you, and this will probably be misquoted, but on 9/11, I think they hit the wrong building. They should have gone into the Capitol building, hit out, knocked out both sides of the aisle, we'd start from scratch, we'd be better off today." I pointed out that "they" did try to hit the Capitol. "Yeah, I know, they missed," he said. "The wrong sequence. If someone had to go, it should have been the Capitol building. On that day I felt differently, but today that's the way I feel."

As hard as Fox News, some big-name conservatives and even the Republican Party tried to make the Tea Parties out to be a mass movement of mainstream Americans, who—not even three months into the Obama administration—had already had enough, the group outside the White House seemed to be coming from the same fringey place. There were somewhere between 500 and 2,000 people in the square throughout the day, which was an impressive turnout considering the weather, but not anywhere near the outpouring of public support that organizers had been promising (or maybe threatening). But almost every sign bore witness that the protester who carried it was well to the right of your average swing voter. "Ameristan—of the gov'nt, by the gov'nt, for the gov'nt, Barack Hussein Obama," read one placard. "Restore the Republic," pleaded another. "They're nothing but Marxist, socialist Communists in there," shouted a man wearing dark sunglasses, in spite of the rain, as he gestured at the White House. Someone standing alone on the grass, about thirty yards from the stage, had a sign calling Obama "Soetero"—the name of his Indonesian stepfather—and telling the president he'd have to get through the guy with the sign if he wanted to destroy the country. But the guy with the sign seemed too busy shouting into his cell phone to stop anyone, much less a president whom nearly two-thirds of the country think is doing a good job.

Though some big corporate lobbyists jumped onto the Tea Party movement, the setup in Lafayette Square did, at least, seem to be truly grassroots. The "stage" was a few planks covered by a sad, drooping blue tarp; the mike wasn't loud enough for anyone standing more than about ten feet away to hear the speakers. With a steady downpour turning the grass underfoot into a thick mud, audio problems, and an ecstatic crowd lapping it all up anyway, the whole thing felt like Woodstock for Ayn Rand disciples. (There was even a telltale scent hanging in the air, though at the Tea Party, it was cigar smoke.) A separate protest was supposed to be held around the corner, featuring establishment conservative types like Alan Keyes, Laura Ingraham, and Grover Norquist, but the Secret Service pulled the permit at the last moment, leaving the big names to share the stage with the faithful.

"While he's trying to deal with the very difficult issues of the day, like where the dog will sleep, I hope that President Obama peeks behind, pushes the curtain open at the White House and looks out, because America refuses to be silent into submission," Ingraham said. The speakers hit the standard conservative grievance politics messages: The media is unfair, the poor don't pay taxes, the liberals have taken over U.S. higher education, etc. "At Wellesley College, Hillary's school, you can take a class called 'feminist economics,'" said Patrick Coyle, the vice president of the Young America's Foundation, which aims to take back college for the conservative movement. "God knows what that's all about." The crowed cheered loudly when Ingraham said they were all "right-wing extremists," referring to a Homeland Security report warning of danger from disgruntled conservatives.

But the people at the Party had a more diffuse set of issues. Holding an American flag with a plastic rattlesnake wrapped around the pole, a "don't tread on me" flag that also featured a rattlesnake and a box labeled "tea," Ed Walsh, an electrician from Fairfax Station, Virginia, said he was most worried about the Federal Reserve. "This government is screwing us over royally," Walsh told me. "The interest that we're paying on the debt that we're generating today—it's going to a private bank, the Federal Reserve. The Federal Reserve is not federal, it's no more federal than Federal Express." That's a vastly oversimplified, mostly inaccurate view of the Fed, which is the central bank for the United States, but it also has very little to do with the stated purpose for the rally.

The irony of the day, of course, was that most people aren't anywhere near as outraged about their April 15 tax bill as the Tea Partiers. A Gallup poll released earlier in the week showed 48 percent of respondents think they pay about the right amount in income taxes. Obama aides, who mostly ignored the Tea Party scene until the tea bags thrown at the White House put the building into lockdown, decided to mark the day by reminding voters that most people have gotten a tax cut because of the economic stimulus bill that passed earlier this year.

"For too long, we've seen taxes used as a wedge to scare people into supporting policies that actually increased the burden on working people instead of helping them live their dreams," Obama said, as the protest raged on outside. "That has to change, and that's the work that we've begun." The president's own 1040 showed he paid $855,323 in federal income tax last year on income of $2,656,902 (mostly from book sales). If the tea business was really the start of a grassroots tax-revolt movement, maybe Obama should have gone out and joined the party.

—April 16, 2009

LOBBYIST MONEY + RIGHT-WING EXTREMISTS = TEA PARTY

David A. Love

The Tea Parties that recently took place around the country were billed as a grassroots, bottom-up groundswell against taxes, big government, and bailouts. Fox News, apparently promoting itself as the official tea-bag network, hopes to grab ratings by embracing the pseudo-populist protests as their own.

Republican politicians tried to hitch onto the mean-spirited Tea Party bandwagon, replete with anti-Obama and racist protest signs. That the GOP wants to associate itself with extremist groups tells you the political party has officially fallen off the deep end. White supremacists, militias, secessionists, conspiracy theorists, and wing nuts—the subjects of a new Department of Homeland Security report—apparently have a seat at the table of the Republican Party. With the moderates and even the reasonable, book learning–oriented conservatives driven from the GOP, the extremists are now the base, the mainstream conservatives. They are all that is left of a party in tatters, of what is now a regional political organization—Southern, Christian, and almost exclusively white.

No more of this going through the motions about diversity, about the big tent. And I think that is fine, because there is no love lost. Many political observers always looked at their overtures to people of color with a jaundiced eye. But the Republicans are playing with fire now as they court the angry lynch mob. And we have been down this road before.

I speak of a time, during Jim Crow segregation, when opportunistic politicians—the White Citizens Council, or the white-collar Klan—appealed to their unwashed racist brethren by standing against desegregation and voting against civil rights. The white-collar Klan gave a good talk. They stood in front of the schoolhouse door to block the black students from attending class, but they kept their hands clean. Meanwhile, the angry mob, Klansmen and other domestic terrorists, did the dirty work. They acted with a wink and a nod from the respectable white-collar Klan, and took matters into their own hands by burning crosses, lynching civil rights workers, and bombing black churches. And this is the arrangement that the GOP appears to be establishing with its base today.

From an organizational point of view, the Tea Parties are a prime example of "astroturfing," top-down machinations operating under the guise of a faux grassroots movement—like a phony, conservative version of MoveOn, but operated by a corporate puppet master. In this case, as was reported in the *Atlantic* and Think Progress, they are being led by corporate lobbyist–run, Republican-affiliated front groups and think tanks: FreedomWorks, a conservative action group led by former U.S. House Majority Leader Dick Armey; the free-market group Americans for Prosperity, and the online-oriented, free-market group DontGo Movement, which was born out of last year's offshore drilling debate in Congress. These organizations are writing the press releases and talking points, thinking up the ideas for the signs, setting up the conference calls, you name it.

Americans for Prosperity operates through the generosity of philanthropies such as the ultraconservative Lynde and Harry Bradley Foundation (which bankrolled Ward Connerly's anti–affirmative action ballot initiatives, and *The Bell Curve* author Charles Murray), and the pro–oil drilling Koch Family foundations.

In accordance with the interests of Armey's client base, Freedom-Works has lobbied for the privatization of Social Security, and the deregulation of the life insurance industry. It supports the status quo in America's use of fossil fuels, and has lobbied against health-care reform. Further, FreedomWorks has received funding from telephone giants Verizon and AT&T, and has opposed net neutrality legislation that would keep the Internet democratic and open. One Freedom-Works funder is the Scaife Foundation, from Richard Mellon Scaife, key patron of the American right.

So, these are the white-collar interests behind the Tea Parties. But what of the angry, disgruntled masses, the violent ones that'll "git 'er done"? Well, the Department of Homeland Security (DHS) just issued a report called "Right-wing Extremism: Current Economic and Political Climate Fueling Resurgence in Radicalization and Recruitment." According to the report, the current economic downturn and the election of an African-American president have provided recruitment opportunities for white-supremacist and radical right-wing groups. As the report warns, "the consequences of a prolonged economic downturn—including real estate foreclosures, unemployment, and an inability to obtain credit—could create a fertile recruiting environment for right-wing extremists and even result in confrontations between such groups and government authorities similar to those in the past."

The current situation is not unlike the 1990s, when angst over a recession fed paranoia, and conspiracy theories about the end times, martial law, and the suspension of the U.S. Constitution. The environment led to the targeting of government buildings and law enforcement, and resulted in the 1995 Oklahoma City bombing. It was the largest terrorist attack on U.S. soil before September 11, 2001: The bombing of the Alfred P. Murrah Federal Building claimed 168 lives and left over 800 people injured.

According to the Southern Poverty Law Center, in 2008 there were 926 hate groups in the United States—more than a 4 percent increase from 888 groups in 2007, and an over 50 percent increase since 2000, when 602 groups were active.

The DHS report notes that disgruntled veterans from the current wars in Iraq and Afghanistan are recruited by white supremacist groups, exploited for the training and skills they acquire in the military. Let's not forget that Oklahoma City bomber Timothy McVeigh was a veteran of Operation Desert Storm in 1990–1991.

These right-wing groups are united by their hatred of immigration and a frustration over perceived government inaction on the issue, and they perpetrate hate crimes against Latinos. And in their hostility toward gun control legislation—such as assault weapons bans and proposed universal handgun registration—they stockpile weapons and ammunition, and engage in paramilitary training.

These extremist organizations are also united by their concern over the election of President Obama, which has translated into new recruits. Can we forget the blood-lust at the McCain-Palin rallies, in which crowd participants called Obama a terrorist and a traitor, carried around Obama monkey dolls and called for his death? During the 2008 presidential campaign, then-candidate Obama received more threats than any other candidate in recent memory, according to the Southern Poverty Law Center. Moreover, several white supremacists were arrested for plotting to assassinate him or threatening to do so.

And the Tea Parties represent another venue, another outlet for racist and extremist sentiment, all funded by right-wing corporate interests. Consider some of the signs that were held by tea-bag protesters:

- At a Madison, Wisconsin, tea-bag rally: "Obama is the anti-Christ!" "Obama's Plan—White Slavery."
- In Chicago: "The American Taxpayers Are the Jews for Obama's Ovens."
- Philadelphia: "Barack Hussein Obama—The New Face of Hitler."

- Fresno, California: "Impeach Osama Obama a.k.a. Hussein."
- In Columbia, South Carolina, an elderly man held a large sign that read, "Barack Obama Supports Abortion, Sodomy, Socialism, and the New World Order."
- At a Washington, D.C., protest, one man held a sign that read, "Stand idly by while some Kenyan tries to destroy America? WAP!! I don't think so!!! Homey don't play dat!!!"

Sadly, under this economic and political climate, some elected officials try to tap into this extremist and racist anger with calls for secession and states' rights, time-tested racist code words for the suppression of civil rights of African-Americans. And the half-baked rejection of the stimulus money by some Republican governors, particularly in Southern states with considerable poverty and large populations of color, smacks of traditional conservative opposition to social programs on the grounds that they'll help black and brown people. It's funny until somebody gets hurt, as they always say.

So, the white-collar Klan and the regular Klan have entered the twenty-first century, and what the government intends to do about it this time around remains to be seen. But it is certain that we can't sleep on this one.

—April 23, 2009

MONGREL POLITICS AND AN AMERICAN MIND

JoAnn Wypijewski

Stranded in Columbia, South Carolina, on tax day, I went up to the state capitol to check out the local Tea Party. It – the Tea Party, that is – was of moderate size, blazingly white. On the capitol steps, facing the Confederate flag on the grounds below, some anarchists sat with a prominent sign, "End the welfare-warfare state." Otherwise, the scene was dominated by Republican politicians and their sign carriers, "Joe (JOBS) Wilson" and the like, raising paeans to "free market capitalism." Some in the crowd appeared to have fared quite nicely off the system, amid others who looked as if they'd got the short end of the stick but had convinced themselves, at least for an afternoon, that the only thing that hindered every one of them from being job-creating small-business dynamos was the socialist tyranny of Barack Obama.

In the shade at the edge of the proceedings, I fell into conversation with a bandy, blue-eyed man who wore a cap that said, "Gun Owners for Paul." He had terrible teeth and a long white beard reminiscent of *O, Brother, Where Art Thou?* and said he was 65. He spoke in a high-pitched country drawl, in a matter-of-fact style with a wild fringe of humor.

Mr. Stewart, as he later identified himself, exists at an angle to the Tea Party's khaki-pants or pencil-skirt headliners, whose packaged vitriol and evasive, radioland-style racism have come to pass for normal. He chimed in with a number of other kibitzers, all of them a little worn at the edges, just as I was finishing a conversation with a fellow called Tom Webb, "Rebel Poet," who was carrying a Confederate flag and dressed in a Citadel cadet's jacket, modified to look like a rebel uniform. Webb had asked for an interview, saying he hoped we could find "common ground." This exchange with Stewart begins as Webb is about to make his exit.

JW: ...I'm all for individual liberty, but I just don't agree with you that this flag isn't about slavery. It's just too hard. The battle flag is a war flag, and the war, while about states' rights and preservation of the union and all that, was ultimately about slavery.

Kibitzer 1: This originally symbolized liberty, but since then it's been twisted, especially by the KKK, which is a shame, and that is how it came to be a symbol of slavery.

JW: Okay, say, for the sake of argument, that the Nazi flag had started really nicely and then it ended up with Hitler.

Kibitzer 2: Now, what was the Nazi symbol?

JW: The swastika.

K2: And that means what?

JW: Well, I guess some Germans might say it's their heritage, but ...

K2: No ma'am, the swastika is a Norse symbol for good luck.

JW: Fine, yes, and you see it also in Native American art, and ...

K2: And it's been twisted.

JW: Well, has it been twisted? I mean, if Adolf Hitler made it his flag, doesn't that sort of trump everything else?

Mr. Stewart: The media define every social issue to suit their agenda. They don't like the Confederate fight for independence; they change the meanin' of the flag so that a fight for freedom becomes a fight for slavery.

JW: But freedom meant freedom to have slaves, freedom to deny a whole lot of other people freedom.

S: Under our Constitution we have rights. I hate slavery. I would have burned the first slave ship myself, personally.

JW: Ok, right on, brother, so …

S: But my ancestors fought for the Confederate flag not because they had slaves; they didn't. They had families, they had farms, and they had a state that had a right to secede, and that did it. I do not approve of war. I blame it on the South, the hotheads that fired on federal troops on federal property. That was a declaration of war, so it's all the fault of hotheads but not the farmers that died in that war.

JW: Absolutely, but the hotheads were the big slaveowners who …

Kibitzer 3: Who is she?

S: I don't know who she is, probably some …

JW: (laughing) Commie symp.

S: Some surreptitious what-is-it, they have that law against people who speak out against the war or somethin', the Alien and Sedition Law. But you look like a good, solid girl to me!

K2: She's my sister, and you're my brother. That's where we stand.

S: Well, this here is my brother. He comes from Scotland. I go by nation. I'm like the Nigroes and the Jews, I stick for my own.

JW: You're Scots-Irish, is that right?

S: I'm a mixture. My ancestors have been here for a long time. Overall, there's no pure race. I'm just part of a nation that happens to have a few other elements, even Hebrew, in it. Over thousands of years, you're naturally gonna end up with genes mixed in. But, so far, I would be a typical white Southerner from South Carolina. My ancestors came from Ireland and Northern Europe. I don't have any Nigro blood, but I do have Indian blood, I think, because most South Carolinians do. That's my race, and I see what my race has done in Europe, in South Carolina, in the United States and North America. They have more peace and prosperity until the government gets 'em into a war. Neighbors respect each other. They don't rape, murder, steal to the same degree that they do in Africa and Latin America, which means it's safe for us to invest in our homes and in our businesses. Our property is respected, unless we fall under Communist government. So, the point is, we're civilized because we come from that nation of people who had created civilization from the very beginning.

JW: Well, not the very beginning. And the Southern Europeans weren't exactly slouches at civilization. The Romans, the Greeks?

S: Those people were originally blonde, blue-eyed Aryan people, who had swastikas and all that as part of their religion, all the way back to ancient Mesopotamia, which is where they originally came from. These were the people who created civilization: the people of ancient Canaan; all the Hittites, which is the language we're speaking right now, the Hittites' language; the Amorites, blond, blue-eyed folks, if you read in the Bible. They established a civilization in ancient Egypt,

Mesopotamia, Sumer – all Aryan people, not Semitic. All these were different nations before they were driven out of the Fertile Crescent, and they ended up in Europe about 4,000 years ago, when the mixed-race Hyksos came in and destroyed ancient Canaan.

So, you had all these Aryans come into Northern Europe. They found new farms, and they had no racial mixture; therefore, civilization could continue. Now, in Southern Europe there was the Cro-Magnon race. The Cro-Magnons lived there before the Ice Age ended. They were heat adapted. They were not tall and thin; they were big, bulky guys, and they were not farmers. They had not been civilized. And when you have a population that hadn't been bred to respect each other, they are just natural savages, like dogs were before they were bred from wolves.

When the Romans and the Greeks came in, they created great civilizations. The Romans had a good cheap work force around the world; they had great ideas to do great things, but they needed that work force. Then, they made the mistake of marrying with these guys, and then they end up mulattos, and you see how mulattos live: go down to the jail here, and look who's there. And those are Nigro juries, mulatto juries, that are lockin' those people up.

So, the Romans fell apart because when you mix a domesticated animal with a savage animal, like a wolf with a dog, you get an animal that is less civilized, less domesticated, more likely to behave like a savage, according to the survival instincts that god puts in every creature.

Now, understand, every race in the world is racist, and they know who the aliens are. That's the law of nature. That's the survival instincts. Pass your genes on, survival of the fittest: that's all a savage knows.

That's been bred out of us. White people aren't even havin' kids anymore. And when we're gone, it's just gonna be another copy of Africa or Latin America, where these people have no compassion, and live in poverty and crime, who will never have science or technology, who will never have a space shuttle. That's what we, in our compassion, are doin' to our civilization: we're destroyin' it.

We're destroyin' it because we don't understand racism. There'll always be Nigroes in Africa. There'll always be Mongoloids in Asia. And I don't blame the Mongoloids. Look, they got space shuttles too. If the white race dies out, that's my only hope for civilization. But Europeans – there won't be any white people left within a generation or two. We still have a few women who want to be mothers. They still have a slight maternal instinct, but they aren't havin' enough kids! Like 1.3 per generation. In Kenya, in Zimbabwe, they're havin' 9 per generation.

I can tell you're a liberal, but you're actually a Republican, I see there [from the elephant charm on my necklace]…

JW: Oh, no, I'm not a Republican. I just like elephants. They're beautiful and they paint. But are you a Republican or more a libertarian, because I see your Ron Paul hat?

S: Ron Paul? I voted for him in the primaries because he stood for peace, which is what Americans wanted and why they voted for Obama. They did not want to redistribute the wealth. All they wanted was No War!

JW: So, you're against the wars in Iraq and Afghanistan.

S: All right, now let me tell you somethin' that'll really blow the minds of whoever listens to this. We do not live in a democracy, even a representative democracy called a republic. We live in a mediacracy.

JW: Meaning M-E-D-I-A?

S: Right. Most people vote according to how they are influenced by the media. Ever since back in the Fifties I could read the newspapers,

I didn't care who won the elections, I was not political, I never voted for 30 or 40 years, but I could tell who was gonna win the elections. All I had to do was open the newspaper, *The New York Times*, and I'd say, well, look, they favor Johnson more than they do Goldwater; Johnson's gotta win. I didn't know why, but ever since then I have been thinkin' about it. Finally, I figured it out.

The people that own the media determine who's gonna get elected because most of the idiots out here are just gonna turn on that TV; they don't have the sense to turn on the Internet and find a different viewpoint. And the people that own the seven or eight big media conglomerates, they start at the primary level, so, by the time you get to the national level – like Obama against McCain – they've already been vetted on both sides. It doesn't matter which one wins, so, in the end, if we had voted for McCain, we'd have gotten the same war that we got from Obama.

I called up a radio station before Obama got elected, I said, "He's not gonna end the war. I know who owns the media, and I know why they put him in there, and they want us in Iraq."

If you look up Who Rules America at the natvan website, www. natvan.com/who-rules-america, you'll see a webpage that shows you the pictures and names of those people who own the media. All of 'em but Murdoch are Jews.

Yeah, I'm against the Iraq war 'cause my flesh and blood that fought every war this country ever had is dyin' over there, fightin' for Israel. Not for me. Not for civilization, but so Israel can do what they're doin' to the Palestinians: a dirty war that you never hear about what goes on, the torture, the genocide, because the Jews own the media.

JW: But the Christians, meaning those organized in churches that produce and elect politicians and are the base of the Republican Party, are probably the most rabid supporters of Israel. I met a big Christian in Kokomo who told me that if Obama ever did a single thing contrary to the will of Israel, he'd know that the president is the Antichrist.

S: Exactly. The first Christians were Jews; they were not Aryans, they were Cro-Magnons, different race, though white people don't understand that. They converted all these civilized, domesticated animals called Celts, Germans and all that. I was talkin' earlier about the swastika that's on their tombstones: it was a holy religious symbol. If you squint in the light, you see a cross, and our ancient people, when they wrote on stone, they just had to be simple. A cross on stone is easy to make, or a circle. That was a symbol of god.

But then the Christians came in, they took the cross and they put a dead Jew on it, and said, He's god. Well, they did the same thing with our winter solstice: they took that and named it Christmas. They converted every holiday we had as pagans, which means "peasants," into a Jewish holiday called Christian. And ever since our kings converted, they took away our religion and gave us a Jew-worship religion, and they have been brainwashin' us ever since. So, we are a lied-to people.

Yeah, I understand why we're fightin' in Iraq, 'cause Israel wants to bomb all those people back to the Stone Age. The reason terrorists are over here is because they are being colonized, the same way that the American Indians fought my ancestors 'cause they were takin' their land. It makes sense. But the Jewish media talks about terrorism, says it ain't got nothin' to do with Palestine. It's 'cause they hate our freedom, all kind of lies, and the American people: yuh, yuh, the Jews are right. Yuh, gotta protect Israel, preacher said so, God's chosen people, hallelujah Israel. I wanna go to heaven, and when the Messiah comes along, I gonna be his man.

JW: So, are you a pagan?

S: I worship god, the same god that my ancestors worshiped for 40,000-50,000 years, and my god is life. Okay, go back to the slavery issue. My ancestors were Christianized, and they'd been taught that the Bible says slavery's okay. The Israelites had slaves. God says you gonna have slaves. So, you got brainwashed civilized people tellin' 'em to enslave these people, it's god's will, this is the Promised Land, kill all the savages if they don't bow down and worship Christ. You know, kill 'em like the Spanish conquistadors did. So, my ancestors were just as brainwashed as people today. They enslaved people, they killed the Indians, you know, but that's not in their heart; they're civilized.

JW: If they did all that, how can you say they were civilized?

S: Well, see, there are two kinds of civilized people. There are two versions of you. There is the version that believes lies, that is insane. They go to church, they're taught lies, they're taught that they're the most evil people on earth until they worship a Jew as lord and savior. So, these people go insane; they try to behave like god told 'em to do, and they end up screwed up, like our ancestors and like people today worshipin' a Jew on a cross, a corpse.

JW: And you don't worship death.

S: You got it! Can I hug you, honey? Oh, lordy, I ain't held a woman in too long.

JW: Now, can I ask you where you're from originally, what you do?

S: My ancestors have been in South Carolina since before the American Revolution. Some of them were in Virginia back in the 1600s, the first settlers. As I say, I think I got some Indian blood …

JW: How about we start with your father …

S: My name is Stewart. I am a Stewart, and my ancestors …

JW: What's your first name?

S: I ain't gonna tell you that. But my genes say I am kin to the same family as the Stewart kings of Scotland. My ancestors were Aryan people: Celts, Germans, no Slavs, all were Northwestern European …

JW: I'm a Slav.

S: Okay, but you look very Germanic, too, you're probably a mixture.

JW: I'm Polish.

S: Okay, but a lot of Germans went into Poland.

JW: Oh, did they ever.

S: Well, you've probably got German blood. But all those races are Aryans.

JW: Hitler didn't think the Poles were Aryans.

S: I can't apologize for Hitler. I've only heard what the Jews have to say about Hitler, and I'd rather see on both sides of the coin before I judge it. I think, he probably chose Poland for propaganda purposes as a justification for German expansion. Poles were next door, and he had to kind of put 'em down, and possibly because the Poles, for some reason, were not as what he considered civilized, in the sense of technologically advanced and whatever. The Germans were great, man, they developed everything you need to build a space shuttle and all of that.

JW: That's the ultimate thing, right? If you have a space shuttle, or, with the Germans, rockets, you're right up there, civilized, no matter…

S: You're civilized if you have compassion for people. And you cannot have great technology and science unless you have compassionate scientists who devote their lives to serving humanity. Excuse me for spitting.

JW: No, no, I was just scratching my eye. But…

S: Well, when people talk, they do spread germs, but, anyway, yeah, the Germans were great people. Slavs, that's R1-something, it's just a little, slightly different, but that's the same race of people. They all came from ancient Canaan.

JW: Why did you learn all this?

S: Because I have the instinct, I was born…

JW: Where?

S: I was born here, in South Carolina. Out in a rural place…

JW: Called?

S: I hate to give all my stuff away because they could trace me down. I don't want to become a hated symbol of the Nazi extermination of the Jews. But I was born in the same county where my ancestors settled in 1767, north of Columbia.

JW: Was your father a farmer?

S: Yeah, all my people been farmers ever since they came from Scotland. I grew most everything I ate, or hunted, up until a few years ago. Gettin' kind of old for a hard workout. Out there diggin' in the soil by yourself is just hard. I do need a wife, someone to take care of an old man.

JW: Are you looking for a wife?

S: Oh, I'd love to have a wife.

JW: Is it hard to find a wife?

S: Well, it was hard when I was young 'cause I was too good for the rest of them. Now I'm too ... none of 'em want me. I never was fit to be married anyway.

JW: Well, you're sort of ornery. You got a smile on your face, though.

S: The people of my family, the Stewarts, are all paranoid. I'm the only one in my family who's been willing to give out his DNA.

JW: On more pedestrian things, what did you think of the rally today?

S: I didn't listen, because I know that all those words aren't gonna do a bit of good, 'cause everybody out here, whatever they do, their vote will be determined by who owns the media. And not one of those speakers, I bet my life, mentioned the word "Jew" or the media, and why we have the government we have. And you can't change anything until you get to the core of the problem.

JW: And on the health care bill, because it was important to this rally today, do you think it was the beginning of socialism in America?

S: No, it's not the beginning. Things started going downhill in this country when they passed the Voters Rights Act of 1965. Until that time, I think 92 per cent of the people in this country were white; that includes the Jews and probably a lot of Hispanics. And then, once they passed that immigration act in the 1960s, then the white race starts dyin' out, you stop havin' compassionate people.

JW: You think it's wrong for black people to be citizens with full rights in this country, and vote and have basic liberties?

S: Well, let me use an expletive. Damn it! You know, the world's a big place. There's nothin' immoral about white people wantin' to live amongst white people, and Nigroes livin' amongst Nigroes, and Jews livin' amongst Jews. There's nothin' wrong with that, and there's nothin' wrong with us havin' an all-white homeland.

JW: Wasn't that dream busted by the first European ship that landed here, and how was it that black people came here in the first place?

S: They were enslaved by Christians, the same guys that exterminated my Indian ancestors! You know, I am a compassionate guy, just like you. I love Nigroes, I love Jews, I love everybody. But I do love civilization, and I realize that, when America becomes like Mexico or Zimbabwe, and whites become a minority, it's gonna be throat-slittin' time.

JW: And did Obama's election have anything to do with your thinking here?

S: Obama, I don't blame him; I don't give him any credit. He wanted to end the war, that was one of his campaign promises, but the Jews ain't gonna let him do that. I predicted that.

I understand the truth. You can be just as smart as me, you won't have to watch the media, you won't have to read anything, once you know who's writin' all that stuff, you gonna know their spin on everything that happens in this world because, if it helps the Jews, they're for it. Doesn't matter whether it's the Republican Party, the

Democratic Party, communism, capitalism. They're racists! Just like Nigroes are racist, that's why they all voted for Obama. I vote for white people 'cause I'm a racist. I don't see anything wrong with racism: it's a healthy survival instinct. I love my race. You're my flesh and blood, let's make some kids!

JW: What if I said I've been in love with a black man?

S: Well, you' d'a been destroyin' our race. You may think this has nothin' to do with anybody but you. Now, we're all mixed a little bit, but the more you mix our race with others, in 100 years or 200 years, that Nigro blood you've got – and the man you'd been with, he ain't black, he's a mulatto, probably 80 per cent black and 20 per cent white, so he's not black, he's like Obama. And you may think he's white, because he's got the same honesty and the same compassion as a white man, but he's mixed. You don't know what's comin' from where. Because you cannot mix a wolf with a domesticated dog and end up with a civilized animal.

JW: So, only white people have compassion?

S: White people are the only race on earth that's been bred to the extent it's been bred to remove those survival instincts from it, and to, to…

JW: To be domesticated dogs.

S: To be so compassionate that they have no racism left. I think everybody should be proud of themselves: Nigro, or part Nigro, or whatever; be proud of yourself. But I'm sayin' let's keep civilization alive by keepin' the race that created civilization as pure as possible, the same way you guard the purity of any breed of animal or plant. That's what benefits civilization, the fact that we have all kinds of diversity of animals, of plants, and the only way you can preserve diversity is not mix the seed. I would rather that the Nigro race be preserved as pure as possible too. I believe, all races should be preserved.

JW: But there is no pure nature, you said it yourself. Look at all the plants around here; none of those hostas there, those with the dark green and the bright green leaves, are pure breeds; that's why they're pretty like that.

S: See, you're a woman. And I don't blame a woman for wantin' to marry a savage race, because they have survival instincts. Now, if I were a woman, my strategy would be, hell, these white people are dyin' out; look at 'em, they're like cattle. I want to get a male that's a savage. I want to get a male that steals, that rapes, that murders, that passes his genes on at all costs, because I want to pass my genes on forever, and I can see these white people ain't gonna do that.

When I was a kid, I didn't know much of what I know today, and I, actually, had a beautiful Nigro girlfriend from – I met her in France, I think she was from Haiti or somewhere. Just a beautiful girl. She was white except for her skin color, but I almost vomited when I kissed her, so, I figured I must be a racist. I think she realized it, because she didn't want to have very much to do with me for too long, either.

JW: What were you doing in France?

S: Oh, I traveled all over the world when I was young.

JW: How? Steamships?

S: Every way you can imagine. I was just a guy who didn't care about makin' a lot of money. You could live for almost nothing, travel for almost nothin' back then. I worked on a ship once. I traveled from Egypt, Suez, I think. And I traveled all around the Horn of Africa, down to Mozambique. I went to Mombasa, Kenya; I went where those pirates are takin' all the ships nowadays. I'm a very compassionate guy. I care about everybody, but I care about civilization too, and I don't want to see the wolves destroy the sheep. That's why I stand up for civilization, and for white people.

JW: Well, I see my battery's about to run out.

S: Oh, I'm sorry I hugged you now. You done turn filthy on me.

JW: That's a sad thing, Mr. Stewart.

S: I'm racist!

JW: You said you loved everybody, and loved everything about life, how can you burden yourself like that?

S: I do love 'em. It's just certain things I don't like.

* * *

Stewart offered a few more denunciations of religion as the root of slavery and the decline of the white race. Before I parted his company, he told me I was okay anyway, a Pole, not as bad as some. "Just enjoy yourself," he said. Then he gave me back the business card I'd given him. "You can take this back. There's a word in your name there; I just can't have that." He paused a beat. "They're probably expensive, these things, anyway; it's just wasted on me."

TEXAS HOLD 'EM, TEA PARTY STYLE

Bob Moser

Texans, as everybody knows, relish nothing more than a big, bloody showdown. And the 2010 Republican primary for governor has long had Lone Star denizens licking their chops. Two-term Governor Rick Perry, the ruggedly handsome successor to George W. Bush, would be squaring off on March 2 against the state's most popular politician, Senator Kay Bailey Hutchison. The two are longtime rivals for supremacy within the Texas GOP, standard-bearers of the party's two competing wings: right and righter.

The stakes looked larger than control of the Texas GOP. With the national Republican Party reeling from the shellacking it took in 2008, Hutchison vs. Perry shaped up as a symbolic battle for the soul—and future—of the party. Hutchison, a former Houston newscaster and state treasurer, embodies the politer, Chamber of Commerce style of conservatism. Nominally pro-choice, she's long talked about building a more "inclusive" party—one that could continue to dominate in a minority-white state. Perry, a Christian conservative ideologue, lucked into the gubernatorial job by serving as lieutenant governor when the U.S. Supreme Court appointed his mentor to the presidency—and he's since shown no interest in giving it up, though he is the longest-serving governor in state history. If he prevailed over Hutchison, who in early 2009 led him by as much as twenty-five points in early polling among likely GOP voters, it would be a victory for the more rock-ribbed "whiter and brighter" wing of the party.

It was gonna be a humdinger. But, as tends to happen in Texas, several funny things have occurred to shift the race in unexpected directions. First, Perry catapulted over Hutchison in the polls after making himself an MSNBC laughingstock—and talk-radio hero—by going all George Wallace at last year's tax day Tea Party rallies, bellowing "states' rights, states' rights, states' rights!" and flirting with the notion that Texas might respond to President Obama's "socialism" by seceding from the Union. Meanwhile, Hutchison fumbled her way through 2009. The lowlight: She announced that she would resign from the Senate in October or November to run full time for governor—and then, with her poll numbers sagging, she informed Texans last fall that she would stay in the Senate after all and campaign part time for governor, because she had discovered a solemn duty to stay put and defeat health-care reform and cap-and-trade legislation. The message: I want to be your governor, kind of.

The funniest twist of all? The long-anticipated two-person race has—almost overnight—turned into a three-person free-for-all, with a first-time candidate, a Ron Paul apostle named Debra Medina, riding a grassroots Tea Party movement from obscurity into contention. Medina, whose two campaign planks are "state sovereignty" and abolishing property taxes (in a state that already has no income tax), has managed the considerable feat of staking out a place to the right of Perry. From 4 percent in November's polls, Medina had surged by early February to within striking distance of Hutchison and a spot in a likely runoff with Perry. Perry's cry for "states' rights" has proven no match, on the vast far right of the Texas GOP, for Medina's call, at a now infamous "Sovereignty or Secession" rally, for the "tree of freedom" to once again be "watered with the blood of tyrants and patriots."

So Texas Republicans' choice on March 2 is now between right, righter and rightest. Thanks to Medina's growing support, a runoff in mid-April is almost guaranteed, since you can't win the nomination without more than 50 percent of the vote. Awaiting the tattered victor in November will be the strongest Democratic candidate the state has seen since the late, lamented Governor Ann Richards: Bill White, a former under-secretary of energy in the Clinton administration and popular mayor of Houston. White, who'd originally been campaigning to replace Hutchison for her Senate seat, announced his switch to the governor's race just after Thanksgiving. Since then, he has out-fundraised both Hutchison and Perry as he cruises to a near-certain landslide victory in the Democratic primary over Farouk Shami, a Palestinian immigrant and hair-care mogul. And then Medina tripped over her momentum the second week of February, telling Glenn Beck that she wasn't convinced the 9/11 conspiracy theory of involvement by the U.S. government had been disproved. The novice candidate quickly began damage control, saying that of course Muslim terrorists had attacked the World Trade Center. But to many, her comments to Beck and the right-wing guru's quick dismissal of her were sure signs that Medina was nuts—and that her ability to build beyond the hard-core right of the base might be limited.

Confused? Welcome, then, to the head-spinning world of Texas politics, circa 2010. Molly Ivins once famously called the state the "national laboratory for bad government." Just as aptly, you could call it America's home of political lunacy. And it's never been more loony than it is right now, especially on the Republican side.

Shortly after 3:00 p.m. on Super Bowl Sunday, far out in the right-wing suburbs of Houston, Rick Perry and Sarah Palin—fresh from her palm-reading appearance at the National Tea Party Convention—took the stage to wild stomps and cheers from a nearly all-white crowd of thousands in a multi–high school arena. Palin, lavishly decked out in a black velvet coat and red suede boots, was on hand to shore up Perry's flagging support among Tea Party types, whom he'd been losing to the upstart Medina, and to amplify the central themes of his campaign: Washington is the worst, and Texas is the greatest!

Perry, warming up the crowd for Palin, cut right to the chase: "Do you want a leader who loves Texas and all it stands for?" he asked. "Or do you want a creature of Washington who tears down Texas at every turn?"

From the beginning of his campaign against Hutchison, Washington-bashing has been Perry's main script. His campaign has been dedicated to painting Hutchison as a "creature of Washington," while he shines as the stimulus-rejecting, Texas-first rebel preventing her from bringing big-spending socialism to Austin.

"Fact is," Perry hollered, "Texas is better off than might near any state I can think of." Campaign videos that had been playing on large screens behind the stage had been making that very case, touting the state's high ranking as a "business friendly" destination (no great surprise, given its low taxes and nearly union-free labor force). While unemployment has risen sharply in Texas over the past two years, it's still lower than the national average—another statistic Perry trumpets at every opportunity. And the state managed to balance its budget in 2009—another thing Perry boasts about, even though the federal stimulus money that he fiercely protested was the only thing that kept Texas in the black.

By all other measures, Perry's tenure as governor has been disastrous for the state. The high school dropout rate has climbed to nearly 30 percent. More than one-quarter of Texans have no health insurance. Thanks to a flurry of deregulation Perry pushed through the legislature, Lone Star Staters pay some of the highest utility and homeowners' insurance rates in the country. Compared with Perry, George W. Bush was a raving liberal as governor.

None of which mattered a whit to the suburbanites who'd come out to see Sarah and cheer Perry's Tea Party–lite message. Introducing Palin, Perry stuck to his theme: "I doubt there is a political figure in our country who gives liberals a bigger case of hives," he said. The folks were delighted by this. "If Keith Olbermann were here today, I bet his head would explode," Perry said, chuckling merrily. "I'm sorry—that image just really tickles me."

Palin—reading from a written script—faithfully echoed Perry's "Washington bad/Texas good" theme, saying that his reelection would "send Washington a message about how things can be done right." The choice is between "the Texas way or the Washington way," she said. "When Washington came calling, he told 'em thanks but no thanks," Palin said, referring to the stimulus funds, which of course came anyway.

This was the message that had lifted Perry above Hutchison throughout 2009. But while Perry still wows 'em in the well-off burbs, he is hardly the ideal candidate for down-and-dirty Tea Partiers, who see him—with plenty of justification—as a "corporate-handout, say-one-thing-and-mean-another candidate," in the words of Phillip Martin, a blogger for the popular liberal Burnt Orange Report.

"Perry has been able to tap into the antigovernment movement that has existed in Texas for a long time," Martin says. "But that support is a mile wide and an inch deep."

Hard-core right-wingers long ago caught on to the fact that Perry's campaigns have been heavily financed by big corporate interests, most notably the state's powerful home-building lobby. And the excesses of his Texas Enterprise Fund, a $363 million "job creation" fund that has doled out huge chunks of money to Perry campaign contributors like Countrywide Financial, the disgraced subprime-mortgage megalith, have been widely reported. The governor suffered another embarrassment in January, when the *Dallas Morning News* reported on a campaign program in which Texans were being paid to set up "Perry Home Headquarters" and round up folks who'd commit to voting for him. One of the most profitable operations, netting $13,440, was being run by an El Paso woman with a rap sheet including a felony drug conviction and a misdemeanor assault.

Hutchison, who has never offered a convincing rationale for her campaign, has been unable to capitalize on Perry's foibles. Her occasional breaks with the right—supporting *Roe v. Wade*, voting to expand the Children's Health Insurance Program, backing some forms of embryonic stem cell research—have made the senator look down-right "pink" to many in the Republican base.

Hutchison is most popular with moderates—not with the folks who'll turn out for a Republican primary. After spending much of 2009 losing ground to Perry with her halfhearted campaign, she had a chance to regain her footing when the candidates met for two tele-vised debates in January. But the senator was tripped up, on both occasions, by the same direct question: Would she support overturning *Roe v. Wade*?

In the first debate, January 14, Hutchison's repeated refusal to answer yes or no prompted gales of derisive laughter from the audience. In the second debate, conducted January 29 without an audience, she was shown a video of her comedic turn—and again refused to answer the question. She had fallen straight into Perry's trap, sounding like a compromised Washingtonian.

"Hutchison has tried to be a big-tent Republican, at least in Texas terms," says Harvey Kronberg, a longtime state-government observer who publishes the online Quorum Report. "Talk-radio doesn't want her, Tea Parties don't want her. The base of the party doesn't want to be a big tent."

All of which should have Perry sitting pretty. Except that, out of nowhere, a far purer champion of the Tea Party right has arisen.

The day before the Perry-Palin spectacle, in the working-class North Texas town of Cleburne, a few hundred folks assembled in the front lot of the Forrest Chevrolet dealership, situated along a butt-ugly stretch of industrial highway, waiting for hours in a cold, whip-ping wind, waving yellow "Don't Tread on Me" flags and cheering any mention of their newly minted hero.

Few Texans had ever heard of Debra Medina before the Janu-ary 14 GOP debate. No surprise there: Her only elected office has been chair of the Wharton County Republican Party. But, given the opportunity to face off with Perry and Hutchison, Medina immedi-ately established herself as the real deal for right-wing Texans. While the senator equivocated and the governor mugged for the cameras and came across as ill informed and ill prepared, Medina—a sturdy-framed, plain-faced homeschooler who runs a small medical-billing business in South Texas—dished up red meat for the Republican right in a straight-shooting and surprisingly confident manner that made her a folk hero overnight.

A debate panelist, noting that Medina was known for carrying a handgun in her car, asked her if she also carried it into the grocery store when she went shopping. "I'd like to, but I don't," Medina responded. When Perry nervously evaded a question about what federal programs he'd like to nullify, Medina said matter-of-factly that she would start with health-care reform if it passed. Throughout the debate, she offered a simple but consistent message, oft-repeated: "restoring true private property rights and gun ownership."

Medina immediately shot into double digits in the polls. It didn't hurt a bit when she subsequently characterized Perry as a "jumpy, fidgety frat boy" or when, before the second debate, she issued a press release calling the governor's claims of fiscal responsibility "bullshit." When she gave another poised, pointed performance in the second (and final) debate, Medina began to edge toward Hutchison in the polls.

The third-wheel campaign has clearly benefited from Perry's and Hutchison's expensive crossfire of attack ads. "She's telling all of Texas how bad *he* is, and he's telling all of Texas how bad *she* is," Medina says. "And I'm going, Yeah, they're right. They're both bad."

Medina's platform is as thin as her political experience. But in the Tea Party universe, there's nothing so appealing as someone who's never held office—and never had to grapple with, or vote on, complicated issues that don't align perfectly with a straight-up ideology. Medina's answer to almost every problem is automatic: Leave it to the free market. At a Dallas forum on the first Saturday in February, before she made the journey to Cleburne, Medina was asked what she'd do to improve the state's wretched public schools. Easy: "We have to have the courage, I think, to tear down the sacred walls that we've erected around the public school monopoly and force competition into that."

And what about her proposal to replace property taxes with sales taxes, another audience member asked. Wouldn't that hurt lower-income folks? "Well, everything is regressive," Medina answered. Food and medicine, she suggested, might be exempted to avoid "creating a taxing structure that is oppressive."

All of which, in the twisted world of Tea Party Texans, makes her a populist. And while Perry's populism is transparently calculated, and Hutchison's is nonexistent, Medina speaks straight to the guts of disaffected Republicans.

At the Chevrolet lot in Cleburne, she showed how it's done. If "we get government off the backs of Texans," Medina said, "we're not gonna have an economic crisis. We're not gonna have an energy crisis. We're not gonna have an immigration crisis."

"Do not allow the seeds of fear and doubt to take root in your life," Medina told the cheering guns-and-camo crowd. "This is a time unlike any other time in our history, where we're gonna stand up and accomplish a revolution without shedding a drop of blood." Unless, of course, bloodshed becomes necessary.

Medina also has an independent streak that alternately perplexes and delights her fans. She supports a moratorium on death sentences in Texas. She talks at length about her disgust with the border wall running through South Texas, which "does nothing but consume private property and waste resources." She speaks passionately about bringing her husband's fellow Hispanics into the Republican fold, saying that Perry's failure to do so "almost makes me cry."

The occasional deviations from Republican orthodoxy don't appear to bother Medina's fans. Her lack of poll-tested positions is what draws them to her. "It's that sense of honesty," says Antoinette Walker of Dallas. "Don't tell us everything is roses," Walker says. "If somebody says it's all nice, and this is the best state—it's a lie. It's a lie."

While Perry will likely withstand Medina's challenge, her candidacy is shifting the Texas GOP even further right. But the state as a whole is moving in the opposite direction, thanks largely to demographic shifts. While John McCain carried Texas in 2008, the State House of Representatives—which had gone whole-hog Republican earlier in the decade—was nearly recaptured by Democrats, who now dominate the state's fast-growing, rapidly diversifying urban areas. In 2010 the Republicans will probably hold on to Texas. But the internecine war among the Tea Party crowd is a grim omen for the party's long-term future. If Rick Perry isn't right enough for Texas Republicans, they're headed straight off an ideological cliff.

—*February 18, 2010*

Editor's Note: Rick Perry did win Texas's gubernatorial primary in March, capturing over 50 percent of the vote and avoiding a runoff with Kay Bailey Hutchison. He heads into the general election to face Bill White.

LABOR AND THE TEA PARTIES

Laura Flanders, Ed Ott, and Michael Johns

Laura Flanders: The turnout was—let's just say it—small, but the scene at the international auto show in Detroit Monday was still interesting. On the one side of the street, Tea Party activists protesting the bailout for the auto industry. On the other side of the street, labor union members organized to protest the Tea Partiers.

Listen in and both agree that the country is in dire straits and folks are in desperate need of jobs. Given that, our question is this: Where exactly do the Tea Party activists and the labor people part ways, and why? If everyone's talking jobs and families and the evils of uncaring elites, where's the divide?

We're joined by one of the organizers of the Detroit Tea Party rally, Michael Johns. He's one of the national founders and leaders of the Tea Party movement. He's also a Heritage Foundation policy analyst and a former speechwriter to President George H.W. Bush.

We're also joined by labor leader Ed Ott, distinguished lecturer at the Murphy Institute School of Professional Studies at the City University of New York and former executive director of the New York City Central Labor Council.

Welcome both; thrilled to have you. Tell us a little bit of background, each of you. Ed, what brings you to where you are today?

Ed Ott: I've actually I've been an activist in the labor movement for forty years, dealing with a lot of the issues that the American working people care about. Everything from taxes to housing to jobs, which is a big concern right now. I'm very concerned with the rights of workers, particularly low-paid workers.

LF: And you grew up where?

EO: I grew up in the Bronx, actually—last twenty years I've been living in Jersey.

LF: And what about you, what brings you to this place?

Michael Johns: Well, I mean, over the last year I've been engaged with the leadership and development of the national Tea Party movement. I've been involved in politics and public policy for about twenty-five years. But I don't think, Laura, that I've seen at any juncture during that duration this level of grassroots angst and opposition to the direction this country's taken.

LF: And where did you grow up?

MJ: I actually grew up in a very blue-collar area myself, Allentown, Pennsylvania, you know, and watched a lot of the manufacturing industry there wither away and never felt good about that, you know. So that was kind of my origin.

LF: A year ago, at the auto show, labor unions were out making their complaints about what was going on. Forgive me if I'm being naïve here, but at least some of what I heard there sounds not unlike some of what I heard from the Tea Party. What's your beef, and how would you distinguish it from theirs?

MJ: Well you know as I've seen this movement develop, I would say there's been disagreement about how to develop prosperity in the country, how to grow jobs. I think you'd find in the Tea Party movement more of an appreciation for the role that the free market can and has historically played in economic growth and job creation. The issue in Detroit really was [as much] with the mortgage bailout as it was with the bank bailout…. We feel this federal government is vastly overextended, and it's setting precedents that become unconstitutional and very damaging and dangerous for the country.

LF: So your fundamental beef is with constitutional overreach, executive overreach.

EO: I think in some cases it's even the same people in both movements, but where we part ways, if you get down to the issue of jobs, from our view, government has abdicated its responsibility to keep jobs in the country. Every year since 1997 this country has lost jobs, they've gone overseas, you can count them. They've destroyed a middle class standard for labor for over 100 years now.

LF: Detroit headlines reveal 50 percent unemployment.

EO: But here's the difference: The difference is, when they talk about free markets and free trade (to be fair, if you look at the Tea Party groups, these ideas vary from place to place; it's not a uniform, highly centralized movement), but a lot of their folks talk about they're for free trade. But it's exactly free trade we oppose. We are looking for fair trade. We're not afraid of trade. This is the city that was Alexander Hamilton's city, we've been a trading city from day one; we'll trade anything from goods to stocks. But the truth of the matter is, we want to have it regulated, so that it's fair to the American worker. The excuse of trading was used to undermine standards that it took us too long to set.

LF: How about that, Michael? I mean FreedomWorks and some of the organizations that work with you and the Tea Party movement are backed by corporations like Koch industries and Scaife who have been advocating for less regulation in corporations and looser labor laws here and around the world.

MJ: There's no denying the underlying, fundamental fact that the middle class of this country is hurting in a significant way. We are losing industries to foreign countries, we are having a very difficult time competing in the global economy and there's a whole bunch of reasons for why that's happening. Number one is that, we just don't make it very easy for companies to do business in this country. And by that I mean, we are a highly regulated society, we are one of the highest taxed countries in the world as far as corporate taxation goes. Obviously I think it's reasonable to expect good wages in this country, but it's a difficult challenge when you're against countries that are paying five dollars and less per hour.

EO: We wouldn't see the issue as taxes. If it was taxes, you couldn't explain the German economy, which kept much more of its productive base. Their taxes were as high or higher than ours over the last twenty years. The truth of the matter is it was corporate greed. I think many corporations in this country have in fact played a seditious role. They have systematically undermined the economic base of their own country so they could make more money, and the problem with government, both parties, was they allowed a set of laws to be instituted that provided incentives to take your capital offshore—take your jobs off shore—and it destroyed things that it took the labor movement and working people years to build. A hundred years ago, industrial jobs were dirty, dangerous, and insecure, and it was organized labor, workers standing up for themselves, that made them a middle class standard. Nobody gave us anything.

LF: But I'm hearing a critique from you too about government over-reach—overreach in helping corporations take jobs abroad.

EO: We've had a net export of jobs. The government was responsible. We both have a healthy distrust of government—the labor movement *and* the Tea Party movement. The difference is we want to define the responsible role of government in the preservation of the things we worked hard to build.

LF: But Michael, there were even people within the Tea Party movement in Michigan who were saying, Well, why are you bringing your complaint to the auto industry? We need jobs and the spending you're complaining about has helped to create jobs right here in Detroit.

MJ: We would definitely question [whether] jobs have been created through this government intervention. One of the great indisputable points of the last year is that the TARP or the stimulus efforts, this is not he way jobs are typically created. Where I do agree, is that certainly there has been an issue of corporate greed, and I don't think, as conservatives, or libertarians or market-oriented people that we need to be bashful in acknowledging that has been damaging to this country. And I don't think our country has properly incentivized American businesses to stay here, meaning on a strictly fiduciary basis…

LF: How do you incentivize employers to pay living wages?

MJ: Well the first thing you do is get away from over-regulating, over-taxing, and entering into unfair trade agreements. I think the Tea Party movement would appreciate the fact that not all trade agreements are good trade agreements.

LF: So the Tea Parties would oppose the next round of free trade agreements?

MJ: No, I think you wouldn't find they would identify trade in and of itself as the problem. However, I think the point that would be conceded is that when we are competing with countries that have substandard labor standards and don't provide wages to their employees, and subsidize their industries—that isn't really fair.

EO: This is where it gets kind of confusing, because the truth of the matter is the solutions to that problem lie in government. It's an international question. Workers shouldn't subsidize free markets with low wages and poverty. And that was what the American labor movement was all about and that was what the European movement was all about.

There are people who argued for free markets and no regulation, and there are places in the world where that pretty much exists: Port-au-Prince, Haiti. None of these guys who advocate for free markets are going there on vacation, they're going to Paris. Good healthy doses of socialism, a little bit of regulation, and clean streets, they really like it. A lot of times you've really got to draw out for people where we're trying to get. I was giving a talk to labor unions last year describing the country as at the intersection between hope and disaster.

LF: One of the things that you said at the time on this program is that working people need to do more than plead with this administration; they need to organize. And I hate to point out statistics, but looking at the polls you've got approval of the labor movement down in the 40s—at least some polls. When you ask people about some abstract concept of a Tea Party movement that would be for cutting taxes and opposing the government stimulus, that brings in about 40 percent too.

EO: Because I think we've gone through about thirty-five years of wage suppression in this country. We have removed the rights of workers to organize and frankly it's been a policy of both business and government, since brother Ronald Reagan, to weaken organized labor, which is the single best protection workers have to keep their standards up. The other piece of that, that's very, very difficult, is our members support tax cuts almost across the board, because it's the only way they can get a raise. If the government is involved in wage suppression, tax cuts make sense. If I can get another $500 a year in my pocket because of tax cuts, I'm going to be for it. And you very rarely see a labor leader, particularly a private sector leader, oppose that notion.

LF: Do you feel that the Tea Parties are stepping into a vacuum left by a labor movement?

MJ: No, I believe what were seeing is just unprecedented national rage toward the direction of the country. I think that's bringing in a whole new political coalition.

LF: One of the groups that's being brought in, Michael, are those who have a beef with Obama because of his race. Those people, coming out there carrying billboards, screaming to the skies, is that in the national interest?

MJ: Absolutely not. I don't think there's any room for that in any political movement. I guess when you bring in 5 million or so to the biggest rallies around the country, and I pointed out earlier it's a heavily top-down managed movement. You're going to have that periodic craziness.

LF: I haven't heard anybody get up there and say, I don't want you here if you're here because you believe in white supremacy.

MJ: I would be the first one to do that. In fact, there's a guy down in Texas who is the only person I've seen who had a sign of that nature, and I really wish he would walk away, because that is not at all what this movement is about. I've been easily outspoken at fifteen Tea Parties, some of the largest ones including here in New York City. I've never seen that sentiment expressed. In fact there's a reasonably growing African-American involvement in the Tea Party movement.

LF: Yet in your own columns, you raise the question of Obama's birth certificate...

MJ: You know, I think that issue is one of transparency, and I think that's a broad concern that many Americans have with this administration. To that extent we spent about $5 million [and] we've got over ten federal courts suppressing documents related to the first thirty years of his life, and I think a lot of Americans legitimately ask what's that about. And that's simply something, I think the onus is on this president and this administration to put to that issue to rest. I haven't heard an explanation as to what they think they're buying with that $5 million in legal fees, in suppressing those documents.

EO: I think it's nonsense when the left brings it up about McCain; I think it's nonsense when the right brings it up about Obama. Both of these guys are qualified Americans and ready to be president. The question for the American people at that point was who's it going to be? I got to tell you, I will not judge these large movements on their fringes, they're going to be judged in the end on what they want to accomplish. It's easy for the right and the left to rally people around what they don't like. Their fun begins as they try to define where they want to go.

LF: Sarah Palin will be one of the keynote speakers at the Nashville Tea Partiers Convention. Palin doesn't scream to me serious commitment to deep thinking about how to move the country forward.

MJ: I think that's probably at the end of the day going to be proven a misperception. I think having worked in the White House and having worked on campaigns, when you come out of a campaign where you lost and you lost big time, and you're [McCain campaign director] Steve Schmidt, and your fingerprints are all over that, the easiest thing to do is turn around and blame other people for it.

LF: Particularly a woman, if you don't mind me saying so.

MJ: That was a legitimate point that was raised… that the two people that took the heaviest hits were Hillary Clinton and Sarah Palin…. To be sure, is Sarah Palin the most distinguished expert on global affairs and national security? No, those are not the issues she's dealt with in Alaska. Those are not the issues that Barack Obama has dealt with, either.

LF: Is there anything here that could ultimately bring these two constituencies, maybe not the leaders, but the constituencies together?

EO: I just want to touch on Sarah Palin. I'm not a hater. I don't think she was ready to be president. But I would agree with you. A whole lot of people started pointing fingers after the campaign. I want to see how Sarah Palin develops, but her popularity has nothing to with her intellectual underpinnings. She's the local girl done good. That's her real appeal on the street, and you feel it even among union women, who look at her and say, Hey, come on, you've had a jerk president up there for eight years named Bush who is dumber than she is, why is she getting unfair treatment?

LF: Looking forward, it seems working people didn't get what they want from health care, they're not getting what they want out of the escalation of the war in Afghanistan, more deployments of their kids. What's going to change this picture?

EO: You saw [AFL-CIO Executive Director] Richard Trumka out there yesterday articulating what's beginning to bubble up from the base of labor movement, which is the sense that *we* put the Democrats in (from the labor side it was almost a universal agreement), if they don't produce they will replicate the disasters of the congressional elections during the Clinton years in 1994—I can see it coming. The problem we have with Republicans is they borrow money with no intentions of giving it back. The Democrats never do what they say they're going to do.

LF: I bet you weren't going to expect this, but you've got the last word.

MJ: I think this has been a bipartisan consensus of blame that goes around Washington. In fact, the big spending issues are the ones you associate with little Democrats. The Tea Party movement is not about a political party. I mean, there is legitimate concern about the Bush administration (that's when this movement came to). To the extent that the middle-income, working men and women of this country are not doing well, I think there is a common denominator to build consensus across the lines.

LF: All right, you heard it here, I thank you both. We're going to send cameras out to your next rally, and I want to see the slap-down of that guy with the racist banner.

MJ: I have to find the guy first.

—January 12, 2010

PART TWO: TOXIC TEA

WHAT'S WITH THE CRYING?

Laura Flanders, Alexander Zaitchik, and Rick Perlstein

Glenn Beck: *Come on, follow me, no matter where you are from, our studio audience here in midtown Manhattan, to the sidewalks outside to the people all over the country. But the show isn't about me; it's not about the president; it's not about parties or politics or anything else. It is about proving that the real power to change America's course still resides with you, you are the secret, you're the answer [crying]. I'm sorry. I just love my country and I fear for it.*
—Fox News, March 13, 2009

Laura Flanders: It's all about you, and what's with the crying? A whole lot of people mocked Glenn Beck for that performance and oh how I personally wish it were that simple. It's not. Glenn Beck has built an empire and it's speaking to millions on television, on radio, through live events and rallies, and through six supposedly bestselling books. Our next guests are going to try to drill down into Glenn Beck. Excuse the expression. One is the author of a brand new, very unofficial, biography, *Common Nonsense*; Alexander Zaitchik is a freelance reporter for AlterNet, among other things. And Rick Perlstein is with us from Chicago: he's the much-famed and award-winning Goldwater-era historian, the author of *Before the Storm* and *Nixonland*. Let's start with you, Alex. What's with the crying?

Alexander Zaitchik: Well, it's a question that maybe isn't as easy to answer as it seems. Clearly there's a theatrical element here, where Beck is hamming it up, it's not quite authentic. He also is a very emotional guy which is one thing that came through from talking to his colleagues over the years, which comes through in the biographical sections of the book.

LF: Did he ever give you an interview?

AZ: No, he never did.

LF: What about that emotional content, Rick? That's familiar for you from a lot of people you studied, [from] forty years ago, fifty years ago now.

Rick Perlstein: It goes back to tent revivals and Billy Sunday and people whose job it is to get lots and lots of people very, very emotional and ready to sign their lives over for a cause. I mean, these are very old tropes, these are very old techniques. He's doing something that's very, very old and very, very time-tested.

LF: Let's go back for those who don't know Glenn Beck, maybe haven't ever checked him out on Fox News channel. What does his empire look like today, Alex? Radio? Television? What else?

AZ: Publishing is the second largest component. People don't realize that. They think of him as the Fox guy, but it's actually radio, publishing, with Fox all the way down at the end of the revenue pyramid of something like $200,000,000 each year out of 32-plus million. So it's extremely diverse. He's also got the stage shows, which you mentioned, he's got this "Insider Extreme" program on his website which streams six different angles every day which people pay extra money for the benefit of viewing. It's this octopus that is constantly growing tentacles out in new, interesting directions. He's very conscious of himself as a media pioneer.

LF: He's also conscious of himself, as I read in your book, as a kind of, well, someone following in the tradition of Orson Welles. Talk a little about his background, his history, where the heck he came from.

AZ: Right. Well, according to his own story, as he tells it, he traces his interest and love for radio back to a collection of classic radio from the golden era, *The Golden Days of Radio* that his mother gave him as a child. He was bowled over by Orson Welles's *War of the Worlds*. That sort of sparked his imagination. When it came time to start his company, he turned to Welles's Mercury to start his own Mercury Radio Arts, so that's a clear nod to Welles. That's something people love to explore, how much of it is just an act, how much of it is dramatic radio. I think that's certainly an element but it would be wrong to chalk it up just to that.

LF: You think it's theater, Rick? Is it as they say, just theater, just performance?

RP: It's fascinating that he should chose *War of the Worlds* as his template, because that was one of the greatest acts of sector feud and flim-flammery, of course. People thought that something that was fake was real. So I think that he's dissolving these lines with a sedulous and careful self-consciousness. There's an interview he gave—which Alexander can speak more on—in *Fortune* magazine, where he talked about how he sees his customers basically as rubes, as marks. A lot of conservatives' demagogues treat their constituency like suckers, like carnival barkers treat people who come up to pay them money and take their chances.

LF: It's interesting that you mention carnival barkers, because maybe a contemporary equivalent to the carnival barker is what Beck was on "morning zoo" radio. Here's a clip from Glenn Beck and his partner on a "morning zoo" show in Phoenix.

[Clip]

The new morning zoo keepers Glenn Beck and Tim Hattrick!

Young Glenn Beck: *We call our bosses right up front. We don't all need gimmicks to sell the new Y95!*

Tim Hattrick: *We've got a better mix of music. Great DJs. That don't yak too much*

GB: *Plenty of easy content for you to win lots of free money.*

TH: *And more continuous music.*

GB: *Visit us, Glenn and Tim, Y95 Airborne Traffic Report. And Special Zoo Guests. With all that talk, who needs gimmicks?*

LF: What did Glenn Beck learn in "morning zoo" radio?

AZ: He learned the art of publicity; it sits in his blood in a way that it only is for someone who has grown up in FM radio. Especially in the 1980s. That period was known for very intense ratings wars because at the beginning of deregulation stations were being bought and sold very quickly for quick profits for the first time ever. So you had people flipping stations and format changes happening overnight. Beck was in the middle of that. He learned that you had to get attention pretty quick if you were going to have a job the next day.

LF: He used some pretty sleazy tactics to get that attention. There's one story that you tell in your book about him calling a rival's wife…

AZ: He was getting clobbered in the ratings by his old friend Bruce Kelly whom he knew from a previous market. And he was trying to get attention from Kelly, hoping to get mentioned on his show. He was pulling all sorts of stunts. At some point, out of desperation, and cruelty, he called his wife live on the air and asked her about her recent miscarriage that she had had. He didn't last too much longer in the market after that. One point I think is important to note is this is the culture that Glenn Beck matured in. For almost twenty years he was successful to varying degrees in what was an aggressively infantile, non-intellectual culture. He did not talk about anything besides Milli Vanilli and Britney Spears raffles until his late thirties.

LF: You can say that maturing in "morning zoo" radio was kind of a contradiction in terms. How did he get into politics?

AZ: He was bottoming out in Top 40 radio and he realized he was not going to reach the level of success that he hoped he would in that format. In the mid-'90s Clear Channel was beginning to enjoy the fruits of deregulation. It was growing rapidly, talk radio was becoming big business, and he decided to switch tracks. Through a couple of lucky breaks he was able to land a radio show in Tampa in 1999 and he started talking politics, which he was awful at, by the way. He was very close to getting fired from his first talk-radio gig.

LF: There was a news event that he realized would be his ticket to the future. That was the election of 2000.

AZ: The recount.

LF: Rick, coming to you, clearly this is a very contemporary story. Is the kind of power that a man like Glenn Beck can wield today comparable to the folks you studied in the '60s, or is it a whole new world of power and influence?

RP: It's interesting you use the word "contemporary." I'm not sure how contemporary it is, actually. It's really more like an eternal return. Ever since the 1920s when you had a nativist movement that seized an enormous amount of power and basically ran the state of Indiana and dictated our immigration policies in the 1920s through McCarthyism in the 1950s through the John Birch Society and those elements in the 1960s. You've had the same sort of right-wing popu-list energies bubbling beneath the surface. Sometimes bursting out to the surface. Now what's different, and what's interesting, is that the rhetoric is the same, the stories are the same (the characters changed: communists then and Muslims now), but what really has changed now from the '60s is the media vectors. Since you have Fox News, and much more importantly, since you have a mainstream media that's basically willing to give a hearing to anyone who repre-sents "one of the sides of the debate," since every media discussion is framed in terms of "he said, she said," they are always on the look-out for those who claim to be the voice of the authentic, right-wing, heartland folks. So that has changed enormously. You have the same sort of energies given much wider currency in the mainstream for two reasons. One is because of the media shifts I have mentioned, but the other is because through most of this [earlier] period, you had people on the right and in the Republican Party who were censoring the extremists. You had the William F. Buckleys who basically were willing to say, This person is an illegitimate voice in our movement. Those people are gone. David Frum tried to serve the role that Wil-liam F. Buckley would serve in the '60s and '70s and '80s and '90s, and he was completely ignored. He was completely laughed off the stage by other people on the right.

LF: So that speaks to the whole idea of same reactionaries, different reaction. Is it Murdoch's doing that Glenn Beck has the power to in-timidate, not just to be laughed off?

AZ: Well, Murdoch certainly has Beck's back. He's gone on record as defending some of his more extreme comments. It flows down from there. Everyone at Fox has Beck's back as do those at Premier Radio Networks, who syndicate him.

LF: Even after Beck's show lost most of its advertisers and 200 companies signed on to boycott advertising...

AZ: It's something like the public television of right-wing ideological media at this point, with foundations and *The Weekly Standard* [as the primary advertisers]. This brings up the question, Exactly what is he viewed as? Is he just a revenue-generating machine or is he viewed as something much more valuable and hard to put a price on?

LF: Well, what do you think?

AZ: I think there is something to be said for Beck's former self-designation as rodeo clown. He is an extremely good distracter, and he's also very good at getting the left to waste a lot of time talking about him. I mean, we're talking about him now.

LF: But that's the question. Rick, how much attention to pay to this guy?

RP: You raise a paradoxical and difficult issue. On the Murdoch thing, I think part of it is when you are a billionaire and you aspire to be one of the rulers of the universe, you don't want to lose space, and you're an arrogant person and you want control, so you don't want anyone else telling you what to do. So some of this might be just sheer stubborn pride. On the other hand, there's the possibility that ultimately the game here is providing a clear shot for unregulated big-business capitalism. Glenn Beck does a very good job, as does Rush Limbaugh, of destroying any kind of constituency—popular constituency—at the grassroots in the heartland for people to resist the rule of money.

I was riding a bus the other day and a guy had [right-wing syndicated talk host] Michael Savage on the bus radio. He was obviously a working class guy and we got into a discussion about Michael Savage. He said, "You're not one of those liberals who thinks rich people and the bosses are all evil?" I was like, well, gee.. Do you get vacation time? Do you get health care? He's working for the man. That really wouldn't happen without the rodeo clowns like Rush Limbaugh and Glenn Beck telling this guy a story about who the enemy is. There's a lot going on. To pretend that it's easy to understand would be very flip.

LF: Glenn Beck is very clear where the threats are. He identifies them for his audience in pretty shocking ways. Take this clip from early August 2010:

[Clip]
Barack Obama: *From all you've done to fight for jobs, to fight for tax cuts for the middle class, to fight for reforms that will reign in the special interests, and the type of policies that will not only rebuild this economy but put us on a long-term path...*

Glenn Beck: *Special interests! What planet have I landed on? Did I slip through a wormhole in the middle of the night and this looks like America? It's like the damn* Planet of the Apes!

LF: Joan Walsh of *Salon* pointed out, Rick, that in your own book on the '60s you write about *Planet of the Apes*. In what context?

RP: Right. Well, white folks are always afraid of the dark hordes taking over and usurping their power. Just as an example I was looking through the archives in the Lyndon Johnson library, and they had a file of all the hate literature that was being circulated [against LBJ] during the 1964 presidential election. You can very easily see the 1964 version of Photoshop, showing Lyndon Johnson shaking hands with some African tribal chief. The same tropes, the same fear of being engulfed by the "dirty hordes." In the case of *Planet of the Apes*, that was a fantasy of what would have happened if the apes ruled the humans, if the blacks ruled the whites. That seems to be part of the cultural unconscious that Beck's accessing. Of course, it's not a particularly sophisticated analysis of *Planet of the Apes*, because in *Planet of the Apes* the apes were civilized and humans were the ones who destroyed the world.

LF: Alex, why does stuff like this cow Democratic politicians and their supporters? It used to be that people understood the nature of a reactionary. A reactionary is going to object to absolutely everything you want to do, get used to it! Democrats with this administration seem to be not sure of themselves. Maybe there's something there that they have to worry about at the polls. Talk about the degree to which you think people who are not looking for Glenn Beck's viewers' votes should work at trying to understand what's going on. Maybe we're just overthinking.

AZ: I think that's a position that's certainly worth taking seriously. The idea that this is a whole lot of sound and fury and ultimately is not going to have a lot of real world impact. The November elections will help clarify that to some extent. Until then I'm sympathetic that this is an overblown media bogeyman. The Tea Party movement maybe doesn't deserve as much energy and critical thought and attention as we've been giving it. At the same time, anytime you have a populist movement that can get tens of thousands of people out into the streets carrying what are very hateful, racist, borderline violent signs, slogans, and imagery, then you have to take that seriously. So we have to find the middle ground.

RP: There's also another very important component: You can't separate it from the history of what's happened in the Democratic Party and the general ideological landscape in the last ten, twenty, thirty years, since the era of Bill Clinton. The world is scary. For an ordinary person trying to make it in America, trying to stay in the middle class, it's always going to be anxiety-producing. There's always going to be anger associated with that. Now, the problem is that traditionally, Democrats, liberals had a populism at hand that they could use to channel that anger into politically progressive directions. The idea was you were being screwed by your boss, that the forces of money were defying you and your family. What's happened with the Democratic Leadership Council world is the Democrats are unilaterally disarming left-wing populism, so if you're angry there is no place for you other than in the Republican Party, other than the Tea Party movement. The Obama world is just about sweet reason, and it doesn't really give you a place to be angry.

LF: Rick Perlstein, thanks so much for joining us; Alexander Zaitchik, thank you both. Lots of books for you to check out. There'll be links at our website, GRITtv.org. Alex's just-out, is *Common Nonsense*, take a look.

—*August 13, 2010*

PUTTING THE SHEETS ON: THE TEA PARTY SHOWS ITS COLORS

Bill Fletcher Jr.

It was just a matter of time, and most black people knew just that. At an anti-health-care-reform rally in Washington, D.C., right-wing demonstrators associated with the so-called "Tea Party" movement verbally assaulted Congressman John Lewis. Calling upon him to vote against the health-care legislation, they chose to use the N-word in describing the congressman.

So now the gloves are off and the sheets are on. The entire pretense regarding an alleged nonracial movement of angry (white) people is gone. What most black people knew all along has been confirmed. Lying only slightly beneath the surface was and is a toxin that has almost nothing to do with health care. One finds one's self reminded of the words of the Rev. Jesse Jackson from more than thirty-five years ago when he was commenting on white opposition to school busing for desegregation: "It's not the bus; it's us." Well, team, the Tea Party opposition, and more particularly the vehemence of it, has more to do with their perception that the USA is no longer in the control of whites, and more specifically, that it does not pay to be white anymore.

Whites' anger about their collapsing lives in the midst of a declining living standard spanning more than thirty years compounded by the immediate crisis of our current Great Recession, has bubbled into all sorts of irrationalist thoughts and behavior, a point I have made in countless columns. Until now, the right-wing Tea Party crowd has attempted to be coy in its crypto-racist attacks on the Obama administration particularly. The use of the so-called Birther movement (those who argue that President Obama was not actually born in the United States and, therefore, is ineligible to be president of the United States) by the right is just one example. The allegations by these lunatics have nothing to do with the facts. It has been demonstrated time and again that Obama was born in the USA. Yet, for the angry white political right, all that matters is that in their minds it is inconceivable that a black person was elected president. Their only answer is that it must have been fraudulent.

Now, however, the Tea Party crowd, in all of its anger and frustration, has let a few things slip. If their opposition to health care had nothing to do with race, then why the use of the N-word? Was it some deep, irresistible impulse that was beyond their control?

Since the gloves are off, progressives, black and nonblack, need to face facts. We cannot treat the Tea Party crowd as simply a set of angry and misled, but otherwise good-natured people. This crowd, as a crowd, constitutes a right-wing, racist movement that must be opposed; in fact, it must be disrupted. Their version of populism may, at times, speak to a legitimate anger felt by many people in the USA as wealth polarizes, and as the Obama administration makes unacceptable compromises with corporate America. But what is really at stake is not that at all. It goes back to the country that they believe they lost.

Here can be found the irony of this situation. We, on the left side of the aisle, recognize that the Obama administration and the majority of the Democratic Congress have been half-stepping in addressing the current economic and environmental crises. In some cases, they have been worse than half-stepping (such as through the escalation of U.S. involvement in Afghanistan). Yet the Tea Party crowd is actually angry about any tendency toward redistribution of wealth in favor of people at the bottom, even when those people at the bottom are themselves or their loved ones. To the extent to which the Tea Party crowd has bought into the notion that health-care reform (in whatever form) is for someone else— specifically, for the so-called undeserving poor, blacks, immigrants, etc.—they line up for war against it. This, it should be noted, is a recurring pattern in U.S. history where large sections of the white population regularly act against their own interests to the extent to which they perceive those interests as being the interests of people of color.

For progressives, the irony increases when we recognize that many of the reforms that the Tea Party crowd opposes are, at best, minimal efforts toward any sort of redistribution, environmental defense, or rule of law. Right-wing populists wish to paint those who have no health care as both undeserving and black or brown, despite the reality of how diverse the health care–less or those with minimal health care may be. Right-wing populists, in general, are not particularly concerned about the deficit either, except and insofar as the deficit is aimed at addressing any of the gross wealth disparities in U.S. society. Their hypocrisy stands tall for all to see whenever there is a war and they are prepared to uncritically support or directly advance the plunging of this country into greater and greater debt, all in the name of patriotism.

What became clear this weekend with the racial epithets as well as the gay-baiting against Congressman Barney Frank by the anti-health-care-reform crowd is that for the right-wing populists the health-care debate was really about the "other America," the one that they believe has come to eclipse them and their dreams.

—June 2010

BECK'S INCENDIARY ANGST IS DANGEROUSLY CLOSE TO HAVING A BODY COUNT

Eric Boehlert

On his Monday radio show, Glenn Beck highlighted claims that before he started targeting a little-known, left-leaning organization called the Tides Foundation on his Fox News TV show, "nobody knew" what the nonprofit was. Indeed, for more than a year Beck has been portraying the progressive organization as a central player in a larger, nefarious cabal of Marxist/socialist/Nazi Obama-loving outlets determined to destroy democracy in America. Beck has routinely smeared the low-profile entity for being staffed by "thugs" and "bullies" and involved in "the nasty of the nastiest," like indoctrinating schoolchildren and creating a "mass organization to seize power."

As Media Matters reported, the conspiratorial host had mentioned (read: attacked) the little-known progressive organization nearly thirty times on his Fox program alone since it premiered in 2009, including several mentions in the last month. (Beck's the only TV talker who regularly references the foundation, according to our Nexis searches.)

So yes, Beck has done all he can to scare the hell out of people about the Tides Foundation and "turn the light of day" onto an organization that actually facilitates nonprofit giving.

And guess what? Everybody in America would have found out about the Tides Foundation last week if Byron Williams had had his way. He's the right-wing, government-hating, gun-toting nut who strapped on his body armor, stocked a pickup truck with guns and ammo, and set off up the California coast to San Francisco in order to start killing employees at the previously obscure Tides Foundation in hopes of sparking a political revolution.

Thankfully, the planned domestic terrorist attack never came to pass, because California Highway Patrol officers pulled Williams over for drunk driving on his way to his killing spree. Williams quickly opened fire, wounding two officers during a lengthy shootout. Luckily, Williams wasn't able to act out the ultimate goal of his dark anger—fueled by the TV news he watched—about how "Congress was railroading through all these left-wing agenda items," as his mother put it. Williams wasn't able to open fire inside the offices of the Tides Foundation, an organization "nobody knew" about until Glenn Beck started targeting it.

And also thankfully, Williams wasn't able to take his place alongside a growing list of domestic, antigovernment terrorists, such as the recent Pentagon shooter, the Holocaust Museum gunman, the kamikaze pilot who flew his plane into an IRS building in Austin, Texas, and the Pittsburgh cop-killer who set up an ambush because he was convinced Obama was going to take away his guns.

All the vigilante attacks appear to have been fueled by an almost pathological hatred for the U.S. government—the same open hatred that right-wing bloggers, AM talk-radio hosts, and Fox News's lineup of antigovernment prophets have been frantically fueling for the last year, pushing doomsday warnings of America's democratic demise under President Obama.

And the sad the sad truth is we're going to see more like Byron Williams. We're going to see more attempts at vigilante violence during the Age of Obama simply because the right-wing media, led by Beck, continue to gleefully (albeit irresponsibly) stoke dangerous fires with the kind of relentlessly incendiary rhetoric that has no match in terms of modern day, mainstream use in American politics or media.

Just listen to Glenn Beck:

- Progressives "are sucking the blood out of the republic" and are "gonna start getting more and more violent."
- "To the day I die, I am going to be a progressive hunter."
- "[Y]ou will have to shoot me in the forehead before you take away my gun" and "before I acquiesce and be silent."
- "This game is for keeps"; "[Y]ou can shoot me in the head ... but there will be ten others that line up."
- "There is a coup going on. There is a stealing of America"; "God help us in an emergency."

And don't forget about the unhinged response when health-care reform was passed in March: "Get down on your knees and pray. Pray. It's September 11th all over again, except that we didn't have the collapsing buildings." After financial reform passed last week, Beck told his audience, "Your republic is over."

Meanwhile, Andrew Breitbart's website recently tagged Obama as the "suicide-bomber-in-chief," while the conservative *Washington Times* just last week published an op-ed—by a former congressman, no less—asserting the president poses more of a threat to America than Al Qaeda.

Note that the radical right's media rhetoric is no longer even political in a partisan sense. Instead, it's purely revolutionary. It isn't, "We think taxes should be lower" or "Obama should be more hawkish overseas." It's, "There's an insidious and deadly plot afoot by Democrats and progressives to strip Americans of their freedom and this country of its greatness." Obama is now the incarnation of evil (the Antichrist?), and his driving hatred for America, as well as for democracy, runs so deep that he ran for president in order to destroy the United States from inside the Oval Office.

Rush Limbaugh: "Our country is being overthrown from within."

And this summer, the latest toxic twist to that line of attack is that Obama is destroying America on purpose in order to exact revenge from white America for the historic sin of slavery. (Think: black *Manchurian Candidate*.) The GOP noise machine is now mixing a vile cocktail by stirring revolutionary rhetoric with hateful race-baiting.

It's impossible to argue that today's avalanche of insurrectionist rhetoric doesn't have a real-world effect. Or that those on the fringes don't find comfort in seeing and hearing their worst fears legitimized on AM radio and Fox News.

The consequences of the doomsday programming seem entirely predictable. As Jeffrey Jones, a professor of media and politics at Old Dominion University, recently explained to the *New York Times* in regard to Beck's rhetoric, "People hear their values are under attack and they get worried. It becomes an opportunity for them to stand up and do something."

Indeed, the relentless message that right-wing audiences hear is unequivocal and inescapable: Do something! Take action!

And last week, Byron Williams, likely inspired by Glenn Beck's Tides obsession, grabbed his guns and set out to do just that.

—July 27, 2010

WHITE POWER USA

Laura Flanders, Rick Rowley, Chip Berlet, and
Jonathan "J.D." Meadows.

A member of the rock group White Knight: *"We already have a president who's out to destroy us and what we stand for. I did not elect a communist to run this country."*

> *from Al Jazeera English report "White Power USA"*
> by filmmakers Rick Rowley and Jacquie Soohen.

Laura Flanders: In April '09, the Department of Homeland Security reported that right-wing extremism was on the rise. The report was roundly ridiculed by the president's critics, but it's worth another look right now. An effigy of President Obama was hung from a storefront in Plains, Georgia, recently—the hometown of former President Jimmy Carter. Is there a perfect storm—of economic turmoil and President Obama in office—ready to start a race war? To discuss this and more, we're joined by independent journalist Rick Rowley, one of the producers of the film you just saw a clip of, *White Power USA*, now being played on Al Jazeera. Also with us: Chip Berlet, senior analyst at Political Research Associates and co-author of *Right-Wing Populism in America: Too Close for Comfort*—he's in the movie. Rick, what drew you to this subject? You're normally in the Middle East, aren't you?

Rick Rowley: That's true, yeah. Well, with Obama's inauguration, there was this feeling and a lot of hype about us entering a post-racial America—and very clearly, we haven't. Not only has there been a measurable rise in hate crimes around the country and a growth in extremist white-supremacist-type organizations, but narratives around race are becoming even more salient, in terms of structuring the discourse around all sorts of different political issues.

LF: Chip, we're just talking about organizing in America—who's gaining momentum, who's losing it. Tell us the data: When Rick says racist organizing is on the rise, what are the numbers? How do they back that up?

Chip Berlet: There's a number of different groups that track hate crimes, outside of the FBI hate crime reporting network, which is delayed many, many months, even years. So there's an ongoing collection of data about the number of groups that appear to be active beyond just one person on a keyboard on an Internet site, as well as attacks—physical assaults—and murders. There have been nine murders since the Obama inauguration that can be tied to some sort of white-supremacist or anti-Semitic conspiracy thinking. So there's something going on, and it can be measured. But it's not just the economy—it's a race/class/gender thing as well. It's a combination of race anxiety, gender anxiety over rights, and abortion rights, and an obviously completely tanked economy for many Americans.

LF: Rick, you connect the fringes to the mainstream. Talk about the "tea-bagging" movement in this context. Is it related? How?

RR: Absolutely. Actually, the day I arrived back from a trip to Iraq, we went down to film the 9/12 protest in D.C., and I have to say it was much more terrifying to me than anything I had seen over there. First of all, there are narrative lines that structure the whole idea—narrative about white disempowerment, about alien immigrant invasion—that are very current inside them, and then there are overt racist appeals. We saw T-shirts and signs saying everything from "Barack Obama's not a real American" to racist pictures—it was visceral and on the surface. (Aside from the fact that the crowd of maybe 75,000 people was almost 99.9 percent white.)

LF: Let's play a clip from *White Power USA*

[Clip]
Man at Tea Party protest speaking: *I think [Obama's] a racist. He's talking about how he's going to bring this country together—if he gets us any more together, we're going to kill each other.*

Woman speaking: *What's the difference between the Cleveland Zoo and the White House? The zoo has an African lion, and the White House has a lyin' African.*

Interviewer: *Do you think Obama is a real American?*

Woman: *No, I do not.*

Man at protest: *I do believe he is trying to change the country to his own image, whatever his image is.*

LF: But I'm confused, Rick. You start the film with people claiming a sort of Nazi identity—don't the Tea Partiers also carry banners that say Obama's a Nazi?

RR: There's no requirement for them to have a coherent and consistent ideology across the spectrum. The same people have signs that have Obama as a Nazi, and as Stalin, and as Lenin, and as Mao. Their incoherence, I think, is actually a source of strength.

[Clip]

White supremacist speaking: *This was founded as a white nation. They call us the fringe, they say this is a fringe movement, but I think what we're saying is very mainstream. We're standing up for the American people—there's nothing fringe about that. The membership has really spiked, especially in the past few years. It's more mainstream now than ever before in our history.*

Clifford Herrington: *This is our blood banner. This flag has flown everywhere in the United States. [Clifford Herrington was the chairman of the National Socialist Movement before they tried to go mainstream—when they still wore Nazi uniforms. As we approach the State Capitol, he starts to state a chant.] No niggers! No Jews! Mexicans must go, too! [Younger members of the leadership quickly silence him, and choose a theme better suited for a mainstream audience: "USA! USA!"]*

LF: Chip, is there any comfort that in that scene there that people didn't immediately start chanting the first of the chants, and that they switched to the second?

CB: Well, hardly comfort. What we're finding is that there is a dynamic where the organized white supremacists—like the neo-Nazis and the Klan, and other such groups—are looking at the "tea-bagging" movement as ripe fruit to pluck for recruitment. But what you also have are people being drawn to the tea-bag movements because of other concerns. And a lot of white people in America are very quick to set aside any idea that they might be racist, but a feeling of white superiority is pretty much embedded in the body politic of the United States. So there's a very complicated set of things going on, involving the Republican Party's anti-Obama stance, this dissident populist movement of right-wing conservatives, and then the ultraright all in play with each other, trying to recruit back and forth, and people trying to pull power out of this rising populist revolt.

LF: Is it important to point out that the language that's used, like "take back America," could be interpreted to mean a wealth of things to all sorts of people, kind of like Obama—and that you can project onto it whatever you want?

RR: Absolutely. First of all, the slogan of the Tea Party movement is "Take Back America." When you're in a crowd of 80,000 white people in front of the White House, or the Capitol, where the first African-American president is sitting, and they're chanting "Take it back!" and they have signs saying "America is a Christian nation," things like that—it becomes clear that the narrative that is being appealed to for a large section of the incoherent and monolithic kind of movement is for a Christian nation that needs to be taken back.

LF: For a little bit more on what is fueling the growth of this and why people are joining up, we spoke to one of the people in the film. We'll start by showing a little more of the movie, and then talk to J.D. Meadows. Take a look.

[Clip]

Tea Party Member of Ripley, Mississippi: The biggest issues right now are the economy, jobs, and illegal immigration. Illegal immigration isn't even really a third issue—it's all about the economy. So that's pretty much driving the graph right now.

[The town of Ripley just formed one of the newest chapters of the Council of Conservative Citizens, and organized its own Tea Party. J.D. Meadows is one of the newest council members. He was receptive to this economic message.]

J.D. Meadows: *My uncle lost his job up here at Bench Craft, and so did my aunt. Their company shut down and moved to China.*

LF: J.D. Meadows, seen there in the film, is a recent recruit to the Council of Conservative Citizens chapter there in Ripley, Mississippi. He's joining us now, on GRITtv. J.D., Glad to have you.

JDM: Glad to be on your show.

LF: For people who have never been to Ripley, can you describe it? What is it that you love about it?

JDM: Here in Ripley, we have about 5,000 people. Geographically, we're somewhat isolated. People here are a lot kinder than they are in most of the larger areas. We have a really, really low crime rate here— maybe one murder every two or three years. It's just a good place to live. A lot of my family lives here.

LF: So it sounds like in some ways it's great. What's the problem?

JDM: Well, when I first moved here, our town was booming—and that was about seven, maybe eight years ago. Two or three years ago, it started to slow down. Bench Craft moved out, and that really hurt us. After that happened, the industrial park started to slowly become empty. A lot of it has to do with Wall Street. Everything that comes down from the federal level affects us here. It's also because our local government is so dependent on the federal government.

LF: Did you personally lose a job?

JDM: No ma'am, I haven't. I've had a lot of family lose jobs. I'm a business owner here. I run a computer repair shop. I work on Windows machines, Macs, and the like. One thing I've noticed: The way it affects my business is that when you have a place like Bench Craft shut down, a lot of those people are out of work, so they can't spend money with local businesses. And eventually that will slow down everybody else, because you have such a large customer base there. That's really how it affects the smaller businesses. Just two weeks ago, we had Sonic shut down here.

LF: What led you to join the Citizens' Council?

JDM: I believe it's a good vessel to speak out against what's going on today. The number one issue right now is the economy. There are a lot of things going on in the media to distract us from that, such as this supposed underwear bomber who set off a fire-cracker in his underwear, or whatever that was about. But the main focus right now is the economy, and that's one thing that Ripley's really been pushing.

LF: Let me ask you to listen to a clip of what the guy who recruited you into CCC has to say about his organization, the economy, and the other issues they care about. Take a look.

[Clip]
CCC recruiter, Brian Pace: *The Council is built like a college. After you get in, and you start reading our beliefs, and you start understanding our platform, you start growing more and more.*
The economy, the bank bailout, and the war get people in the door, he says. *Once inside, the group tries to educate them about racial threats to America.*

BP: *A mixing of cultures—it could be ethnic, it could be religious, it could be language…we want to preserve the Caucasian Christian culture that has made up the United States, in the South, traditionally.*

LF: So, J.D., as you heard there, you might have joined for economic reasons, but Brian Pace says the group's about race.

JDM: It's not really about race, I would say. Most of the racial issues, per se, come out of Washington, D.C. There are a lot of people out there who are pushing the race issue. Most of the time it's just going to end up being a distraction away from what's really going on in the government.

LF: So how do you feel about what Brian Pace said there, which is that you're being recruited on the economic issues, but if you stick around, you'll be "educated" on the racial stuff?

JDM: I know Brian, I've known him for about three years. He's not that type of person, to be honest with you. But there are a lot of race problems out there, and the government has been playing people off against each other.

LF: Do you have a problem with Barack Obama?

JDM: I think it's not just with Obama. Obama is a spokesman for Wall Street. I don't think it lies specifically with one president—it's been going on for probably the past fifty years. Look at the presidents we've had. Look at Bush—he's probably one of the most racist presidents we've ever had.

LF: And one of the biggest expanders of federal government. I've got a question. Was there any other group interested in having you join, there in Ripley, that was focused on the economy, focused on layoffs? Did any other group reach out to you?

JDM: Well, actually I'm a member of several groups. The Council of Conservative Citizens, for one. Another one is the Concerned

Citizens' Group—we have a club here that goes out in the community, trying to improve the community. We recently had an election on the board of directors of the Tippah County Power Association. We're trying to get some new people in there, to try to get the electric rates lowered.

LF: So it sounds like you're very active, J.D. If you showed up at a CCC meeting and people there with swastikas and "Hail Hitler" signs, would you speak out? Would you stick around?

JDM: I've never heard of such, but from what I understand of history, the swastika is a symbol of the Nazi Party, and the Nazis stood for the National Socialist German Worker's Party.

LF: Yeah, but you and I know what it's come to signify. If people started wearing those patches, and talking that language, would you stick around at the meetings?

JDM: I wouldn't.

LF: J.D. Meadows, it's great to talk with you. Chip Berlet, you heard why J.D. says he's joining a group like the Citizens' Council—he says he would leave if it became blatantly, explicitly racist.

CB: It already is blatantly and explicitly racist, but the issue here is, because of the anxiety over the economy and race and gender, there are people who join movements that offer to help them out in some way, and they're quite able to sincerely say, "I'm not racist." And that's part of the dilemma of this idea that it's a post-racial America—it's not. The Conservative Citizens Council is part of a white nationalist movement. The dilemma here is that there's a range of people being drawn into these white supremacist movements that are very quick to deny that any racism is involved, because they're grabbing onto these movements because of fear of falling in economic or social status. So it's very complicated—it's not as simple as the liberal press would have it, that there's a wonderful and divinely ordinate center of Republicans and Democrats, and that dissidents on the left and right are somehow on a slippery slope toward terrorism or supremacy of some sort. It's simply not true. It's a way of reaffirming the status quo. So many of these folks who join these movements, like J.D., could have been organized by a left organization that had found a new way of reaching out to folks worried about their families and their communities.

LF: Let me ask you about that, Rick, in another part of the program, we talked about what organizing was looking like on the other side of the spectrum. In the towns that you went to in Arizona and elsewhere, what did you find on that?

RR: Progressives are going to be completely out-organized by the populist right. We sat down for lunch with the Council Chapter in Ripley. J.D.—he's motivated by the economy. We pushed him to talk about racial segregation and things that the council says on its website that it's in favor of. It says that it's against race mixing, that it's against forced integration. But yet, J.D.'s joining because it was the only group that was standing up against a bank bailout on Wall Street while Main Street died. Another interesting thing was that the other passionate person at the table was there because of the war. He said, "I've been a Republican my whole life, I was going to vote for McCain until he said that we were going to be in Iraq for a hundred years. I switched, and was going to vote for Obama, but then he said he was just going to move everything to Afghanistan." So that was the only place he had left.

LF: Rick Rowley, Chip Berlet, thank you so much.

—January 7, 2010

IMAGINE: PROTEST, INSURGENCY, AND THE WORKINGS OF WHITE PRIVILEGE

Tim Wise

Let's play a game, shall we? The name of the game is called "Imagine." The way it's played is simple: We'll envision recent happenings in the news, but then change them up a bit. Instead of envisioning white people as the main actors in the scenes we'll conjure—the ones who are driving the action—we'll envision black folks or other people of color instead. The object of the game is to imagine the public reaction to the events or incidents if the main actors were of color, rather than white. Whoever gains the most insight into the workings of race in America by the end of the game, wins.

So let's begin.

Imagine that hundreds of black protesters were to descend upon Washington, D.C., and Northern Virginia, just a few miles from the Capitol and White House, armed with AK-47s, assorted handguns, and ammunition. And imagine that some of these protesters—the black protesters—spoke of the need for political revolution, and possibly even armed conflict in the event that laws they didn't like were enforced by the government. Would these protesters—these black protesters with guns—be seen as brave defenders of the Second Amendment, or would they be viewed by most whites as a danger to the republic? What if they were Arab-Americans? Because, after all, that's what happened recently when white gun enthusiasts descended upon the nation's capital, arms in hand, and verbally announced their readiness to make war on the country's political leaders if the need arose.

Imagine that white members of Congress, while walking to work, were surrounded by thousands of angry, screaming black people, one of whom proceeded to spit on one of those congressmen for not voting the way the black demonstrators desired. Would the protesters be seen as merely patriotic Americans voicing their opinions, or as an angry, potentially violent, and even insurrectionary mob? After all, this is what white Tea Party protesters did recently in Washington.

Imagine that a black rap artist were to say, in reference to a white politician and presidential candidate: "He's a piece of shit and I told him to suck on my machine gun." And what would happen to any prominent liberal commentator who then, when asked about that statement, replied that the rapper was a friend and that he (the commentator) would not disavow or even criticize him for his remarks. Because that's what rocker Ted Nugent said in 2007 about Barack Obama, and that's how Sean Hannity responded to Nugent's remarks when he was asked about them.

Imagine that a prominent mainstream black political commentator had long employed an overt bigot as executive director of his organization, and that this bigot regularly participated in black separatist conferences, and once assaulted a white person while calling them by a racial slur. When that prominent black commentator and his sister—who also works for the organization—defended the bigot as a good guy who was misunderstood and "going through a tough time in his life," would anyone accept their excuse-making? Would that commentator still have a place on a mainstream network? Because that's what happened in the real world, when Pat Buchanan employed as executive director of his group, America's Cause, a blatant racist who did all these things, or at least their white equivalents: attending white separatist conferences and attacking a black woman while calling her the N-word.

Imagine that a black radio host were to suggest that the only way to get promoted in the administration of a white president is by "hating black people," or that a prominent white person had only endorsed a white presidential candidate as an act of racial bonding, or blamed a white president for a fight on a school bus in which a black kid was jumped by two white kids, or said that he wouldn't want to kill all conservatives, but rather, would like to leave just enough— "living fossils" as he called them—"so we will never forget what these people stood for." After all, these are things that Rush Limbaugh has said, about Barack Obama's administration, Colin Powell's endorsement of Barack Obama, a fight on a school bus in Belleville, Illinois, in which two black kids beat up a white kid, and about liberals, generally.[1]

Imagine that a black pastor, formerly a member of the U.S. military, were to declare, as part of his opposition to a white president's policies, that he was ready to "suit up, get my gun, go to Washington, and do what they trained me to do." This is, after all, what Pastor Stan Craig said recently at a Tea Party rally in Greenville, South Carolina.

Imagine a black radio-talk-show host gleefully predicting a revolution by people of color if the government continues to be dominated by the rich white men who have been "destroying" the country, or if said radio personality were to call Christians or Jews nonhumans, or say that when it came to conservatives, the best solution would be to "hang 'em high." And what would happen to any congressional representative who praised that commentator for "speaking common sense" and likened his hate talk to "American values"? After all, those are among the things said by radio host and bestselling author Michael Savage, predicting white revolution in the face of multiculturalism, or said by Savage about Arab Muslims and liberals, respectively. And it was Congressman Culbertson, from Texas, who praised Savage in that way, despite his hateful rhetoric.

Imagine a black political commentator suggesting that the only thing the guy who flew his plane into the Austin, Texas, IRS building did wrong was not blowing up Fox News instead. This is, after all, what Anne Coulter said about Tim McVeigh, when she noted that his only mistake was not blowing up the *New York Times*.

Imagine that a popular black liberal website posted comments about the daughter of a white president, calling her "typical redneck trash," or a "whore" whose mother entertains her by "making monkey sounds." After all that's comparable to what conservatives posted about Malia Obama on freerepublic.com last year, when they referred to her as "ghetto trash."

Imagine that black protesters at a large political rally were walking around with signs calling for the lynching of their congressional enemies. Because that's what white conservatives did last year, in reference to Democratic Party leaders in Congress.

In other words, imagine that even one-third of the anger and vitriol currently being hurled at President Obama, by folks who are almost exclusively white, were being aimed, instead, at a white president, by people of color. How many whites viewing the anger, the hatred, the contempt for that white president would then wax eloquent about free speech, and the glories of democracy? And how many would be calling for further crackdowns on thuggish behavior, and investigations into the radical agendas of those same people of color?

To ask any of these questions is to answer them. Protest is only seen as fundamentally American when those who have long had the luxury of seeing themselves as *prototypically* American engage in it. When the dangerous and dark "other" does so, however, it isn't viewed as normal or natural, let alone patriotic. Which is why Rush Limbaugh could say, this past week, that the Tea Parties are the first time since the Civil War that ordinary, common Americans stood up for their rights—a statement that erases the normalcy and "Americanness" of blacks in the civil rights struggle, not to mention women in the fight for suffrage and equality, working people in the fight for better working conditions, and LGBT folks as they struggle to be treated as full and equal human beings.

And this, my friends, is what white privilege is all about. The ability to threaten others, to engage in violent and incendiary rhetoric without consequence, to be viewed as patriotic and normal no matter what you do, and never to be feared and despised as people of color would be, if they tried to get away with half the shit we do, on a daily basis.

Game Over.

—April 25, 2010

Notes

1. *Denver Post*, December 29, 1995.

HOW MORMONISM BUILT GLENN BECK

Joanna Brooks

Glenn Beck leans forward on his elbows. His voice hushes. His eyes grow red at the corners. He presses his lips together and clears his throat. He cannot speak. The tears fall, and just for a moment the brashest voice in American conservatism today falls silent.

This is what happens when Beck tells the story of his 1999 conversion to Mormonism.

"I was friendless, working in the smallest radio market I had ever worked in... a hopeless alcoholic, abusing drugs every day," Beck said in an interview taped last fall. "I was trying to find a job and nobody would hire me... couldn't get an agent to represent me."

That's when Beck's wife-to-be Tania suggested that the family go on a "church tour," which finally led (after some prodding from Beck's longtime on-air partner Pat Gray, a Mormon) to his local Mormon wardhouse. Six months later, the Beck family joined the Church of Jesus Christ of Latter-day Saints.

"I was baptized on a Sunday, and on Monday"—Beck's throat tightens again; he wipes tears from his eyes with his index fingers—"an agent called me out of the blue." Three days later, Beck was offered his own political talk-radio show at WFLA-AM in Tampa, Florida, the job that put him on the road from "morning zoo" radio prankster to conservative media heavyweight.

Spiritual narratives of the I-once-was-lost-now-I-am-financially-sound variety are commonplace within Mormonism, which, like most of American Protestantism, has never been allergic to wealth. The institutional culture of the Mormon Church is strongly corporate, down to the dark suits, white shirts, and red or blue ties church leaders wear instead of vestments; Mormonism's most powerful public figures, like Mitt Romney, Jon Huntsman Jr., and Bill Marriott Jr., come from the business world.

But whether or not one believes that God rewards baptism with fortune, it is clear that Glenn Beck's conversion to and education in the Mormon faith after 1999 corresponds precisely with his rise as a media force.

Beck, who was raised Catholic in Washington State, has produced, with the help of Mormon Church–owned Deseret Book Company, the DVD *An Unlikely Mormon: The Conversion Story of Glenn Beck* (2008); Mormon fansites invite visitors to learn more about Beck's beliefs by clicking through to the official website of the Church of Jesus Christ of Latter-day Saints. But what these fansites don't reveal is the extent to which Mormonism has given Beck key elements of his on-air personality and messaging.

TEARY TIRADES AND MORMON MASCULINITY

Before 1999, Glenn Beck told jokes and pulled on-air stunts for a living. He developed the content of his current conservative messaging (an amalgam of anticommunism, United States–founder worship, and connect-the-dots conspiracy theorizing) after his entree into the deeply insular world of Mormon thought and culture. A significant figure in this world is the late W. Cleon Skousen (1913–2006), the archconservative and fiercely anticommunist Brigham Young University professor, founder of the Freeman Society, and author of fifteen books, including *The Naked Capitalist*, *The Making of America*, and *Prophecy and Modern Times*. Beck, who first cited Skousen in his 2003 book *The Real America: Messages from the Heart and the Heartland*, later started pitching Skousen's 1981 book *The 5,000 Year*

Leap on air in December 2008. He wrote a preface for a new edition of the book issued a few months later and in his March 2009 kickoff of the 9/12 movement declared Skousen's book to be "divinely inspired." In a recent article for *Salon*, Alexander Zaitchik suggested that Beck "rescued [Skousen] from the remainder pile of history." But Cleon Skousen was never remaindered among the most politically conservative Mormons, for whom he has been a household name since the 1960s.

It is likely that Beck owes his brand of founding father–worship to Mormonism, where reverence for the founders and the United States Constitution as divinely inspired are often-declared elements of orthodox belief. Mormon Church President Wilford Woodruff (1807–1898) declared that George Washington and the signers of the Declaration of Independence appeared to him in the Mormon Temple in St. George, Utah, in 1877, and requested that he perform Mormon temple ordinances on their behalf. Many Mormons also believe that Joseph Smith prophesied in 1843 that the U.S. Constitution would one day "hang by a thread" and be saved by faithful Mormons; this idea was given new life in the 1960s by former U.S. Secretary of Agriculture Ezra Taft Benson, who cited Smith's 1843 prophecy from the pulpit while speaking as a member of the Church's Quorum of Twelve Apostles.

Many key elements of Beck's on-the-fly messaging derive from a Mormon lexicon, such as his Twitter-issued September 19 call: "Sept 28. Lets make it a day of Fast and Prayer for the Republic. Spread the word. Let us walk in the founders steps." This call to fasting and prayer may indeed have been an appropriation of the Jewish holy day of Yom Kippur, but it is also rooted in the traditional Mormon practice of holding individual, familial, and collective fasts to address spiritual challenges.

Even the overt sentimentality Beck now indulges from time to time was formed within the cradle of Mormon literary culture. Take, for example, his novel *The Christmas Sweater* (2008) (co-authored by

Mormon writer Jason Wright) and its accompanying children's picture book, which tell the story of an impoverished twelve-year-old boy who rejects a "handmade, ugly sweater" his widowed mother knits him for Christmas, only to watch his mother die in a fiery car crash hours later. This punishing sentimentality is a consistent feature of Mormon storytelling from church-produced cinematic classics like *Cipher in the Snow* (1973) and *The Mailbox* (1977) to the *New York Times* bestselling novel *The Christmas Box* (1995) by Mormon author Richard Paul Evans.

Finally, Beck's oft-ridiculed penchant for punctuating his tirades with tears is the hallmark of a distinctly Mormon mode of masculinity. As sociologist David Knowlton has written, "Mormonism praises the man who is able to shed tears as a manifestation of spirituality." Crying and choking up are understood by Mormons as manifestations of the Holy Spirit. For men at every rank of Mormon culture and visibility, appropriately timed displays of tender emotion are displays of power.

PEACE ON THE RELIGIOUS RIGHT BETWEEN MORMONS AND EVANGELICALS?

Indeed, Beck, who grew up without a father, narrates his conversion and personal transformation around a series of tearful bonding moments with Mormon men, from the Sunday School teacher who first taught him about the Mormon concept of Zion—"Tears started to roll down his cheeks, and he said, 'It can only happen if I truly love you and you love me'"—to his baptism by immersion by his longtime friend Pat Gray, who was so choked up, according to Beck, that "he couldn't get the words out."

Not typical of Mormon masculinity are Beck's high-decibel swings between bombast and self-deprecation. Such demonstrative excesses are socialized out of most Mormon men during a regimented process of masculine formation that begins with entry into the lowest ranks of

Mormonism's lay priesthood at age twelve, intensifies during compulsory missionary service from age nineteen through twenty-one, and continues throughout a lifetime of service within hierarchical priesthood quorums. A textbook example of the traditional Mormon "man of steel and velvet" is Mitt Romney, whose inability to connect with the Republican base may have as much to do with his lack of familiar jocularity and chest-thumping outrage as it does with the perceived weirdness of his Mormon beliefs. As a convert, Beck missed out on crucial early years of Mormon male socialization. Consequently, his renegade persona may endear him even more to his Mormon male fans who might like to comport themselves as he does, but feel they cannot.

It's true that his Mormonism sometimes gets Beck into trouble with evangelical Christians, who have long antagonized Mormons by denying the authenticity of their belief in Jesus Christ and deriding the Mormon Church as a cult. Last December, James Dobson's Focus on the Family website pulled a Beck column, citing concerns about his Mormon ties. Still, Beck's spectacular rise suggests that evangelical conservatives (especially those under forty who may not remember the anti-Mormon cult crusades of the 1980s) are increasingly willing to set aside their reservations about Mormons when it suits their pragmatic and political interests.

Glenn Beck marks an unprecedented national mainstreaming of a peculiar strand of religious political conservatism rooted in, and once isolated to, the Mormon culture regions of the American West. That Mormons are capable of leveraging disproportionate political influence with decisive results was one of the great lessons of California's 2008 election season, wherein readily mobilized Mormons, who make up 2 percent of California's population, contributed more than 50 percent of the individual donations to the successful anti–marriage equality Proposition 8 campaign, and a sizeable majority of its on-the-ground efforts.

How much traction Glenn Beck can muster remains to be seen.

But if the American religious right has sometimes been imagined as a monolithic product of the evangelical Deep South and Bible Belt, the rise of Glenn Beck suggests that those who would understand American conservatism might also look west, toward Salt Lake City.

—October 7, 2009

GUN OWNERSHIP: 'AN OBLIGATION TO GOD'

Sarah Posner and Julie Ingersoll

Herb Titus, a lawyer for the far-right Gun Owners of America, is jubilant over last week's Supreme Court decision in the case *McDonald v. City of Chicago*, finding that state and local regulation of gun ownership must comport with the Second Amendment right to bear arms.

The decision has also pleased the National Rifle Association, which sees it as ammunition for challenging gun control laws across the country. But for Titus, who thinks the NRA "compromises" on gun rights, the Second Amendment isn't solely about "firepower," he says. "You have to see it in its spiritual and providential perspective."

That perspective is about far more than hunting and self-defense. For Titus, the Court's 2008 recognition of an individual right to bear arms, and its application of that principle to the states in the *McDonald* case, are crucial steps toward arming Americans against their own government. Titus cites the "totalitarian threat" posed by "Obamacare" and "what Sarah Palin said about death panels." People need to be armed, he said, "because ultimately it may come to the point where it's a life and death situation."

Titus, who filed an *amicus* brief on behalf of the GOA, an organization that claims 300,000 members, told Religion Dispatches that "the ultimate authority is God."

"[I]f you have a people that has basically been disarmed by the civil government," he added, "then there really isn't any effectual means available to the people to restore law and liberty and that's really the purpose of the right keep and bear arms—is to defend yourself against a tyrant."

If this sounds like standard-issue Tea Party fodder, it's because the Tea Party movement emerges out of the confluence of different strands of the far right, including Christian Reconstructionism. Titus has long been a player at the intersection of Christian Reconstructionism, the standard religious right, and other far-right groups in which the Tea Party finds its roots. He was a speaker at the Reconstructionist American Vision's annual "Worldview Conference" in 2009, has been a member of the Council for National Policy, and is a longtime homeschooling advocate from a Reconstructionist perspective. In the 1996 presidential election he was the running mate of conservative icon (and Christian Reconstructionist) Howard Phillips for the far-right U.S. Taxpayers Party (now called the Constitution Party), whose platform included the restoration of "American jurisprudence to its biblical premises" and, notably, opposition to every gun law in the United States.

Now a lawyer with the firm William J. Olson, P.C., Titus was a founding dean of Pat Robertson's Regent University Law School, where he was the chair of a three-member committee that supervised Virginia Governor Bob McDonnell's now-notorious graduate thesis. In it, a recitation of the religious right's agenda, McDonnell called working women and feminists "detrimental" to the family, argued for policy favoring married couples over "cohabitators, homosexuals, or fornicators," and called the 1972 legalization of contraception by married couples "illogical." During his 2009 campaign, McDonnell tried to distance himself from his own work, but Titus told the *Washington Post* that McDonnell's thesis was "right."

In 2004, after Judge Roy Moore, another Titus client, was stripped of his position for defying a federal court order to remove his 2.6-ton monument to the Ten Commandments from the rotunda of the Alabama Supreme Court, he joined Titus in drafting the Constitution

Restoration Act. The bill, had it passed, would have deprived federal courts of jurisdiction to hear cases challenging a government entity's or official's "acknowledgment of God as the sovereign source of law, liberty, or government."

This clear articulation of the religious right's dominionist aims, framed as a challenge to what the right asserts is the excessive power of the federal government, did manage to receive Republican support. It had nine co-sponsors in the Senate and was introduced in the House by Alabama Republican Robert Aderholt, who had fifty co-sponsors, including now–Minority Whip Eric Cantor, now–Louisiana Governor Bobby Jindal, and Representative Mike Pence, who is thought to be considering a 2012 presidential run.

PARTNERS IN ARMS: MILITIAS, THE RELIGIOUS RIGHT, AND BIBLICAL LAW

The militia movement and Christian Reconstructionism both contend that our current civil government, most especially the federal government, is illegitimate: that it has overreached the limits of its divinely ordained authority, and that it continues to do so. At this intersection of the religious right and the militia movement, gun ownership is portrayed as a religious issue. "When we're talking about firearms," GOA executive director Larry Pratt told Religion Dispatches, "we're not really talking about a right but an obligation, as creatures of God, to protect the life that was given them."

Many in the militia movement, the Tea Party movement, and Christian Reconstruction also share the view that civil government should be reformed according to the dictates of biblical law.

In describing the "fundamental issue" as "God's authority," Titus echoes themes from Christian Reconstructionist founder R.J. Rushdoony, including the notion that civil government has certain limits established by God. Although Titus, who earned his law degree from Harvard in 1962, claims he is not a Reconstructionist, he doesn't deny its influence on his thinking, acknowledging how, after he was saved in 1975, his new jurisprudence was shaped by Rushdoony's seminal text, *The Institutes of Biblical Law.*

Like Rushdoony, Titus argues that government is by covenant; that authority is distributed by God among three institutions with distinct (and distinctly limited) jurisdictions: family, church, and civil government. To root this view in the American constitutional system, Rushdoony and Titus both read the secular language of the Constitution in the context of the invocation of "the Creator" in the Declaration of Independence: "Inalienable rights are endowed by the Creator." These rights, both Rushdoony and Titus contend, are not granted by either document, only recognized in them; these rights exist only because they were granted by God.

Because Supreme Court nominee Elena Kagan refused to acknowledge the divine source of the Constitution, and in particular the Second Amendment, Titus believes she is not qualified to serve on the Court. (Titus's law partner testified on behalf of the GOA against Kagan's confirmation, one of several witnesses called by the Republicans.) Echoing the Christian Reconstructionist view, Senator Charles Grassley asked Kagan, "Did the Second Amendment codify a preexisting right or was it a right created by the Constitution?"—something Kagan, not surprisingly, said she'd never contemplated.

"Here's a woman who's being nominated to sit on the United States Supreme Court and she's never thought about the question whether rights are given by God or given by men," Titus exclaimed incredulously. "She's never even considered it!"

GOD AND GUNS: THE CHRISTIAN DUTY TO TAKE UP ARMS AGAINST THE GOVERNMENT

While many gun advocates are concerned with preserving access to firearms for hunting, and others argue that the right to possession of firearms is essential for self-defense against criminals,

Reconstructionists have a loftier argument: so Christians can exercise their duty to take up arms against a government that has exceeded its bounds as established by God.

In this view, when the civil government oversteps the authority given to it by God, citizens have a right and an obligation to resist. Titus insists it is "the basis upon which this nation was founded. We were a well-armed people, and when the call came to come out and to fight the redcoats, people were armed—pastors, and their parishioners. They came out and defended their liberties."

The view that gun ownership is a Christian duty, rooted in the overlap between Reconstructionism and the survivalist/militia movement, has become common in both. In his "Bring Your Pieces to Church" Sunday essay, Reconstructionist Joel McDurmon makes this point, suggesting that believers should organize target practice after church:

> Christians should be aware that the use of force in preservation of life is a biblical doctrine (Ex. 22:2–3; Prov. 24:10–12; Est. 8–9; Neh. 4; cp. John 15:13–14). Likewise, those who possessed weapons in Scripture are often said to be well skilled in the use of them (Judg. 20:15–16; 1 Chron. 12:1–2, 21–22). We can only surmise that 1) God gave them talent in this regard, and that 2) they engaged in target practice regularly. Further, under biblical law, to be disarmed was to be enslaved and led to a disruption of the economic order due to government regulations and monopolies (1 Sam 13:19–22).

Reconstructionists are critical of those who defend the Second Amendment only in terms of hunting. They believe that the protection of a sporting activity would not have been the basis of an amendment to the Constitution intended to protect basic rights that were fundamental to liberty. McDurmon also points to widespread gun ownership as a defense against tyranny, tracing the colonial laws that required gun ownership and arguing that "in the context of the War for Independence, ministers saw guns as tools of liberty and defense against tyranny." In fact, he argues that gun ownership by individuals should be the basis of national defense and that a standing army is unbiblical.

THE TEA PARTY–CHRISTIAN RECONSTRUCTIONISM–MILITIA CONNECTION

Representative Ron Paul, a godfather of sorts to the Tea Parties, calls the GOA "the only no-compromise gun lobby in Washington." Indeed, Pratt, GOA's executive director, told Religion Dispatches that he has spoken at Tea Party events, calling his group "a natural match for the folks in the Tea Party." Pratt believes the federal government is largely unconstitutional, and that all federal agencies save the Department of Justice and the Department of the Treasury (which should be "a lot smaller") should be abolished. (The Internal Revenue Service is a part of the Treasury that Pratt would like to see abolished.)

GOA's political action arm has endorsed Paul's son, Rand, in the Kentucky Senate race, as well as other Tea Party favorites for Senate Sharron Angle (Nevada), Marco Rubio (Florida), J.D. Hayworth (Arizona), David Vitter (Louisiana), Tom Coburn (Oklahoma), and Jim DeMint (South Carolina), as well as eight House candidates. The Angle campaign embraced the endorsement, with her spokesperson saying, "Not only is Mrs. Angle unafraid of guns, but she is also unafraid to stand up against those who would attempt to deny the legal rights of other gun owners."

Pratt, whose advocacy has led him to intersect not only with the Tea Partiers, but also with neo-Nazis and white supremacists, sees the revitalization of the Tenth Amendment movement—far-right agitators who believe the federal government is largely unconstitutional— as evidence of states "pushing back federal authority." Pratt believes that states should be "reactivating" militias, which should be at their disposal "instead of relying on the [federal] government to come and screw things up... these things should be given new life."

Pratt refuses the label "Christian Reconstructionist," telling Religion Dispatches he prefers to identify as a "Biblical Christian." He advocates for militias, which he describes as "the sheriff's posse," and believes that the "availability of it will further cool their [the federal government's] jets. No more Wacos. Because if you try something like that again, we're not going to stand around and watch. We're going to put you in our jail. Which is what the sheriff in that county should have told the thugs in Waco."

This is predicated, Pratt insists, "on the actual meaning of the word *militia*, as it was put into the Constitution and into the Bill of Rights."

Citing Romans 13, Pratt said the "magistrate is a servant of God. He's supposed to be a terror to evildoers and a comfort to the righteous. So we talk in terms of protecting the people's liberties. That's really the same concept."

In an essay posted on the GOA website, "What Does The Bible Say About Gun Control?" Pratt argues that "resisting an attack is not to be confused with taking vengeance, which is the exclusive domain of God," citing Romans 12:19. That domain of God, he maintains, "has been delegated to the civil magistrate" who is "God's minister, an avenger to execute wrath on him who practices evil."

Likewise, Titus, in his interview with Religion Dispatches, referred to this notion of legitimate civil uprising or resistance resting on the support of "lesser magistrates." This concept derives from Calvin but is a concept central to Reconstructionism—that Christians are obligated to obey civil authority because it is delegated by God; they can only resist one civil authority when in submission to another one. Put in secular terms, this dovetails with their longstanding support for "states' rights" and their desire to see organized militias that can be called up by state governors (who are "lesser magistrates") for the defense of a state against what they claim is the tyrannical over-reach of the federal government.

With the receptivity of the Tea Party movement to arguments against supposed excessive federal power, Christian Reconstruction-ist–inspired militias could find new converts. Pratt said that when he speaks about his militia idea at Tea Party rallies, "it's very well re-ceived." It may be "a new idea in the details," he added, "but it cer-tainly resonates instantly with them."

—July 6, 2010

PART THREE:
THE PEDAGOGY OF SHOCK (AND LUNACY)

IS THIS THE BIRTH OF A NATION?

Melissa Harris-Lacewell

In response to the imminent passage of health care reform protesters spat on Representative Emmanuel Cleaver.[1] They hurled homophobic obscenities[2] at Representative Barney Frank. They shouted racial slurs[3] at Representative John Lewis.

Democratic leadership responded by marching to the Capitol[4] in a scene that looked more like a 1960s demonstration than a morning commute for the majority party.

The attacks on black and gay members of Congress immediately mobilized lefty mainstream media. On Monday night both Keith Olbermann[5] and Rachel Maddow drew parallels between the health-care battle and the civil rights movement. I like, respect, and appear frequently on both programs, but I think both have missed the mark in their racial analysis.

Crafting a metaphor that connects the civil rights movement and the bigoted language of this weekend's protesters is seductive. It seems so obvious given that Representative John Lewis plays a critical role in both. A young Lewis was severely beaten forty-five years ago when he tried to lead a group[6] of brave citizens across the Edmund Pettus bridge in an effort to secure voting rights for black Americans.

This weekend he graciously rebuffed his detractors in a perfect example of nonviolent, direct resistance. Representative Lewis said he harbored no ill will against those who called him names and insisted that we are all citizens of this nation and that we must learn to live peacefully and respectfully together. It was the kind of response that makes Lewis a hero to many.[7]

But there is a very important difference between Bloody Sunday of 1965 and Health Care Reform Sunday of 2010. In 1965 Lewis was a disenfranchised protester fighting to be recognized as a full citizen. When he was beaten by the police, he was being attacked by the state. In 2010 Lewis is a longtime elected representative. When he is attacked by protesters, he is himself an agent of the state. This difference is critically important; not because it changes the fact that racism is present in both moments, but because it radically alters the way we should understand the meaning of power, protest, and race.

I often begin my political science courses with a brief introduction to the idea of "the state." The state is the entity that has a monopoly on the legitimate use of violence, force, and coercion. If an individual travels to another country and kills its citizens, we call it terrorism. If the state does it, we call it war. If a man kills his neighbor it is murder; if the state does it is the death penalty. If an individual takes his neighbor's money, it is theft; if the state does it, it is taxation.

To the extent that a state is challenged as the sole, legitimate owner of the tools of violence, force, and coercion, it is challenged at its core. This is why "states' rights" led to secession and Civil War. The legitimacy of the central state was challenged, then reestablished. It is also why the civil rights movement was so powerful. The overt abuse of state power evidenced by the violence of Southern police called into question their foundational legitimacy. The federal government had to act or risk losing its authority as a state altogether.

Which leads us to March 2010.

The Tea Party is a challenge to the legitimacy of the U.S. state. When Tea Party participants charge the current administration with various forms of totalitarianism, they are arguing that this government has no right to levy taxes or make policy. Many GOP elected officials offered nearly secessionist rhetoric from the floor of Congress this weekend. They joined as co-conspirators with the Tea Party protesters by arguing that this government has no monopoly on legitimacy.

I appreciate the parallels to the civil rights movement drawn by the MSNBC crowd, but they are inadequate. When protesters spit on and scream at duly elected representatives of the U.S. government it is more than act of racism. It is an act of sedition.

John Lewis is no longer just a brave American fighting for the soul of his country—he is an elected official. He is an embodiment of the state.

Commentators and observers need to move their historical lens back a little further. The relevant comparison here is not the mid-twentieth century civil rights movement. The better analogy is the mid-nineteenth century period of Reconstruction. From the end of the Civil War in 1865 until the unholy Hayes-Tilden compromise of 1877, black Americans enjoyed a brief experiment with full citizenship and political power sharing.

During this decade black men voted, held office, and organized as laborers and farmers. It was a fragile political equality made possible only by the determined and powerful presence of the federal government. Then in 1877 the federal government abdicated its responsibilities to new black citizens and withdrew from the South. When it did so it allowed local governments and racial terrorist organizations like the KKK to have the monopoly on violence, force, and coercion in the South for nearly 100 years.

As I watch the rising tide of racial anxiety and secessionist sentiment I am not so much reminded of the Bloody Sunday protests as I am reminded of D.W. Griffith's *Birth of Nation*. This 1915 film depicts the racist imagination currently at work in our nation as a black president first appoints a Latina Supreme Court justice and then works with a woman speaker of the House to pass sweeping national legislation. This bigotry assumes no such government could possibly be legitimate and therefore frames resistance against this government as a patriotic responsibility.

There are historic lessons to be learned. But they are the lessons of the nineteenth century, not the twentieth. We must now guard against the end of our new Reconstruction and the descent of a vicious new Jim Crow terrorism.

—March 22, 2010

Notes:

1. http://www.washingtonpost.com/wp-dyn/content/article/2010/03/20/AR2010032002556.html

2. http://www.ontopmag.com/article.aspx?id=5457&MediaType=1&Category=26

3. http://news.yahoo.com/s/mcclatchy/3457015

4. http://www.democraticunderground.com/discuss/duboard.php?az=view_all&address=389x7972612

5. http://www.thepoliticalcarnival.net/2010/03/video-keith-olbermanns-special-comment.html

6. http://memory.loc.gov/ammem/today/mar07.html

7. http://www.huffingtonpost.com/cynthia-boaz/to-john-lewis-an-open-let_b_507869.html

THE MAD TEA PARTY

Richard Kim

Leftists like to say that another world is possible, but I was never quite sure of that until I started reading Tea Party websites. There, a government of leftists is not only possible, it's on the cusp of seizing permanent power, having broken American capitalism and replaced it with a socialist state. Down that rabbit hole, Barack Obama and Rahm Emanuel are communists, and "The Left"—which encompasses everyone from the Democratic Leadership Council to Maoist sectarians—is a disciplined and near-omnipotent army marching in lockstep to a decades-old master plan for domination called the "Cloward-Piven strategy" or, as of January 20, 2009, "Cloward-Piven government."

What is this plot? According to David Horowitz, who apparently coined the expression, Cloward-Piven is "the strategy of forcing political change through orchestrated crisis." Named after sociologists and antipoverty and voting-rights activists Richard Cloward and Frances Fox Piven, who first elucidated it in a May 2, 1966, article for *The Nation* called "The Weight of the Poor: A Strategy to End Poverty," the Cloward-Piven strategy, in Horowitz's words, "seeks to hasten the fall of capitalism by overloading the government bureaucracy with a flood of impossible demands, thus pushing society into crisis and economic collapse." Like a fun-house-mirror version of Naomi Klein's Shock Doctrine theory, the Cloward-Piven strategy dictates that the left will exploit that crisis to push through unpopular, socialist policies in a totalitarian manner.

Since Obama's election and the financial crash of 2008, Horowitz's description has been taken up by a clutch of Tea Party propagandists—from TV and radio hosts Glenn Beck, Rush Limbaugh, and Mark Levin to *WorldNetDaily* editor Joseph Farah, *National Review* editor Stanley Kurtz, and *The Obama Nation* author Jerome Corsi—to explain how both events could have happened, here, in the U-S-A. In their historical narrative, it was Cloward and Piven's article that gave ACORN the idea to start peddling subprime mortgages to poor minorities in the 1980s, knowingly laying the groundwork for a global economic meltdown nearly thirty years later. Beck calls Cloward and Piven the two people who are "fundamentally responsible for the unsustainability and possible collapse of our economic system." It was Cloward and Piven who had the diabolical idea of registering (illegal or nonexistent) poor and minority voters through Project Vote and the Motor Voter Act, thus guaranteeing Obama's "fraudulent" victory. And it is the Cloward-Piven strategy that guides the Obama administration's every move to this day, as it seeks to ram through health-care reform, economic stimulus and financial regulation (all of which, in reality, have enjoyed majority support in many polls taken during the last two years).

As proof, Beck & Co. point to what they see as a shadowy web of associations: Cloward and Piven worked in alliance with welfare rights organizer George Wiley, who mentored Wade Rathke, who went on to found ACORN, which sometimes coordinated registration drives with Project Vote (whose board of directors Piven just recently joined), a previous incarnation of which employed Obama to run a Chicago chapter in the early '90s. They also repeatedly cite Emanuel's statement, made in November 2008 after the passage of TARP but before the stimulus, that "you never want a serious crisis to go to waste." From *The Nation*'s pages to the White House's brains and muscles—it took only forty-four years!

All of this, of course, is a reactionary paranoid fantasy. Rahm Emanuel is no more Frances Fox Piven's stooge than Obama is a Muslim. But the looniness of it has not stopped the Cloward-Piven conspiracy theory from spreading across Tea Party networks. And the left's gut reaction upon hearing of it—to laugh it off as a Scooby-Doo comic mystery—does nothing to blunt its appeal or limit its impact. In order to respond, alas, we have to understand, and that means going through the looking glass.

Horowitz first wrote of the Cloward-Piven strategy on his website discoverthenetworks.org, which claims to be "a guide to the left." His description is a crude and false account of what Cloward and Piven argued. For example, the words "capital" and "capitalism" never appear in their article. The piece is about precipitating a crisis in the welfare system by legally enrolling masses of eligible recipients, which the welfare bureaucracy could not handle, thus creating a demand for more radical reforms, like a guaranteed minimum income—a proposal that Nixon, of all people, floated in 1969 and that, in fact, Democratic-majority Congresses voted down through 1972. Moreover, as Piven recently explained to me, although the article was written as a strategic thought experiment, in many ways it described and reacted to changes already sweeping the nation, chief among them the civil rights and welfare rights movements, which created newly politicized constituencies to which the Democratic Party had to respond. "The mainstream," Piven says, "was responsive to the idea that we could end poverty because of these movements." In short, the stresses placed on the welfare system were caused by a confluence of factors, of which an article published in *The Nation*, it is safe to say, was but one, and most likely a minor one at that.

Nevertheless—history and facts be damned—it is Horowitz's caricature of Cloward-Piven that is now the Rosetta stone of American politics for the Tea Party's self-styled intellectuals. Glenn Beck has brought up Cloward and Piven on at least twenty-eight episodes of his show over the past year. Beck is sometimes aided by a blackboard on which he has diagramed something called "The Tree of Revolution," which links Che Guevara, SEIU, and ACORN's Wade Rathke to Saul Alinsky, the Sierra Club's Carl Pope, Bill Ayers, and, perhaps most improbably, to White House senior adviser Valerie Jarrett. In the center of the tree's arching trunk, above SDS and Woodrow Wilson (!?) but below Barack Obama, who adorns the tree's crown, Beck has scrawled "Cloward & Piven."

Beck's tree, however, is derivative of and pales in comparison with the flowchart created by Jim Simpson, a self-described businessman and former George H.W. Bush White House budget analyst and the leading proponent of the Cloward-Piven conspiracy theory. Cribbing from Horowitz, but adding his own very special embellishments, Simpson has penned an 18,000-word, six-part exposé of the "Cloward-Piven strategy," which can be found on the websites Americanthinker.com and Americandaughter.com. I have read it so you don't have to. The central innovations of this wild and woolly compilation of right-wing myths, published in installments during the summer and fall of 2008, are to attribute nearly every past, present, and future crisis to Cloward and Piven and to link them to Obama's political past and agenda. Among the schemes Simpson credits to the Cloward-Piven strategy are health-care reform, the Employee Free Choice Act, cap and trade, immigration reform, hate crimes legislation, and public financing of elections. For Simpson, the Cloward-Piven strategy is vast, vast—"a malevolent overarching strategy that has motivated many, if not all, of the most destructive radical leftist organizations in the United States since the 1960s." And beyond: Somehow, Gorbachev's Crimean dacha is implicated, as are Saddam Hussein's palaces.

Most integral to Simpson's theory, however, and where his rather impressive skills as a collagist descend into the orthodoxy of Fox News, is ACORN, which he says has been "the new tip of the Cloward-Piven spear" since 1970. In what is by now a familiar right-wing story line, ACORN is responsible for the global economic crisis. By using the 1977 Community Reinvestment Act—itself a conspiratorial response to the bogus crisis of housing discrimination—ACORN enrolled masses of low-income people in subprime mortgages, creating a housing bubble that caused stock markets around the world to crash, paving the way for bank nationalization and socialism via the bailout and the stimulus. Whew! There are, of course, more than a few pages missing in this whodunit—for instance, that it was ACORN that tried to warn Congress about risky and predatory lenders; that it was too-big-to-fail banks and complex financial instruments that spread the contagion across the worldwide economy; and that in fact the banks have not been nationalized. (For a debunking of this myth, see Peter Dreier and John Atlas's "The GOP's Blame-ACORN Game," *The Nation*, October 22, 2008.)

If Simpson's chain of events is not particularly original, his theory of intentionality is: According to him, the left, guided by the Cloward-Piven strategy, was fully aware that subprime mortgages would produce a calamitous financial bubble; it supported subprime lending not to help minorities become homeowners but to sabotage capitalism from the inside. "*The failure is deliberate,*" he writes repeatedly in italics.

Like others on the right, Simpson sees Obama's election itself as a machination of ACORN, which registered millions of felons, illegal aliens, and dead citizens to vote through Project Vote and the Motor Voter Act, which Cloward and Piven championed and which Bill Clinton signed in 1993. (Voter fraud seems to be Simpson's enduring preoccupation and the subject of an early 2007 article on Cloward-Piven.) By the logic of the Cloward-Piven strategy, he suggests, voter registration efforts were aimed at corrupting democracy, not expanding it. This argument depends on the denial of several key realities: that changing demographics have altered the balance of party power, that legally increasing the voting rate of key constituencies is a common and legitimate practice of both parties, and that the Republican Party consistently fails to win over minorities because of the policies it promotes. What Simpson and Beck want to cast doubt on is that the democratic process could elect Obama, or that democratic majorities would endorse the agenda Obama has proposed. In the months before the 2008 election, Simpson wrote, "It is not inconceivable that this presidential race could be decided by fraudulent votes alone."

Beck and Simpson have played the Tea Party's Paul Reveres, warning the masses of the Cloward-Piven assault. But nearly the entire orbit of Tea Party luminaries have taken it up in some way. In October 2008 the *Washington Times* ran an op-ed by Robert Chandler called "The Cloward Piven Strategy," and Stanley Kurtz wrote about it in *National Review* Online. Mark Levin, author of the bestseller *Liberty and Tyranny: A Conservative Manifesto*, has discussed it on multiple occasions on his radio program, as did Rush Limbaugh on the March 4 broadcast of his show. In a January 13 interview, Beck asked Sarah Palin if she had seen and believed in the case he had been making on Cloward and Piven. Palin replied, "I do. I do believe it.... It has to be purposeful what they are doing. Otherwise—otherwise I would say, Glenn, that there is no hope, that there are no solutions."

In February, Kyle Olson, a GOP hack who runs an ersatz education nonprofit called the Education Action Group, posed as a student and requested a videotaped interview with Piven, which she gave in her home. Olson posted a portion of the interview on biggovernment. com, a website run by Andrew Breitbart, who released the "prostitute and pimp" undercover ACORN sting in 2009. Olson captures nothing so dramatic: Piven lucidly discusses homeowner civil disobedience during the Great Depression as a model for how foreclosed homeowners today could refuse to leave their homes and thus create pressure on banks to renegotiate mortgages—a strategy advocated by Ohio Congresswoman Marcy Kaptur and, yes, ACORN.

Suffice it to say, if Beck and crew believe half of this crap, they belong in an asylum in the middle of Shutter Island, where they can tend to their survival seeds and sleuth out imagined conspiracies apart from the rest of the human population. The danger, however, is that they will maroon a sizable portion of the electorate there with them. Since Obama's inauguration, references to the Cloward-Piven strategy have popped up with increasing frequency in op-eds and letters to the editor of local newspapers, including those in Florida, Ohio, Pennsylvania, and New Mexico. Snippets of Simpson's tome or Beck's rants appear frequently in the comments section of blogs and articles; a search for the term "Cloward-Piven strategy" generated more than 255,000 Google hits.

Why does the Cloward-Piven conspiracy theory hold such appeal? And what, if anything, does it accomplish? On one level it's entertainment. It allows believers to tease out the left's secrets and sinister patterns. Since none of the evidence that supposedly confirms the existence of the Cloward-Piven strategy is, in fact, secret, this proves rather easy to do, and so the puzzle is both thrilling and gratifying.

On another level, the theory is an adaptive response to the Tea Party's fragmentation. As Jonathan Raban pointed out in *The New York Review of Books*, the Tea Party is an uneasy conclave of Ayn Rand secular libertarians and fundamentalist Christian evangelicals; it contains birthers, Birchers, racists, xenophobes, Ron Paulites, cold warriors, Zionists, constitutionalists, vanilla Republicans looking for a high, and militia-style survivalists. Because the Cloward-Piven strategy is so expansive, it allows Tea Party propagandists to engage any one—or all—of the pet issues that incite these various constituencies. For some, the left's "offensive to promote illegal immigration" is "Cloward-Piven on steroids." For others, it is the Cloward-Piven "advocates of social change" who "used the Fed, which was complicit in the scheme" to "engineer" the 2008 fiscal crisis. In his speech at the Tea Party convention in Nashville, WorldNetDaily's Joseph Farah notes that Obama was just four when the Cloward-Piven strategy was written. "We *think*," Farah said. He paused dramatically before adding, "Without the birth certificate we really just don't know," as a sizable portion of the audience broke into applause.

Racial and class resentments, however, are never far from the surface, no matter which subject is slotted into the great Cloward-Piven conspiracy machine. The word "radical," for example, is almost always preceded by the word "black" when it can be (George Wiley), but nobody is ever called a "white radical" (Bill Ayers). Whenever grammatically possible—and sometimes even when it is not—Cloward and Piven are identified as "Columbia professors" and Obama as a "Harvard graduate." (Beyond just heaping Nixonian scorn on elites, the Cloward-Piven conspiracy credits the left with an almost divine intelligence.)

And as of now, the Cloward-Piven strategy is most often used to put two classes of people on the Tea Party's enemies list: those who work for the Obama administration and those who work to increase the political power of poor people of color. (Doing both—as was the case with Van Jones—can be fatal.) It is the latter target that is particularly appalling: Here is a so-called populist movement promulgating a master narrative that holds poor people to blame for the world's woes. The precise impact of this conspiracy theory and the broader movement it incites on Obama's legislative agenda is, as of now, unclear. But the toll it has taken on organizations that advocate for poor people of color could not be more stark. On the weekend the health-care reform bill cleared the House, Tea Party activists descended on Washington to decry "the end of America"; their bitter pill was soothed by front-page coverage of the end of something else—ACORN announced it was on the verge of bankruptcy, the victim of what CEO Bertha Lewis called "a series of well-orchestrated, relentless, well-funded right-wing attacks."

Perhaps most critical, the Cloward-Piven conspiracy theory pushes the Tea Party's kettle closer to a boil. In its obsession with voter fraud and the potential illegitimacy of the 2008 election—and the democratic process itself—the conspiracy suggests a tit-for-tat strategy for victory: If the left is going to cynically manipulate the system to produce tyranny, then so will we. How? To begin, there's the tried-and-true tactic of suppressing the poor minority vote—which would next place Project Vote in the Tea Party's crosshairs. But why stop there? Like every good conspiracy theory, this one too is a call to arms.

—April 15, 2010

TEA PARTIERS SAY SLAVERY NOT RACE-RELATED

Julie Ingersoll

For those who wonder about the religious dimensions of the Tea Party movement, an event earlier this month at Faith Baptist Church in Deltona, Florida, looked pretty much indistinguishable from the 1980s-era church-based political organizing efforts of the religious right. As each local candidate spoke at the Deltona 9/12 Patriots event, it was clear how profoundly conservative, Republican, and Christian (in the exclusivist conservative sense of Christian) this gathering was.

But there was a twist, born of the Tea Party's efforts to run from the racist and violent imagery and rhetoric in its ranks. The banner on the Florida Tea Party website read: "9-12 Project: not racist, not violent, just not silent anymore."

The event was in a more rural part of Florida than where I live and I passed a number of Confederate flags on my way there. I expected an all-white crowd making arguments about "reverse discrimination," libertarian arguments against violations of state sovereignty, especially with regard to the Civil Rights Act, and maybe even some of the "slavery wasn't as bad as people say" arguments. Not so much.

DON'T LIKE HISTORY? MAKE UP SOME OF YOUR OWN

The keynote speaker was Frantz Kebreau of the Florida-based National Association for the Advancement of Conservative People of all Colors (that's right: NAACPC), who has been traveling the Tea Party circuit with his alternative history of racism and slavery in America. The NAACPC maintains that the "once-great NAACP has become a negative, shameful tool of the left: overseers committed to keeping their fellow blacks dependent and subservient to the Democrat party."

According to the NAACPC's website, Kebreau believes "Identity Politics, race, white guilt, political correctness and racism are the means by which Socialism through entitlements will bring our Country down." In his lectures, the site promises, Frantz exposes the hidden history that the radical left, progressives, and Democrats do not want you to know about. Hold on, because the information you will receive is virtually impossible to find in the history books. Kebreau's biography warns that the progressives and socialists are "are rewriting history as we speak" so they can "bring Socialism to the United States of America," and promises that his truth-telling "will set you free!"

His audience at Faith Baptist was not unaccustomed to revisionist history. Sitting in the sanctuary decked in patriotic trimmings—eight big flags on the wall, bunting covering the altar area, and a collection of small flags on the altar itself—the assembled activists discussed homeschooling, David Barton's seminal revisionist work on "America's Christian heritage," all while Copeland's *Fanfare for the Common Man* played over the sound system.

There didn't seem to be any of those secular, libertarian Tea Partiers here. In fact, if the people at Faith Baptist abandon the Republican Party, it will likely be for the Reconstructionist-oriented, more conservative Constitution Party.

The Tea Party–supported candidates for local office all invoked "Christian American history" and the "religion of the founders." The "principles" of the 9/12 Project, the brainchild of Glenn Beck, are a distillation of those found in W. Cleon Skousen's 1981 book, *The 5,000 Year Leap*, to which the speakers repeatedly referred. Although Beck has been responsible for its recent resurgence, the book has long been a favorite for Christian schools and homeschoolers (and among

Reconstructionists—though Skousen himself was a Mormon, free market, Austrian school guy).

SO, SLAVERY WAS NOT ABOUT RACE?

As I understand it, the fight over the degree to which America was "founded as a Christian Nation," is a fight over our mythic understanding of ourselves. I don't mean myth in the popular sense—as in "myths are widely held to be true but actually are not." Rather, I mean myth in the technical sense: narratives though which groups of people construct a sense of themselves and perpetuate that sense throughout the culture and to successive generations.

Kebreau's presence at this event signaled a new development in the religious right's mythmaking. In Kebreau's narrative, racism is a legacy of slavery but not a cause: Instead, racism was a socially constructed mechanism by which people in power divided, threatened, and manipulated both blacks and whites to support slavery. Many of the pieces of historical data he marshals in favor of this thesis are not unfamiliar to those of us who have studied this aspect of American history, although they are probably not as well-known among Americans in general: Some slave owners were also black, not all slaves were black, black Africans played a huge role in the slave trade, very few Southerners actually owned slaves. Most often, though, I hear these points made in argument from white Southerners—in a way that preserves the "us" and "them" division among black and white Americans—who just want the issue of slavery and racism to just go away.

These points are usually presented with a specific subtext: Some slave owners were also black (so why are you blaming us?); not all slaves were black (and white people experience just as much racism today); black Africans played a huge role in the slave trade ("they" did it to "us" too); very few Southerners actually owned slaves (so why does it have to be such a big deal?).

But Kebreau's subtext is different: he argues that slavery was not really about race. He says some slave owners were also black (so it wasn't about race); not all slaves were black (so it wasn't about race); black Africans played a huge role in the slave trade (so it wasn't about race); very few Southerners actually owned slaves. So how did they convince the rest of them to go to war and die to defend the "property" of a few rich people? They did so, according to Kebreau, by developing and perpetuating racial divisions among people who wouldn't, otherwise, have had an interest in the fight.

He traced the ways in which the institution of slavery developed in the colonies, becoming increasingly race-based over time and accompanied by racist laws and customs that preserved it. Or to put it the way he does, how the "color line got darker and darker," all in the interest of fostering racism to preserve the power, wealth, and status of a few.

Kebreau convinced a white Southern audience, who would likely insist that the "war of Northern aggression" was not about slavery, to be "proud of America" in which nearly two-thirds of a million people gave their lives in a war to end slavery. He took an audience of Southerners and led them to claim the vision of the North. He took an audience of white Christians who would have opposed a Martin Luther King Jr. holiday, and had them shouting "Amen!" and cheering him on from the pews like members of the AME Church as he talked about Martin Luther King Jr.'s dream and the March on Washington. He moved the audience from the view that the Civil Rights Acts were an intrusion of government into realms in which it did not belong, to the view that they should be proud to be Republicans because Republicans introduced those bills and passed them, over the opposition of Democrats! (You could almost hear them saying, "Damn those Democrats." Of course, the Democrats that opposed these measures have long-since moved to the Republican Party and, though the Republican Party of another era freed the slaves, more contemporarily they also launched the divisive "Southern strategy.")

So while explicit, traditional "God and Country" religion was everywhere at this event, so was the less explicit construction of a new "creation myth" for the Republican Party's American civil religion. I couldn't help but marvel at power of myth to unite a group of people in agreement about what's wrong, whose fault it is, and how an election could be used to fix it.

—June 22, 2010

PROGRESSIVES AND 'BITTER' WHITE AMERICA

Kai Wright

Frank Rich, as always, does his trade honors in Sunday's *New York Times* column on the real source of Tea Party anger. (The column pairs nicely with Richard Kim's dissection of Tea Party conspiracy theories in *The Nation* this week.) But understanding this movement's emotional and mental core is only part of the battle. We also have to respond to it, and that's where progressive and Democratic Party leadership alike continue to fail. Progressives consistently meet Tea Partiers with sneering outrage. What we need, with increasing urgency, is leadership that explicitly aligns working-class white folks and people of color.

Rich points out the reality that America is undergoing one of the most deep, significant changes in its history. No, it's not health-insurance reform. Nor is it our economic collapse, though that's surely part of it. Frankly, it's not even the fact of a black president. The change is far deeper and probably far more consequential: White people will shortly lose their status as *normative* Americans. Whatever else does or doesn't change, by the time Millennials are adults, no one will equate white skin with the phrase "all-American"—assuming the phrase carries meaning at all.

Rich cites this stat: Nearly half of all babies born in the 12 months preceding July 2008 were born to black, Asian, or Latino moms. He'll be able to fill his column with similar stats when we get results from the 2010 Census. Already, the demographics of public schools in the

South and the West defy the notion of "minorities." And while the absolute number of white Americans will shrink over the next generation, the Latino community will nearly triple.

All of this will eventually shape every aspect of American life. Young, colored folks will drive the economy, the culture, the politics—and the country's rapidly shrinking, white-dominated enclaves will grow increasingly defensive about that fact. As Rich writes:

> If Obama's first legislative priority had been immigration or financial reform or climate change, we would have seen the same trajectory. The conjunction of a black president and a female speaker of the House—topped off by a wise Latina on the Supreme Court and a powerful gay Congressional committee chairman—would sow fears of disenfranchisement among a dwindling and threatened minority in the country no matter what policies were in play. It's not happenstance that Frank, Lewis and Cleaver—none of them major Democratic players in the health care push—received a major share of last weekend's abuse. When you hear demonstrators chant the slogan "Take our country back!," these are the people they want to take the country back from.

They can't.

But they can rip our polity to shreds in the process of trying. And if they do, it will be as much the fault of national progressive leaders as it is of the conservatives we're rightly holding accountable for the recent violence. Progressive leaders remain reluctant to confront the meaningful anxieties working-class white people face. Profiteering demagogues like Sarah Palin are filling the void.

As I've written previously, I'm consistently reminded of Martin Luther King Jr.'s most astute, if rarely cited, analysis. "The Southern aristocracy took the world and gave the poor white man Jim Crow," he declared during the 1965 march on Selma, Alabama.

That pact has come apart. Our manufacturing economy is gone, along with the inequality that reserved the best jobs within it for whites. The face of our politics is forever altered, by both Barack Obama and Nancy Pelosi. And Millennials are redefining the very idea of an American. The Glenn Becks of the world peddle the notion that sheer anger can reverse these trends. What's the progressive response? Sneering's not it.

The upheaval of our times presents a unique opportunity to dismantle a centuries-old tool of oppression: pitting working-class whites against people of color. Either we seize the moment by addressing the "bitterness" Obama so infamously identified on the campaign trail, or we watch the public square devolve into a mob of spit and bricks. Worse, we squander a rare opening for real change.

—March 29, 2010

THE PEDAGOGY OF SHOCK (AND GRANDIOSE LUNACY)

Lisa Duggan

Glenn Beck wants you to *think*. He wants you to *read*. He wants you, most of all, to *question*. Standing before his trademark blackboard, he draws connections between ideas, public figures, organizations, political *consequences*. He wants you to understand large forces at work in your world, so you will grasp what is at stake, so you can *act* responsibly.

Glenn Beck mobilizes the tools and rhetoric of the classroom on his 5:00 p.m. weekday Fox television program. More than any other TV pundit, he brings the blackboard, the syllabus, the challenging historical interpretation of current events, into the approximately 3 million households where his show is watched each day. But there's something distinctly off kilter about this classroom experience. It reminds me of Father Guido Sarducci's "Five Minute University," Donald Trump's surprisingly named Trump University (now Trump Education, after a challenge to the use of the term "university" by the State of New York), or the famed McDonald's Hamburger U. The trappings of the college classroom surround an enterprise that combines entertainment, narcissistic grandiosity, and a very narrow and specific kind of "knowledge" organized to produce fear and eager compliance with the teacher's agenda.

Beck is deploying the pedagogy of shock and awe to sell a B-movie plot as if it were history, a version of history that engages deep currents of paranoia in the American body politic. He repeats the plot summary like a mantra as he lays out its details:

> What are we looking for? We are looking for a group of people, a small group, global.... [T]hey believe that there is a threat to the Earth and that...rich countries are the problem. They will collapse the industrialized system.... They will collapse the system and they also need to control it, every aspect of it.

The quest is to identify the people, the organizations, the ideas and the institutions that are collaborating in this elite plot to destroy the nation's wealth and freedom. Toward this end, Beck identifies the core conspiracy as "progressivism," and provides a syllabus and an historical analysis to explain the dangerous projects behind the 2008 economic collapse, in particular.

Beck's version of the history of progressivism is based largely on Ronald Pestritto's *Woodrow Wilson and the Roots of Modern Liberalism*, among other similar tomes. This view presents progressivism as a betrayal of U.S. constitutional principles, and its proponents from Woodrow Wilson on as advocates of elite control over an ever-expanding state. As Glenn Beck expounds it, this historical argument is a kind of fun-house-mirror version of a longstanding New Left critique of early twentieth century progressivism as a force for undemocratic, paternalistic, "expert" control of state policy. But if the left critique was developed in the interests of egalitarian radical democracy, Beck's critique leads his viewers toward the alternative of an unregulated "free market," presided over by a theocratic version of the founders' republic.

In order to disseminate this historical analysis and political program more widely, Beck has expanded his $32 million empire of publications (six books and the magazine *Fusion*), radio, digital media, speaking events, and television to include the new online Beck

University. As a $9.95-per-month member of Beck's Insider Extreme, "students" may listen to live lectures and podcasts on faith, hope, and charity by the three "professors": notorious right wing theocrat David Barton of Wallbuilders, business consultant and motivational speaker David L. Bruckner, and James R. Stoner, a professor of political science at Louisiana State University and the sole academic teaching at Beck U.

These courses were been organized to begin during 2010, leading up to Beck's grand call to "Refound America" on the steps of the Lincoln Memorial on August 28, the anniversary of Martin Luther King Jr.'s "I Have a Dream Speech."

This brings us to another key aspect of Glenn Beck's "pedagogy"— his grandiose lunacy, an X-factor that revs up the kind of paranoia and conspiracy mongering that have marked American politics on the right and left from the John Birch Society to Lyndon LaRouche's incessant campaigns. If the historical analysis presented via Beck's TV classroom is not *totally* off the wall, in that it includes provocations that are worth considering along with far-fetched or simply erroneous claims, he surrounds his "lectures" with the kind of nutball high jinks he developed earlier in his career as a "morning zoo" radio D.J. As recounted by Beck biographer Alexander Zaitchik, many of the audio and visual tropes Beck employs—the Muppet voices, the outrageous claims, the props, skits and stunts, the goofy supporting cast— have their roots in zoo and post-zoo radio. As Zaitchik recounts it, Beck's radio career went on the skids after he simply went too far with fat jokes, racial impersonations, and cruel practical jokes (including calling a competitor's wife at home to make fun of a recent miscarriage). His new career as a conservative talk-show host did not take off until he sobered up from his years of alcohol and drug abuse, joined the Mormon church, and acquired a new, transformed identity as a convert.

The cruel and crazed Beck of his radio days folds into the transformed and teary Beck as he names individual policy makers and social justice advocates (including Van Jones, John Podesta, and Frances Fox Piven), connects them to conspiratorial plots to undermine the nation, and insists that they are all *connected*, basically to Stalin's Gulags and the Holocaust. He calls the web of connections he concocts on his blackboard "Crime, Inc." and asks, teary face in the camera lens, "How do you expose this and live?" He morphs from earnest pedagogue to full-out crackpot. As Matthew Continetti points out in the conservative *Weekly Standard*, Beck's list of the "Top Ten Bastards of All Time" lists Pol Pot (#10), Adolf Hitler (#6), and Pontius Pilate (#4) beneath FDR (#3) and Woodrow Wilson (#1).

How does this lunacy draw in 3 million viewers to his TV program, not to mention his other listeners, readers, and online "members"? Analyzing his appeal actually *can* provide his audiences with an education in American history and politics. The combination of a classic conspiracy theory, with an account of personal conversion and transformation, along with a religious vocabulary and a vision that plays so many strings in the historical American political symphony, it immerses audiences in overlapping, deeply familiar flows of imagery, language, and emotion. As the historian of American religion Joanna Brooks points out, Beck draws quite specifically on a range of Mormon ideas and images, as he also embeds his religiosity in his recovery from decades of alcohol and drug abuse. And his transformation could be yours! From the Great Awakenings through the many contemporary modes of fusing personal redemption, religious commitment, and political belief, Beck calls upon the weary, the lost, the confused, the angry, the wounded, the desperate, to wake up, stand up, and find the strength to Stop the Madness!

The antidote to this intoxicating brew is not simply to ridicule it, or point out the myriad contradictions and inaccuracies in his shtick. The strongest response would be to expand the syllabus and place Beck's performance in historical context. Instead of simply parodying Beck's act (which Jon Stewart, Stephen Colbert, and the *South Park* crew have done brilliantly), those who wish to deflate his impact might place Beck squarely within the history of American paranoid politics, updated now since Richard Hofstadter's classic historical account, and outline the sources of his spiel. I've often had the fantasy that, with Beck's blackboard and his audience, I could persuade half his viewers to engage the counter-syllabus of radical democratic left history and politics. The frustrations and emotions that Beck taps can lead in that direction at least as easily, as Michael Moore once demonstrated on a TV Nation episode on which he convinced the ragged white male members of the Michigan Militia that greedy corporations were more to blame for their travails than black people (and they held hands and sang "Kumbaya" with him at the end too!).

Of course, no corporate broadcaster is going to offer that platform to a radical/left Democrat any time soon. But perhaps something of that counter analysis can find its way onto a blackboard on another station—say, MSNBC? Rachel Maddow, with Jeff Sharlet? Laura Flanders on GRITtv? Or perhaps Beck will just self-destruct on national television with no assistance first...

—August, 2010

GLENN BECK, AMERICA'S HISTORIAN LAUREATE

Greg Grandin

Americans, it's been said, learn geography when they go to war. Now, it seems, many get their history when they go to a Tea Party rally or tune in to Glenn Beck.

History is a "battlefield of ideas," as Beck recently put it, while looking professorial in front of a blackboard filled with his trademark circled names connected by multidirectional arrows, his hands covered with chalk dust. In this struggle, movement historians like Beck go all in, advancing a comprehensive interpretation of American history meant to provide analytical clarity to believers and potential converts alike. As paranoid as it may be, this history is neither radical nor revisionist, since the Tea Party activists and their fellow travelers pluck at some of the major chords of American nationalism.

It's easy to dismiss the iconography of the movement: the wigs and knee breeches, the founding-father fetishism, the coiled snakes, and, yes, the tea bags. It's no less easy to laugh at recent historical howlers like the claims[1] of Dick Armey, who heads FreedomWorks, a corporate Tea Party front,[2] that Jamestown was settled by "socialists" or the Texas School Board's airbrushing[3] of Deist Thomas Jefferson from its history textbooks. It's fun to ridicule Beck, as Jon Stewart recently did,[4] when he goes all *Da Vinci Code*, and starts connecting[5] Woodrow Wilson, Mussolini, and ACORN[6] in order to explain 2008's economic collapse.

But historical analysis is about making connections, and there is, in fact, coherence to the Tea Party version of history, which allows conservative cadres not just to interpret the world but to act in it. And yes, it *is* all about race.

THE 1040 ARCHIPELAGO

At the heart of Tea Party history is the argument that "progressivism is fascism is communism." Conceptually, such a claim helps frame what many call "American exceptionalism," a belief that the exclusive role of government is to protect individual rights—to speech, to assembly, to carry guns, and, of course, to own property—and not to deliver social rights like health care, education, or welfare.

At Tea Party rallies and on right-wing blogs, it's common to hear that, since the time of President Woodrow Wilson, progressives have been waging a "hundred-year-long war" on America's unique values. This bit of wisdom comes directly from Beck, who has become something like the historian laureate of American exceptionalism, devoting many on-air hours to why progressivism is a threat equal to Nazism and Stalinism.

Progressives, he typically says, "started a hundred-year time bomb. They planted it in the early 1900s." Beck has compared himself to "Israeli Nazi hunters," promising,[7] with language more easily associated with the Nazis than those who pursued them, to track down the progressive "vampires" who are "sucking the blood out of the republic."

As Michael Lind pointed out[8] in a recent essay in *Salon*, behind such Sturm-und-Drang language lurks a small group of relatively obscure historians, teaching in peaceful, leafy liberal arts colleges, many of them influenced by the late University of Chicago political theorist Leo Strauss.[9] They argue that the early-twentieth-century progressive movement betrayed the very idea of universal natural rights invested in the individual, embracing instead a relativist "cult of the state." As a result, a quest for "social justice" was elevated above the defense of "liberty"—a path that led straight to the Gulag and the 1040 short form. From there, it was an easy leap to history's terminus: the Obamacare death panels.[10]

These historians and their popular interpreters, especially Beck and Jonah Goldberg, the author of *Liberal Fascism*, naturally ignore the real threats to individualism that the turn-of-the-twentieth-century progressive movement was responding to—namely a massive concentration of corporate political and economic power and Gilded Era "wage slavery." Instead, they present history as a zero-sum, all-or-nothing "battlefield of ideas," with the founding fathers, Abraham Lincoln, and Winston Churchill on one side, and Jefferson Davis, Wilson, Franklin Roosevelt, Stalin, Hitler, and Obama on the other. The individual versus the state. Freedom versus slavery.

In such an epic view of American history, there is, however, a fly in the ointment or, more accurately, a Confederate in the conceptual attic—and that's the inability of the Tea Party and affiliated right-wing movements to whistle past Dixie.

IS THE TEA PARTY RACIST?

Of course[11] it is. Polls confirm that Tea Party militants entertain deep-seated racial resentment. In April, a *New York Times*/CBS News study revealed[12] that most Tea Partiers tend to be over forty-five, white, male, affluent, and educated, and think that "too much has been made of the problems facing black people." A high percentage of them also believe that Obama favors blacks over whites.

But to say the movement is racist based only on the spit and vitriol hurled[13] at African-American congressmen and civil rights activists like Emanuel Cleaver, or on the placards depicting Obama as a monkey or a pimp, allows for rebuttal. The minute the reality of the spitting incident is challenged and "Don't Tread on Me" is substituted for "Go Back to Kenya," voilà, the movement is instantly as wholesome as apple pie.

A debate over a recent University of Washington poll helps us understand why the movement is racist no matter which slogans and symbols it chooses to use. The poll found[14] that "support for the Tea Party remains a valid predictor of racial resentment." When right-wingers offered the criticism that the pollsters' methodology conflated racism with support for small-government ideology, they reexamined their data and found themselves in agreement (of a sort) with their critics. "Ideology," they wrote in a follow-up, was indeed an important factor, for "as people become more conservative, it increases by 23 percent the chance that they're racially resentful." In other words, it wasn't membership in the Tea Party movement per se that predicted racism, but conservatism itself (though the Tea Party does have a higher percentage of members who displayed racism than conservatism in general).

This should surprise no one. After all, the founding fathers cut Thomas Jefferson's description of slavery as an "execrable commerce" and an "assemblage of horrors" from the final draft of the Declaration of Independence, and race has been crucially embedded in the conception of the patriot ideal of the sovereign individual ever since. As Harvard historian Jill Lepore has written[15] about the original Boston Tea Party, the colonists had a choice: "either abolish slavery... [or] resist parliamentary rule. It could not do both." Many in Virginia, of course, didn't want to do both. Instead, they simply defined the defense of slavery as part of American liberty.

While Jefferson, himself a slaveholder, failed in his effort to extend the notion of individual inalienable rights to blacks, he was successful in setting two rhetorical precedents that would continue to influence American political culture. First, he used chattel slavery as a metaphor for British tyranny, equating the oppression of Africans with the oppression of the white colonists. At the same time, he stoked racial fears to incite rebellion: King George III, he wrote,[16] was "exciting" blacks to "rise in arms among us, and to purchase that liberty of which he has deprived them by murdering" whites. One could draw a straight line from these words to George H.W. Bush's infamous[17] 1988 Willie Horton ad.[18]

From then on, the ideal of the assertion and protection of individual rights was regularly bound up with racial demonology. Anglo genocidal campaigns against and land theft from Native Americans, for instance, contributed[19] to the influential theories concerning property of John Locke,[20] who before Beck arrived on the scene, was considered "America's philosopher," the man most associated with the notion of God-given inalienable individual rights and restricted government.

Once such theories were formulated, they were then used to further justify dispossession, contributing, as law professor Howard Berman put it,[21] to the "Americanization of the law of real property." The nineteenth century was known for a frenzied speculative capitalism that generated staggering inequality. At the same time, eliminationist wars that drove Indian removal, the illegal invasion of Mexico by the United States in 1846, and the ongoing subjugation of African-Americans helped stabilize the Daniel Boone–like image of a disciplined, propertied, white male self—and did so by contrasting it with racial enemies who were imagined to be unbridled (like the speculative capitalists) but also abject and propertyless.

The Civil War cemented the metaphor whereby the free individual was defined by (and endangered by) his opposite, the slave, and has been used ever since to frame conflicts that often, on the surface at least, don't seem to be about race at all. It's a point nicely illustrated recently by Dale Robertson, a prominent Tea Party organizer, who carried[22] a sign at a rally that read: "Congress = Slaveowner, Taxpayer = Niggar." Beck, for his part, has identified[23] ACORN, the Service Employees International Union or SEIU, the census, and the health-care bill, among other threats, as laying the foundation for a "modern-day slave state" in which, of course, his overwhelmingly white following could be reduced to the status of slaves. As to progressives, he has said[24] that, "back in Samuel Adams's day, they used to call them tyrants. A little later I think they were also called slave owners, people who encourage you to become more dependent on them."

Sometimes, though, it really is just about race: "Obama's Plan," announced[25] one placard at a Wisconsin Tea Party gathering, would lead to "White Slavery."

LOCK-AND-LOAD POPULISM

When Tea Partiers say "Obama is trying to turn us into something we are not," as one did recently on cable TV, they are not wrong. It's an honest statement, acknowledging that attempts to implement any government policies to help the poor would signal an assault on American exceptionalism, defined by Beck and likeminded others as extreme individualism.

The issue is not really the specific content of any particular policy. As any number of frustrated observers[26] can testify, it is no use pointing out that, say, the health-care legislation that passed is fundamentally conservative and similar to past Republican health-care plans,[27] or that Obama has actually lowered taxes[28] for most Americans, or that he gets an F rating[29] from the Brady Campaign to Prevent Gun Violence. The issue is the idea of public policy itself, which, for many on the right, violates an ideal of absolute individual rights.

In other words, any version of progressive taxation, policy, and regulation, no matter how mild, or for that matter, of social "justice" and the "common good"—qualities the Texas School Board recently deleted from its textbook definition of "good citizenship"—are not simply codes for race. They *are* race. To put it another way, individual supremacy has been, historically speaking, white supremacy.

This helps explain why it is impossible for the anti-Obama backlash to restrain its Tourette's-like references to the Civil War to frame its fight, or its rhetorical spasms invoking secession and nullification, or its urge to carry Confederate flags as well as signs equating taxpayers with slaves. That America's first black president's first major social legislation was health care—something so intimately, even invasively about the body, the place where the social relations of race are physically inscribed (and recorded in differential mortality rates)—pushed the world-turned-upside-down carnival on display every night on Fox News, where the privileged fancy themselves powerless, another step toward the absurd.

The deepest contradiction may, however, lie in this: The tea-baggers who reject any move by Big Government when it comes to social policy at home remain devoted, as Andrew Sullivan recently wrote,[30] to the Biggest Budget-Busting Government of All, the "military-industrial-ideological complex" and its all-powerful commander-in-chief executive (and surprising numbers of them are also dependent on that complex's give-away welfare state when it comes to their livelihoods).

As James Bovard, a consistent libertarian, has observed, "many 'tea party' activists staunchly oppose big government, except when it is warring, wiretapping, or waterboarding." For all the signs asking[31] "Who is John Galt?" the movement has openly embraced[32] Arizona's new "show-me-your-papers" immigration law and mutters not one complaint over the fact that America is "the most incarcerated society on earth," something Robert Perkinson detailed in Texas Tough,[33] his book on the Lone Star roots of the U.S. penitentiary system. The skin color of those being tortured, rounded up, and jailed obviously has something to do with the selective libertarianism of much of the conservative movement. But this passion for pain and punishment is also an admission that the crisis-prone ideal of absolute individualism, forged in racial violence, would be unsustainable without further state violence.

Behind the lock-and-load populism and the kitsch calls to "rearm for revolution" is a recognition that the right's agenda of corporate deregulation—the effects of which are evident in exploding coal mines in West Virginia and apocalyptic oil spills in the Gulf of Mexico—can only be achieved through ceaseless mobilization against enemies domestic and foreign.

Here's an example: "I know that the safety and health of coal miners is my most important job," said[34] Don Blankenship at a corporate-funded Friends of America rally held in West Virginia last Labor Day, where speakers such as Ted Nugent and Sean Hannity spoke out[35] against tyrants, regulation, "Obama and his cronies," taxes, cap-and-trade legislation, unnamed "cockroaches," China, green technology, and, naturally, gun control. Blankenship just happens to be the CEO of Massey Energy, owner of the Upper Big Branch mine where twenty-nine workers recently lost their lives.

He is also famous for waving the banner of individual rights even as he presides[36] over a company that any totalitarian state worth its salt would envy, one that intimidates "its workers into a type of lock-step compliance that most often takes the form of silence," including threats to fire workers who take time off to attend the funerals of the dead miners. Wrapping himself in the American flag—literally, wearing[37] a stars-and-stripes shirt and baseball cap—Blankenship told that Labor Day crowd that he didn't "need Washington politicians to tell" him about mine safety. Seven months later, twenty-nine miners are dead.

THE END OF AMERICAN EXCEPTIONALISM

And here's the irony, or one of them anyway: In the process of defining American exceptionalism as little more than a pitchfork loyalty to individual rights, Beck and other right-wingers are themselves becoming the destroyers of what was exceptional, governmentally speaking, about the United States. Like John Locke's celebration of inalienable rights, founding father James Madison's distrust of the masses became a distinctive feature of American political culture. Madison valued individual rights, but in the tripartite American system of government he worked hard to help fashion, a bulwark meant to contain the passions he knew they generated. "Liberty is to faction what air is to fire," he wrote in 1787, and in the centuries that followed, American politicians would consistently define their unique democracy against the populist and revolutionary excesses of other countries.

Today, though, not just Fox News Jacobins like Beck and Hannity but nearly the entire leadership of the Republican Party are fanning those flames. Newt Gingrich hopes [38] the Tea Party will become the "militant wing of the Republican Party," looking to hitch his political fortunes to a movement now regularly calling[39] for a "second bloody revolution." It is hard to think of another time in American history when one half of the political establishment has so wholly embraced insurrectionary populism as an electoral strategy.

Considering the right's success at mimicking the organizing tactics of the left, it would be tempting to see recent calls for rebellion and violence as signs that the conservative movement is entering its Weathermen phase—the moment in the 1960s and 1970s when some left-wing activists succumbed to revolutionary fantasies, contributing to the New Left's crackup. Except that violence did not really come all that easy to the American leftists of that moment. There was endless theorizing and agonizing, Leninist justifying and Dostoevskian moralizing, from which the left, considering the ongoing finger pointing and mea culpas, still hasn't recovered.

In contrast, conservative entitlement to the threat of violence is so baked into American history that, in moments like this, it seems to be taken for granted.[40] The Tea Party crowd, along with its militia, NRA, and Oath Keeper friends, would just as easily threaten to overthrow the federal government—or waterboard Nancy Pelosi[41]—as go golfing.[42]

On the fifteenth anniversary of the bombing of the Oklahoma Federal Building, which left 168 people dead and 600 wounded, gun-rights militants held a rally at the Mall in Washington, along with a smaller, heavily armed one across the Potomac, where speaker after speaker threatened revolution and invoked the federal siege of Waco[43] to justify the Oklahoma bombing. This is the kind of militancy Gingrich believes the Republicans can harness and which he tenderly calls a "natural expression" of frustration.

Where all this will lead, who knows? But you still "don't need a weatherman to know which way the wind blows."

—May 13, 2010

Notes:

1. http://www.charlotteobserver.com/2010/04/04/1354655/the-right-takes-on-history.html

2. http://www.alternet.org/economy/145459/public_is_ready_to_raise_taxes_on_corporations_and_the_rich,_oregon_vote_shows

3. http://www.nytimes.com/2010/03/13/education/13texas.html

4. http://www.thedailyshow.com/watch/thu-march-18-2010/conservative-libertarian

5. http://www.thenation.com/../../../../../../doc/20100412/kim

6. http://mediamatters.org/research/200908050038

7. http://mediamatters.org/research/201001220026

8. http://www.salon.com/news/opinion/feature/2010/04/05/glenn_beck_s_historians

9. http://leostrausscenter.uchicago.edu/

10. http://politifact.com/truth-o-meter/article/2009/dec/18/politifact-lie-year-death-panels

11. http://www.youtube.com/watch?v=S38VioxnBaI&NR=1

12. http://www.nytimes.com/2010/04/15/us/politics/15poll.html

13. http://www.washingtonpost.com/wp-dyn/content/article/2010/03/20/AR2010032002556.html

14. http://depts.washington.edu/uwiser/racepolitics.html

15. http://hnn.us/roundup/comments/126019.html

16. http://www.ushistory.org/declaration/document/compare.htm

17. http://en.wikipedia.org/wiki/Willie_Horton

18. http://www.youtube.com/watch?v=Io9KMSSEZ0Y

19. http://books.google.com/books?id=KmIqnHquHhIC&printsec=frontcov
er&dq=the american indian in western&cd=1#v=snippet&q="
wild woods and uncultivated waste of america"&f=false

20. http://en.wikipedia.org/wiki/John_locke

21. http://books.google.com/books?id=IVvU_yWHOFEC&pg=PA94&l
pg=PA94&dq="Americanization of the law of real property"&sour
ce=bl&ots=u1-ngqFwb_&sig=bCShMmDY_L31kxhI68muY6mb4n
Q&hl=en&ei=TenmS6GrNZGENMqr0IQI&sa=X&oi=bo
ok_result&ct=result&resnum=1&ved=0CBcQ6AEwA

22. http://img.wonkette.com/wp-content/uploads/2010/01/dalerobertson.jpg

23. http://mediamatters.org/mmtv/200907230017

24. http://www.huffingtonpost.com/2009/10/20/glenn-beck-smears-progres_n_
327860.html

25. http://www.amconmag.com/headline/1737/index.html

26. http://andrewsullivan.theatlantic.com/the_daily_dish/2010/04/from-the-co-
coon.html

27. http://www.mlive.com/opinion/kalamazoo/index.ssf/2010/04/column_
health_care_reform_legi.html

28. http://mediamatters.org/research/201004150075

29. http://www.politicsdaily.com/2010/01/19/obama-gets-failing-grades-from-
gun-control-group

30. http://andrewsullivan.theatlantic.com/the_daily_dish/2010/04/why-im-pass-
ing-on-tea.html

31. http://en.wikipedia.org/wiki/John_Galt

32. http://arizonateaparty.com/

33. http://www.amazon.com/dp/0805080694/ref=nosim/?tag=tomdispatch-20

34. http://www.loe.org/shows/segments.htm?programID=10-P13-00015&
segmentID=1

35. http://www.youtube.com/watch?v=3ceDL1NayQg

36. http://washingtonindependent.com/82941/in-coal-county-a-culture-of-fear

37. http://understory.ran.org/wp-content/uploads/2010/04/rally12_
i090907204958.jpg

38. http://tpmdc.talkingpointsmemo.com/2010/04/gingrich-tea-party-move-ment-will-be-militant-wing-of-the-republican-party.php

39. http://www.csgv.org/issues-and-campaigns/guns-democracy-and-freedom/april-19-second-amendment-rallies/speakers-at-second-amendment-rallies

40. http://www.youtube.com/watch?v=Nr-0088ZLno

41. http://www.youtube.com/watch?v=WYyBX_fVa_g

42. http://www.thenation.com/../../../../../slideshow/20091005/slideshow_rightwing/8

43. http://en.wikipedia.org/wiki/Waco_Siege

MORE POODLE THAN PANTHER: A REVIEW OF GLENN BECK'S *THE OVERTON WINDOW*

Barry Eisler

The most surprising aspect of Glenn Beck's novel *The Overton Window* is the banality of its politics. Coming from an entertainer whose trademark is blackboard diagrams connecting Nazism, the Lincoln penny, Woodrow Wilson, and the impending destruction of America by organizations promoting social justice, and with a back cover promise "to be as controversial as it is eye-opening," in the end the book posits nothing more than a boilerplate conspiracy run by an evil New York public-relations magnate. Could Beck have taken on a less controversial player? Perhaps he initially considered risking everything by vilifying Wall Street bankers, or telemarketers, or child molesters, before gritting his teeth and pledging his life, his fortune, and his sacred honor to outing such a powerful and well-defended foe.

But on second thought, Beck's choice of conspiracy villain makes a kind of sense. After all, has Beck ever gone after a player who could actually hit back? Whether it's a politically powerless organization like ACORN or the Tides Group; a peripheral bureaucrat like Van Jones or a politician so prominent he's already a lightning rod for criticism, like Obama; or concepts so broad or amorphous that railing against them is as dangerous as screaming into a pillow, like "progressives" or "the liberal media"—Beck's villains are always carefully screened to guarantee the only repercussions he'll endure for choosing them is a boost to his ratings. This is true for his television and radio shows, so it stands to reason it would be true in his first attempt at a novel, too.

In fact, a reasonable rule of thumb for testing the seriousness of anyone's claim to the role of underdog in the fight against vast, powerful forces, is this: What actual damage has the claimant sustained? Ask this question of Glenn Greenwald, or Jeremy Scahill, or Marcy Wheeler, or of any other real journalist, and you'll learn of doors closed and financial opportunities lost. Ask it of Glenn Beck, and you'll learn of multimillion-dollar television contracts and book advances. Ah, the sacrifices this man has made in exposing the powerful forces that secretly control America.

The safe silliness of Beck's villain aside, progressive readers would be hard-pressed to disagree with the novel's main premise: A misinformed and apathetic populace has allowed America to be captured by oligarchic elites, elites who masterfully manipulate public opinion to perpetrate the system by which they engorge themselves on the citizenry. Not such a different conception, in fact, from the one that undergirds my own recent novel, *Inside Out*. We both even include an author's note and list of sources to help readers sift out the fact upon which we base our fiction. And we both clearly intend for our novels not just to entertain but to elucidate.

Which makes it all the stranger to consider that the author of this earnest book is the same man *The Daily Show* hilariously demonstrated to be in the grip of Nazi Tourette's, whose obsession with race led him to declare that Obama "has a deep-seated hatred for white people or the white culture," and who has composed virtual love letters to President Bush and Sarah Palin. If I hadn't known Beck the television huckster before encountering Beck the novelist, I would have thought that, politically, at least, we might have much in common.

But similar premises don't necessarily lead to a confluence of conclusions. A sobering thought for anyone hopeful that, say, the Tea Party's small-government rhetoric provides possible common ground for some sort of progressive outreach. Progressives think government is too big and therefore want to reduce secrecy and prevent the president from imprisoning and assassinating American citizens without due process; Tea Partiers think government is too big and therefore want to prevent universal health care. Progressives think the national deficit and debt are out of control and therefore want to shrink the military; Tea Partiers think the national deficit and debt are out of control and therefore want to eliminate Social Security. The differences in such worldviews are far more significant than the similarities, and an attempt to minimize the differences and try to build on the similarities is apt to lead to extremely disappointing results.

The good news, I suppose, is that whatever readership *The Overton Window* finds, the book's impact is apt to be benign. Most of its readers are probably already Beck's fans, in which case the damage is done. Those who get through the book without first knowing Beck will likely be distracted from deep thought by the one-dimensional characters, unending political speeches masquerading as dialogue, and absurdity of the conspiracy Beck posits. *The Overton Window* is dull and disjointed more than it is dangerous or disquieting, and therefore, as both political primer and political thriller, ultimately, inert.

—August, 2010

BECKONOMICS

Richard Wolff

When Glenn Beck's show invited me for a May 2008 TV interview with him, I accepted with curiosity and skepticism. At his Manhattan studio, I asked the makeup person preparing me whether this was a set-up. "Am I the sacrificial lamb," I asked, "skewered to amuse Beck and his audience?" Not at all, she had said.

Before going on air, Beck explained the interview's planned topic. He wanted to discuss how elite, rich universities evade paying taxes—especially to their host local communities—and thereby increase the tax burdens of others in those communities far less able to pay. Feeling that was unfair and outrageous, Beck wanted a televised discussion with an economist. Beyond repeating that he loved capitalism and that I was someone who did not, Beck stayed on topic throughout the interview.

He knew that I had studied Yale University's economic relationship to its host, New Haven, Connecticut. I had a Yale PhD in economics and lived many years in New Haven. I had criticized Yale's refusal to pay local property taxes (or make payments in lieu of taxes, or "pilots") on its educational property. Even Harvard, Princeton, and other such billion-dollar institutions made modest pilots (always at far lower rates than most local residents and businesses had to pay). Since elite, rich universities consume local public services (schools for their employees, police, fire, health, etc.), when they don't pay taxes, the rest of their communities must pay higher taxes to cover the delivery of *free* public services to those universities.

New Haven, one of the nation's ten poorest large cities, has thus been subsidizing one of the world's richest universities: Robin Hood in extreme reverse for decades. Before a nationwide TV audience, Beck and I largely agreed that tax exemptions for such universities affronted basic notions of democracy and fairness.

We identified an economic reality that angered our audience. Taxes—like reduced wages and job opportunities and rising prices— were economic walls closing in on that audience. But as Americans seem conditioned to do, his viewers did not blame their economic problems on the institutions that actually determine hiring, firing, wages, and prices: the corporations. Rather they attacked politicians, the traditionally much more allowable object of anger and derision.

Thus, Beck's expressive outrage against taxes focused on the evil government unjustly imposing them. That built a bridge of solidarity to his viewers. Beyond his speech, his entire TV persona mixed rage, tears, and the intensity of aroused, explicit anger. In championing abused taxpayers, Beck invited them to identify with him as he railed against threatening economic forces. I suspect he understood that his audience believed it was powerless and had no other way to fight back. His viewers had either given up on labor unions as unable or unwilling to fight government and taxes, or they had succumbed to a demonology that positioned unions as major causes of their economic plight. His viewers likewise expected nothing positive from most politicians or either party. Without traditional organizations through which to be politically effective, feeling isolated, victimized, and weak, they vibrated to Beck's (as to the parallel Tea Parties') theatrics as their only available political weapon.

Beck carefully avoided connecting their abuse to the larger economic system. In contrast, I provided details, economic implications, and history suggesting how rich universities' tax exemptions linked to the larger, systemic context of *capitalism*. He knew that I occupied the other end of the political spectrum. Nonetheless, he interviewed me to help build *his* bridge to the audience. Notwithstanding our different goals, we both sought to reach that audience around a shared issue.

In hindsight, I would have liked to take the interview where Beck would not—by showing, for example, how large corporations elude far more taxation than rich universities. I would have stressed how those universities rely on and support capitalism as a system via rationalizations and legitimations built into their curricula. Perhaps most importantly, I would have stressed how U.S. capitalism's profits provide the means to secure a compliant, subservient governmental apparatus and its policies.

I had spoken to the anger that Beck cultivated, but connected it to very different root causes. Much evidence—including that interview and subsequent reactions thereto—suggests that my analyses, if given air time, would have resonated well with most of our shared audience. But Beck's control of the interview precluded such an outcome.

Many Glenn Becks are working today's economic crisis to revive traditional rightist attacks on their usual targets. Corporate profits they can tap for resources to reach that shared audience are not available to us. Yet we have the analytical ways and means to do so. We lack chiefly the organizations and political self-confidence as left alternatives to mobilize a serious, well-financed counterweight to today's rightist forces.

—*August 2010*

REPUBLICANS AND THE TEA PARTY OF NO

Arun Gupta

As much as they may grumble, there is a legitimate reason why the Republicans have been labeled the "Party of No." For decades, the party's knee-jerk stance has been to oppose any legislation or policy involving social, economic, or political progress.

You name it, the right has opposed it: civil rights, school desegregation, women's rights, labor organizing, the minimum wage, Social Security, LGBT rights, welfare, immigrant rights, public education, reproductive rights, Medicare, Medicaid. And through the years the right invoked hysterical rhetoric in opposition, predicting that implementing any such policies would result in the end of family-free-enterprise-God-America on the one hand, and the imposition of atheism-socialism-Nazism on the other.

Republicans are obstructionist for one simple reason: It's a winning strategy. Opposing progressive policies allows the right to actualize the ideals that both motivate and define their base. Rightist ideologies are not without sophistication, but right-wing politicians and media figures boil them down to a crude Manichean dualism to mobilize supporters based on group difference: good versus evil, us versus them. By demonizing and scapegoating politically marginal groups, the right is able to define "real Americans," who are good, versus those defined as parasites, illegitimate, and internal threats, who are evil.

There is a critical paradox at work. The Republicans have deftly turned being the "Party of No" into a positive stance: They signal to their base they are working to defeat an alien ideology while defending real Americans and traditional values and institutions.

Ideologues and opinion-makers spin any redistributive policy as a zero-sum game; progressive policies give to undeserving groups by taking wealth from or denying rights to deserving Americans and institutions. Since Obama took office, the rise of the Tea Party has made the Republicans even more strident in their opposition. The GOP fights against every Democratic policy—including the stimulus bill, jobs programs, aid to local governments, court appointees, more labor rights, health care, financial regulation, net neutrality, unemployment benefits, expanding access to food stamps and Head Start, action on global warming and immigrant rights—because it claims some sort of theft of money or rights is involved.

Sara Diamond neatly summarizes the politics behind the right's obstructionism in her book, *Roads To Dominion*. She writes, "To be right-wing means to support the state in its capacity as *enforcer* of order and to oppose the state as *distributor* of wealth and power downward and more equitably in society" (emphasis in original). These principles, in turn, flow from four interrelated political philosophies that animate the modern right: militarism, neoliberalism, traditionalism, and white supremacism.

The heart of the right's agenda is neoliberalism, which is the rule of the "free market" above all else. It demands that everything be a commodity, all actions be judged according to cost-benefit analysis, every realm be opened to capital's predations, all human needs subjugated to those of finance. If neoliberalism were left unchecked, argues David Harvey in *A Brief History of Neoliberalism*, it would result in market anarchy and the dissolution of social solidarities. British Prime Minister Margaret Thatcher famously summed it up in her view, "There is no such thing as society but only individuals."

Faced with market nihilism, "some degree of coercion appears

necessary to restore order," writes Harvey. Enter the neoconserva-
tives, who play a crucial role resolving the contradictions between neoliberalism and traditionalism through militarism. Harvey explains
that they "emphasize militarization as an antidote to the chaos of individual interests. For this reason, they are far more likely to highlight
threats, real or imagined, both at home and abroad, to the integrity
and stability of the nation."

Militarism is just the means, however. To mobilize support for
repressive methods the right stokes the passions and fears of its base
by posing traditional values as under attack: the family, God, marriage, America, private property, law and order, and freedom itself.
These values are often linked to neoliberalism and contrasted in opposition to "collectivism," which is presented as a looming danger to
both property and God. This also bridges the ideological gap between
the religious right and the free-market right.

For example, the Christian right is stridently antiunion. While
the Bible can easily be read as a socialist document, the central role
of money-driven ministries and televangelism has oriented evangelicals toward free-market ideology that is expressed in its "prosperity
theology"—"the belief that God rewards signs of faith with wealth,
health and happiness." As many evangelicals are actual or would-be
entrepreneurs, this doctrine is readily accepted. It's a small step to
convince them that unions promote secular collectivism that threatens private religious values, thus creating a theological rationale for
neoliberal policies.

I use "the right" instead of "Republican" or even "conservative" to
describe the movement and its ideas. Until recent years, there was a
breed of socially liberal, fiscally conservative Republican that retained
a foothold in the GOP. These Republicans provided critical support
for civil rights and other progressive legislation. This segment, which
tended to concentrate in the North, has largely shifted to the Democratic Party (with the result of pushing the Democrats further to
the right). So while the right may now overlap significantly with the

Republican Party, it wasn't always so. More important, as shown by the Christian right in years past and the Tea Party today, the right will try to purge those Republicans deemed not sufficiently orthodox, making the party more and more extreme.

The Tea Party is the latest chapter in the history of the Republicans as the "Party of No." Its existence depends on continuous promotion from Fox News, organizing by Republican consultants, front groups such as Americans for Prosperity and FreedomWorks, and the GOP itself. Much of the Tea Party's funding comes from right-wing foundations through the front groups, and its politics are antigovernment, anti-labor, pro-corporate, and often socially conservative, which is the same agenda the right has been pushing for more than thirty years.

The roots of right-wing obstruction are represented by three pivotal historical figures: William F. Buckley Jr., Barry Goldwater, and George Wallace. "The father of modern conservatism," Buckley proclaimed his intention to stand "athwart history, yelling Stop!'" in founding *National Review* in 1955. He knit together traditionalism, free market ideology, and anticommunism, and his politics were a textbook case of opposing distribution of power and wealth and for imposing social order. In the 1950s, he dismissed civil rights legislation because Southern whites were "the advanced race." This wasn't a passing fancy; he defended this position as "absolutely correct" in 1989 on NPR. He inveighed against the 1965 Voting Rights Act as threatening "chaos" and "mobcratic rule." While opposing basic freedoms for all people because it threatened the traditional order, he was for using force to impose Gulag-like policies such as quarantining drug addicts and tattooing people with AIDS on their buttocks, and he suggested "relocating chronic welfare cases" to "rehabilitation centers."

Buckley was not alone in believing progressive policies eroded traditional mores and institutions. Barry Goldwater, who as the Republican presidential nominee was trounced in 1964, voted against the

1964 Civil Rights Act, calling it "unconstitutional." He fought school desegregation, and the desegregation of public accommodations, claiming it "tampers with the rights of assembly, freedom of speech, freedom of religion and freedom of property." He railed against federal aid to schools, the minimum wage, Medicare and the entire welfare state because "socialism can be achieved through welfarism." He opposed the progressive income tax because it artificially "enforce[ed] equality among unequal men." One of Goldwater's informal advisers in 1964 was the economist Milton Friedman, who saw nothing wrong with racial discrimination in employment because it was a matter of "taste." Many campaign volunteers came from the conspiratorial John Birch Society, which labeled integration a communist plot. Within Goldwater's campaign one can see how various segments of the right united in opposing racial equality, but each for different reasons.

In contrast to Buckley, Goldwater was no religious traditionalist, but he did combine libertarianism and anticommunism. He hewed to a secular traditionalism forged from patriotism, the Constitution, and frontier mythology, and was far more open-minded on social issues. His wife Peggy helped found the Arizona chapter of Planned Parenthood, and he made clear his contempt for and opposition to the Christian right when it began to take over the Republican Party in the 1980s.

A contemporary of Goldwater was the unapologetic racist, former Alabama Governor George Wallace, who swept the Deep South in the 1968 presidential election running on a segregationist platform. He represented yet another form of traditionalism, one that stoked fears that "blacks were moving beyond their safely encapsulated ghettos into 'our' streets, 'our' schools, 'our' neighborhoods," according to Dan Carter, author of *From George Wallace to Newt Gingrich: Race in the Conservative Counterrevolution*.

Wallace pioneered the race-based appeals that still excite the populist right today. But he was also a deft cultural warrior who, writes Carter, "knew that a substantial percentage of the American electorate despised the civil rights agitators and antiwar demonstrators as symptoms of a fundamental decline in the traditional cultural compass of God, family, and country, a decline reflected in rising crime rates, the legalization of abortion, the rise in out-of-wedlock pregnancies, the increase in divorce rates, and the proliferation of 'obscene' literature and films." Add gay marriage, Islam, and immigration, and you pretty much have the right's culture war agenda of today.

The right's need for enemies is coded in its political DNA. Without enemies to defeat, vanquish, and even destroy, the right would suffer an existential crisis. For Goldwater it was the communist menace; for Wallace, integrationists and intellectuals; for Nixon, liberals, antiwar activists, and black radicals; for Reagan, labor, welfare queens, and the Evil Empire; for Gingrich and his cohorts it was gays, feminists, welfare mothers, and Democrats; during the Bush years it was Islam, immigrants, gays, and abortionists; For the Tea Party, Glenn Beck, and Sarah Palin, it's all of the above.

There is one final step in how the right mobilizes grassroots support behind an obstructionist agenda. Few people mull over philosophical concepts when making political decisions. That's why mobilizing group resentment and solidarity simultaneously is so effective. It gives people a way to see both enemies and allies in their daily lives. In the case of immigrants, the narrative is about "illegals" stealing jobs and social services from taxpayers. In the case of the Obama administration, the story is that taxes are being stolen from hard-working Americans to support parasites ranging from welfare recipients to Wall Street bankers.

Chip Berlet, a scholar at Political Research Associates, describes this as "producerism." He defines it as "a world view in which people in the middle class feel they are being squeezed from above by crippling taxes, government bureaucracies, and financial elites while simultaneously being pushed around, robbed, and shoved aside by an underclass of 'lazy, sinful, and subversive freeloaders.' The idea is that unproductive parasites above and below are bleeding the productive middle class dry."

Segments of the right use producerism differently, explains Berlet. "Economic libertarians blast the government for high taxes and too much regulation of business. Anti-immigrant xenophobes blast the government for letting 'illegals' steal their jobs and increase their taxes. Christian fundamentalists blast the government for allowing the lazy, sinful, and subversive elements to ruin society." In recent history, Wallace and Nixon used producerist rhetoric to mobilize white working-class resentment against blacks.

Producerism is premised on other techniques. First, argues Berlet, a group of people are dehumanized so they are seen as objects and then they are demonized as evil. Next, the group is scapegoated irrationally for specific problems. Lou Dobbs mastered this process in defining undocumented immigrants as "illegal," then spouting dubious claims about immigrants being responsible for crime waves and disease outbreaks, and finally blaming them for stealing jobs and social services. Another example is Fox News and its hit job on ACORN. The group was caricatured as so nefarious and omnipotent, a poll last year by Public Policy Polling found that 52 percent of Republicans believed ACORN had stolen the 2008 election for Obama.

The Tea Party movement—which the Republicans have helped create and exploited to oppose the entirety of the Obama administration—is the latest political variant of the right's themes. Much of the right's anger is directed at immigrants, African-Americans and social welfare and equality in general. Among Tea Partiers, 73 percent think "Blacks would be as well off as whites if they just tried harder"; 73 percent believe "Providing government benefits to poor people encourages them to remain poor"; 60 percent believe "We have gone too far in pushing equal rights in this country"; 56 percent think "Immigrants take jobs from Americans"; 92 percent want a smaller government with "fewer services"; 92 percent think Obama's policies are moving the country toward socialism; only 7 percent approve of

Obama's performance as president; and a combined 5 percent identify themselves as black, Asian, or of Hispanic origin.

One survey found that identifying as a conservative or a Tea Party supporter was an accurate predictor of racial resentment. Additionally, only one-third were opposed to the government tapping people's telephones and racial or religious profiling, and barely half opposed indefinite detention without trial. This is a movement that thrives on opposing the distribution of power and wealth more equitably in society and supporting the imposition of a repressive social order.

With nearly 60 percent of Tea Partiers believing Obama is foreign-born or saying they are not sure, it becomes clear why so many on the right have adopted violent and revolutionary rhetoric. The thinking is he's a foreigner or a Muslim or stole the election, so he is alien and illegitimate. As such, it makes sense he is pushing an alien idea like socialism that may be part of some grand conspiracy like the New World Order, the North American Union, the Bilderberg Group, or Satan. (In a poll last September of New Jersey residents, not known for being prone to right-wing radicalism, 29 percent of Republicans thought Obama was the Antichrist or were unsure.)

However irrational this position may be, the logical consequences are not: Anything Obama and the Democrats do must be opposed because it is a life-and-death struggle. In opposing the health-care plan, the right is not just trying to deny services to the undeserving, it is affirming and protecting free choice, family, the sanctity of life, the market, God, country, the Constitution—all arguments trotted out in the last year.

Like the Clinton years, no matter how much Obama tries to appease Republicans, he will remain under attack and be held responsible for bizarre crimes and conspiracies, because the right has nothing to gain from compromise. In fact, Republican opposition has devolved from the philosophical to the tactical. The right-wing noise machine frames Obama and the Democrats as the source of all evil, making compromise virtually impossible. Republicans now assail Obama policies they used to champion, from the market-friendly health-care law and huge tax cuts in the stimulus bill to the bipartisan deficit commission and pay-as-you-go budget rules.

At the same time, the Obama administration has stoked support for the Tea Party by providing aid and comfort to Wall Street rather than Main Street. The Republicans have exploited legitimate anxieties over high unemployment, a shrinking economy, and onerous taxes by scapegoating the weak and marginal for policies that are structural and historical in nature.

The lesson for Obama and Democrats is not that they went too far to the "left," it's that they went too far to the right. Obama had the political capital and the leverage over the banking and auto industries to push for a "Green New Deal" that could have restructured the transportation and energy sectors and created millions of new jobs. By slashing the bloated military budget while fighting for some type of single-payer health care—instead of a plan that uses public money to subsidize the for-profit health-care industry—budget deficits could have been constrained while reducing the financial burden of medical bills for most American households. Implementing such an agenda could have created a mass constituency that would fight for a progressive vision and against the right's repressive politics.

The right has well-thought-out ideologies, a specific agenda, clearly defined enemies, and ruthlessly pursues power to achieve its goals. And it's fighting a Democratic White House and party that stand for nothing, which is why being the "Party of No" will continue to be a winning strategy for Republicans.

—May 17, 2010

GLENN BECK:
OUT-ORGANIZING THE ORGANIZERS

Sally Kohn

Glenn Beck gained attention with apocalyptic warnings about the dangers of community organizers, which is ironic—since Beck is a community organizer, too.

In essence, community organizers do three things. First, they identify a community that is disempowered in the current hierarchy of decision-making and power. Second, they help the community identify and analyze the issues at the core of their concerns. Third, they build public campaigns to dramatize the injustice against the marginalized community on the part of decision-makers, often in a polarizing way that casts the status quo power-holders as "the enemy" or the bad guys (or, once in a while, the bad women).

Of course, in the classic example, you have a community of poor people—often people of color—who, all of the sudden, find out that a toxic fume–emitting paint factory is being built in their backyard. The paint company and the government that zoned the factory don't seem to care about the health and environmental impacts on this already pretty polluted and decrepit community that, by the way, lacks the political pull to do anything about it anyway. For the community, the paint factory is just one more thing on a long list of problems and what could they do to change any of it? Enter the community organizer. She meets with families in the community, hears about their needs, and helps them see the paint factory as a larger symbol of the official poisoning of their neighborhoods. The community forms a group, holds meetings, understands how the paint-factory zoning decision was made, who was responsible in government, even how the paint company's research on toxic emissions is scientifically flawed. They launch a campaign, they embarrass the paint company and press government to be accountable to all its citizens, and plans for the paint factory are scrapped.

If you watch Glenn Beck regularly, it doesn't take long to know that, according to him, organizers like these are the devil and campaigns like this undermine capitalism. Which sounds like a neat and tidy distinction until Beck brings out his chalkboard...

How is Glenn Beck a community organizer? First, he's identified a community that looks, well, much like himself—working-class and middle-class white folks who feel the pangs of growing economic uncertainty but are unsure whom to blame. Beck has constructed for them the perfect alibi. Lazy people of color and immigrants are stealing their taxes and changing America to a socialist/Marxist paradise, led by the scary (and, coincidentally, black) Community Organizer in Chief Barack Obama. Of course, this narrative is nothing new. The conservative right has been working for decades to draw a wedge between working class white people and people of color who might otherwise unite to rupture the conservative status quo. But Beck's real innovation is what he does with this white, Middle America constituency.

The issues Beck tackles range from cap-and-trade legislation to financial reform to health care, but the organizer part is the chalkboard. Beck doesn't just rant and rave. He educates. Any community organizer can tell you about power analysis—the process by which organizers work with grassroots leaders to methodically dissect an issue: Who's behind it? Who will gain? Who will lose? How could we change it for the better? This is what Glenn Beck does five nights a week, chalk in hand, for millions of Americans who are feeling frustrated and hopeless and looking for guidance.

And like poor folks in church basements of community organizations, intoxicated by the suggestion that they could be powerful and together make their lives and community better, Beck's audience—who for too long have rightly felt disregarded by government and big business—are dizzy with the idea that they, too, could matter in America. For an audience that has sensed the American dream slipping further from their grasp for decades, Beck offers the alluring possibility that white working-class America can have its cake and eat it too—implicitly by denying immigrants and poor people and people of color a seat at the table. For a desperate community unfortunately all-too-primed with racial anxiety, Beck paints a picture of white heaven on Earth.

Then Beck indeed builds public campaigns of polarization—from his attacks on ACORN and Van Jones to his creation of the 9/12 Project and joining forces with FreedomWorks and the Tea Party fringe. Beck very intentionally and methodically helps his audience translate their angst into action.

This from the man who said about community organizers, "We have no idea how dangerous these people can become."[1] Looked in a mirror lately?

Yet what's really disconcerting is not the duplicity with which Beck is condemning community organizers on the one hand while clearly acting like an organizer on the other—it's that, in many ways, Beck is organizing better than the community organizations against which he rails. First, audacious though we might like to think President Obama and his progressive allies are, Glenn Beck exudes a bravado that we can only envy. Beck's extraordinary confidence about the righteousness of the right-wing agenda and the truth of his convictions—including those that are blatantly false—reflects a better understanding of what it takes to inspire legions of Americans than do the rational argument and data on which progressives remain too reliant for persuasion. Yes, Beck uses numbers and details (the word "facts" would often be a stretch), but they're merely adornments sewn to a richer tapestry of narrative and vision. He tells America a story, supported by some facts. Progressives tell some facts and hope people can discern the story.

Beck has also surpassed the modern progressive movement in terms of scale. His 5:00 p.m. EST show on Fox News reaches at least 1.7 million viewers per night. That's far more than most progressive organizations and has a reach comparable to liberal megastars like MoveOn and the Service Employees International Union. Yet with his 1.7 million people, give or take, Beck isn't just asking for signatures on a petition or calls to Congress. He is effectively building a legion of politically educated ordinary Americans to spread right-wing analysis and ideology through the Heartland—and he's doing it at scale. Some of the best grassroots organizations that engage in similar political education reach maybe a few hundred people at a time in their trainings. Beck is building the consciousness of millions.

The good news is, Beck's ratings are half of what they used to be and advertising for his show is also falling—thanks to unpopular comments that President Obama is a racist Nazi.[2] Still, Glenn Beck is a one-man organizing empire, supporting himself to the tune of $32 million–plus last year without any foundation grants and reaching millions of Americans. Though Beck's prominence in the media is hard to match for grassroots organizers of color, whose issues and opinions rarely receive the same coverage as those of the white working and middle classes, even the existing liberal powerhouses on television, in Hollywood, and in Washington could better step up to the plate. Jon Stewart makes us laugh. Rachel Maddow makes us think. But Glenn Beck makes America act. And Glenn Beck, the organizer, is winning.

On his July 26, 2010, show, Beck said, "You have to think like an activist.... Now you're involved, and not because you want to be but because you now realize you have to be. I know the last thing you want to do is take a day off and join a protest.... This is exactly the time *not* to give up.... You cannot give up. You have to build on every small victory at the local level." Spoken like a true organizer. Now we have to out-organize Glenn Beck.

—August 2010

Notes:

1. http://www.glennbeck.com/content/articles/article/196/28528/

2. http://www.bnet.com/blog/advertising-business/glenn-beck-cost-fox-millions-and-lost-half-his-audience-but-news-corp-stands-behind-him/5135

TEA PARTY TECH

Deanna Zandt

Progressives have long held the leadership crown when it comes to technology and activism. And by "long," I of course mean, "a few years"—as long as anyone's been taking a serious look at how developments in blogging, social networking, and more are playing out in the political arena.

Conservatives are starting to catch up. Many theories are bandied about on why social technologies didn't catch on with the right as quickly as they did with progressives; one of the more likely reasons relates to how conservative ideologies rely greatly on top-down organizing tactics. Empowering people on the ground with free-wheeling communication and organizing tools doesn't fit this worldview, and thus might have led to a delay in adoption.

Which makes the case of Tea Party's use of social networking and other tech tools all the more intriguing—many claim the relative success of this small number of ideologues is due to their savvy use of Facebook and blogs. If bottom-up, grassroots organizing doesn't fit into the conservative model, how could this be the case?

Perhaps it's indicative of a larger set of fissures within the conservative movement, fissures that stem from dissatisfaction with the leadership, and the lockstep required to participate in the conservative leadership's vision. Social networking tools provide a means for bypassing traditional leadership and advancing alternative agendas. In the past, organizers of all political stripes have had to rely on a traditional hierarchical system of information distribution, in which ideas and issues are pushed up from the bottom onto leadership, who then pick and choose which ones are important enough to adopt and broadcast out to the rest of the community. With social networks becoming more dominant, our communities of friends, family, and colleagues are connected to one another as overlapping spheres of influence, and information travels through those spheres rapidly—without as much of a need for the traditional means of distribution.

No doubt about it: Social-networking tools are firmly planted in our culture. In the summer of 2010, Facebook announced its 300 millionth user, and Twitter's icons have become ubiquitous in advertising and journalism. And yes, we all know that we can get the word out about a product or service, or raise money for a cause we care about, but that's only the beginning of the story.

No matter what end of the political spectrum we fall on, something very fundamental about social change has not changed at all during the last several thousand years. Before we get to any organizing tactics—whether that's door-knocking, lobbying, petition-signing, or a "meetup"—change starts with stories. Our stories. Storytelling has been the most powerful building block for social change since the beginning of time—think about how long humans have been sitting around the campfire telling each other what's going on. Social networking gives us unprecedented power to share our stories with more people than we ever imagined.

On the one hand, we see how storytelling moves us in the direction of progress.[1] But the Tea Party also illustrates the power of storytelling and social change—changing *back* to a more restrictive, more racist paradigm. Nonetheless, the connections made through sharing and empathizing with each other's burdens, perceived or real, have laid the groundwork for a political platform that's gained (a perhaps unreasonable amount of) attention in mainstream America.

True Tea Partiers—not necessarily the politicians trying to carry the banner—are also beginning to understand the power of structureless, flexible organizations, which social networking tools facilitate well. Ken Vogel, in a story for *Politico*, noted the current popularity of one of 2006's lefty-darling books, *The Starfish and the Spider*, amongst Tea Party activists.[2] *Starfish* basically states that organizations that have strong leadership, which can easily be taken out (chopping off the head of the spider), will fail in the coming years. But organizations with loose organizations and little hierarchy can survive attacks and nimbly reorganize for success (splitting a starfish doesn't kill it; it creates two new starfish).

Next thing you know, they'll pick up Clay Shirky's *Here Comes Everybody*, and we'll have a real social-networking war out there. All right, enough with the jabs. I digress.

The rejection by Tea Party groups of candidates and politicians that attempt to run on a Tea Party platform is further indication that a Tea Party activists aren't ready to fold into a larger conservative, or even Republican, top-down agenda. Representative Jason Chaffetz (R, Utah) tweeted in July 2010, "If any one person(s) tries to co-opt it, the Tea Party will lose its identity and effectiveness. Go Tea Party! But not with D.C. 'leadership.'"[3] Buoyed by the sense of community and camaraderie found on Facebook, Twitter, and elsewhere, they are withholding their support for leaders that want to ride the wave.

Well, except for Sarah Palin. She's still everyone's darling in Tea Party land, but her use of social-networking platforms belies her true top-down leadership style. To understand this nuance, it's important to note that social technologies are designed to inspire conversations, not replicate broadcast-style media, where messages are only sent in one direction. Think of social networks as an ad hoc get-together that's always happening. Just as you wouldn't get up on a chair at a cocktail party and yell at everyone everything that's been happening with you, you shouldn't do that on social networks, either. Instead, you're supposed to have conversations—ask people what's up with them, respond to things they say, as well as share your own news and opinions as part of the mix.

Sarah Palin didn't get the memo, evidently. Looking at her Twitter page, and there is little to no mention of other Twitter users (a no-no in that culture, the equivalent of the standing-on-the-chair thing), or responding to anyone else. She's adopted this as a medium of broadcast, and arguably, that's working for her—it fits neatly within the conservative worldview of top-down, listen-to-what-I-say messaging. While some of those messages will resonate with Tea Partiers, I wouldn't be surprised if there were some eventual backlash... as we're starting to see with how things run on her Facebook page.

It turns out that Camp Palin spends a lot of time "scrubbing" undesirable elements from her fan page on Facebook. "Scrubbing" is an Internet term for whitewashing, and is considered a big no-no in social communities. Just google "Wikipedia scrubbing scandal" for a few examples of people that have tried to get away with modifying their (or someone else's) entry, and you'll see how well that kind of behavior is received.

In the case of Palin and her fan page, John Dickerson in *Slate* did a thorough investigation of what kinds of comments get scrubbed, and came up with some interesting results:

- Mean comments about Sarah Palin.
- Mean things about the people who say mean things about Sarah Palin.
- Racial or ethnic slurs.
- Polite disagreement.
- Too much agreement.
- Criticism of her children.
- Anything about Obama's birth certificate or conspiracies related thereto, even in muted form.
- Complaints about her endorsements of so many female candidates.
- Excessive use of religious prophesy or imagery. [4]

Of course, most commenting communities moderate participation in one way or another, and that's OK—it's what keeps the conversation going. But what Palin is doing is creating a very carefully crafted portrait of her community, using this small slice of participation to inaccurately reflect the whole kit and caboodle. Not such a die-hard "populist" after all, eh, Sarah?

The question of removing undesirable elements from the discourse brings up other questions about how to deal with extremist attacks online from Tea Party members and other far-right activists. It's often the knee-jerk reaction for progressives to request bans on hate speech online. That may be what's required when the speech escalates to heights that call for violence,[5] but we shouldn't be so quick to dismiss extremist speech when we see it.

The Internet is many things to many people, and one of the main things we forget is that it's not just a place to vent prejudice, but also often a mirror on the society and people that create that prejudice. We can use social technologies especially as a lens into subcultures that have certainly not disappeared with progress—only gone underground, until now. Rinku Sen, executive director of the Applied Research Center, talked about hate speech as a tool:

The Applied Research Center (ARC), a nonprofit racial justice organization that publishes *ColorLines* magazine, gains insight from monitoring and listening to responses—both positive and negative—to their work. "In a non-web world, we can be disconnected and isolated from each other," Sen notes. "It's not that hard to do progressive racial justice work [in that context] and never have to deal with racial conservatives. It allows people to pick and choose who they deal with."

Certainly the Wild West frontier nature of the Internet can sometimes leave progressives feeling confused and angry when it comes to reacting to opponents' strategies. But the rise of social networking across the political spectrum has given rise to conversations that otherwise might not have happened in large public spheres even just a few years ago. We have a huge opportunity at hand both to shape the direction of these public conversations that ultimately inform policy decisions and to shift cultural standards, as well as to use these tools as insight into the inner workings of ideologies that threaten a future that benefits *all* people, from diverse backgrounds, and not just a chosen few.

—August 2010

Notes:

1. In fact, I wrote a whole book about this. Check it out at http://sharethischange. com.

2. http://www.politico.com/news/stories/0710/40492.html

3. http://latimesblogs.latimes.com/washington/2010/07/social-media-wrap-bachmann-rallies-support-for-tea-party-caucus-in-dc.html

4. http://www.slate.com/id/2262544/pagenum/all/

5. Facebook groups and pages have been set up to directly call for the murder of President Obama, http://thenextweb.com/2010/01/05/facebook-group-openly-calls-murder-president-obama/, to praying for his death, http://abcnews. go.com/Technology/facebook-page-prays-obamas-death/story?id=10451069, and more.

PART FOUR: MAMA GRIZZLIES

SEX AND THE GOP

Betsy Reed

In the media spectacle that is the 2010 midterm elections, women of the GOP are playing starring roles. They have figured prominently in nearly every plot and subplot that holds any real interest or potential for debased amusement: from Indian-American Nikki Haley's triumph over her mudslinging male rivals for the GOP gubernatorial nod in South Carolina, to Carly Fiorina's catty open-mike swipe at her opponent Barbara Boxer's hair in the first-ever contest between two women for a California Senate seat, to WWF founder and Connecticut Senate hopeful Linda McMahon's gifts to oh-so-lucky Democratic ad firms (including video of the candidate physically attacking a buxom, scantily clad woman purporting to be her husband's lover), to the daily dose of clips revealing Christine O'Donnell's youthful preoccupations with witchcraft and masturbation. Remember when politics was boring?

Before the new GOP women entered the picture, the Republican Party was like Kansas in *The Wizard of Oz*: colorless, defined by a white male old guard along with a lackluster lineup of "young guns" cut from the same drab cloth. Now the party is dancing down a yellow-brick road to what it hopes is victory in November. As Minnesota Governor Tim Pawlenty, a 2012 presidential aspirant, proclaimed, "It's going to be a new day, a new era in terms of the face and voice and tone of the Republican Party, and I think that's really good." A movie just released by the conservative group Citizens United tells this happy tale: *Fire From the Heartland: The Awakening of the Conservative Woman* features Michele Bachmann and Ann Coulter, among others.

The "GOP Year of the Woman," a label tossed out by pundits in the wake of some primaries in June, has been zestfully adopted by party operatives. "I like strong women," wrote strategist Mark McKinnon in the *Daily Beast*. "Agree with them or not, it's the women of the GOP…who are tough enough to say exactly what they think. And their words are resonating with an increasingly vocal electoral bloc."

But are they? Has the party truly cultivated and supported its women candidates, and is it, as a result, poised to bring more women to Washington and more women voters into the fold? Or, as it lurches to the right, is the GOP in fact alienating women, including voters and potential leaders, who tend to be less conservative than men in their partisan identification and ideological views? Is the party's embrace of the current array of female candidates really about enhancing its appeal to men?

Before turning to these questions, let's be precise: If 2010 is the year of anything other than antiestablishment rage, it is the year of the right-wing woman, a type that has prospered at the expense of moderates, male and female alike. It is true that a record number of women filed to run for office this year as Republicans—some of whom may have been inspired by Sarah Palin's example. But it is also true that a record number lost: Of the 128 women running for the House, eighty-one were defeated in their primaries, leaving forty-seven still in the running. In the Senate, seventeen filed to run, but only five won. That's a much higher rate of primary loss for Republican women than in the previous six election cycles. With some exceptions, the female candidates who survived are very, very conservative. Debbie Walsh, director of the Rutgers Center for American Women and Politics, says, "This is something quite far from a year of the woman. From the past, I would have assumed that the Republican women who are elected tend to be more moderate than Republican men. In this crop, we saw some very conservative women running and winning." It may well be that the Tea Party, with its bottom-up structure, provided an opening for ultraright women, like Christine O'Donnell, who had been grassroots activists but were hungry for a larger role in the electoral arena.

But to understand where GOP gender dynamics really are, it's important to consider not only the women who won this year's primaries but those who lost, and why. The picture that emerges is one of a national party that, at best, takes its women candidates for granted even as it plays up its new female-friendly image. Take Alaska's Lisa Murkowski and Colorado's Jane Norton, both mainstream Republican women who saw little support from the party as they struggled to fend off their hard-right male challengers. While the party whacked away at O'Donnell in its futile attempt to save moderate Mike Castle in Delaware, it failed to respond with such alacrity when the Palin-endorsed Tea Partier Joe Miller took aim at Murkowski—emphasizing her relative liberalism on abortion rights—in the Alaska Senate primary. "The national party seemed conflicted about Murkowski," noted another GOP woman who has had her own conflicts with the party, former New Jersey Governor Christie Todd Whitman, in an interview for this article.

When, after her primary loss, Murkowski launched a write-in campaign targeting Miller—a climate-change denier who favors abolishing Medicaid and Social Security—as an extremist, the party's wrath was unleashed upon her, with minority leader Mitch McConnell threatening to strip her of her position as ranking member of the Energy Committee and declaring that she "no longer has my support for serving in any leadership roles." As Senate vice chair, she had been the party's sole female in a top leadership position. Karl Rove called her a "spoilsport" and her write-in campaign "sad and sorry."

As for Norton, the GOP establishment candidate for Senate in Colorado, after being recruited by the party, she was largely on her own in a nasty contest with Tea Partier Ken Buck—who opposes abortion even in cases of rape and incest along with many forms of birth control and asked for voters' support because "I don't wear high heels." A much hoped-for Palin endorsement never came through for Norton.

Even though moderate Republican female candidates are more in sync with women voters, they are not faring well in the present environment, in which the passion is with the angry Tea Party voters who are "sick and tired of what is going on" but are less clear about what they are for and are unmoved by women who "don't voice the same kind of passion but want to get things done," Christie Whitman observed. But Whitman still sees "an enormous place" for moderate women in politics and peril ahead for the GOP if they continue to be sidelined. "Purity is a nice thing in concept, but in a country as diverse as ours, [the party] risks becoming irrelevant" if it pursues its present course.

It was not always thus. The first female senator to be elected in her own right (as opposed to inheriting a seat after the death of her husband) was the pro-choice Kansas Republican Nancy Kassebaum in 1978, who famously worked with Ted Kennedy on health care legislation. In the '80s, Republican women actually outnumbered Democratic women in Congress, and many of them stood in the middle of the road ideologically. Over the succeeding three decades, however, Republican women in Congress have moved steadily to the right, according to a study by the Hubert H. Humphrey Institute of Public Affairs at the University of Minnesota—to the point where in 2009 they were voting more conservatively than 77 percent of the House as a whole, a modern record. At the same time, their overall numbers relative to Democratic women have diminished; today, of a total of seventy-three female House members, just seventeen are Republicans. In the Senate, just four of seventeen women are Republicans, making Maine moderates Olympia Snowe and Susan Collins members of a rare species indeed. One reason for the paucity of Republican women in office is that qualified candidates are much less likely than their Democratic counterparts to have been recruited to run for office by party leaders and activists, according to research by Jennifer Lawless of American University and Richard Fox of Loyola Marymount University.

Among the very few institutional forces dedicated to fostering Republican women's leadership is the Susan B. Anthony List Candidate Fund. (It was at an SBA breakfast that Sarah Palin gave the "mama grizzlies" speech heard round the world.) But the fund, which says it promotes pro-life women in politics, allotted 25 percent of its Congressional endorsements this cycle to antiabortion men, highlighting how several such candidates could unseat pro-choice women in Congress. "Have you heard about the wonderful SBA-list endorsed men candidates who are running against women who have been backed by pro-abortion groups?" asked one fundraising appeal titled "More Nancy Pelosis?"

Then there are groups like the Republican Majority for Choice, which are facing a tough slog right now. "I would be very careful marketing all Republican women candidates as Sarah Palin. I actually think that's insulting to these women—they should be seen on their own terms," says RMC co-chair Candy Straight, who observes how rough the electoral environment is for moderate women, who are seen as more ready to collaborate than convey the voters' anger to Washington. (Moderate GOP women running in governor's races appear likely to fare better in November, perhaps because voters are more apt to support a perceived problem-solver in an executive role.) To put the "GOP Year of the Woman" in further perspective, keep in mind that some of the most conspicuous Republican women candidates, like Carly Fiorina, Linda McMahon, and Meg Whitman (who has spent a record-shattering $119 million), are self-funders—meaning that their campaigns do not reflect any significant investment of resources by the national party.

Just as the "stampede of pink elephants" that Sarah Palin warned

Washington to expect in November may not amount to more than a modest new presence in Congress, the "mama grizzlies," as an electoral bloc, do not pose a tangible threat to Democrats, strategists say. The gender gap, in which women voters consistently favor Democrats, is holding steady this year, at anywhere from 16 to 20 points, depending on the poll. Says a high-level Democratic operative working on the midterm election campaign, "Do we have a battle on our hands? Yes. But am I concerned that in particular we have the mama grizzlies, lots of really conservative women, coming to the polls? No. That is a branding strategy, not an electoral strategy."

Although the electorate in general is more conservative this year, and conservative voters are more energized, there has been no relative growth in the proportion of women who describe themselves as conservative—it's around one-third, compared with 44 percent of men. That doesn't mean that the passionate female following described in so many breathless stories about the mama grizzlies is imaginary, just that its size and significance have been inflated. "Palin does have appeal among really conservative women, but it is a very small group. They do a great job of marketing it, to make it look bigger than it is," says Molly O'Rourke of Hart Research Associates.

Women, by and large, are leery of the new right-wing female politicians, but men are far more receptive. Palin has a much larger gender gap than her ideological persuasion would predict: men are split 44 to 45 between those who hold favorable and unfavorable views of her; for women, the split is 35 to 58, according to a *National Journal* poll. Says Christie Whitman, "Palin appeals to more men than women. It was the white men in the party who put her on the ticket [in 2008], thinking that women who would have voted for Hillary would vote for her. That was dumb. They weren't going to buy into that." In a recent survey presenting respondents with a hypothetical matchup between Palin and Obama, Obama beat Palin by 13 points among women, but men preferred Palin by 2 points. In other words, if it were up to men, Palin might very well become president in 2012 (if it were up to white men, she'd be a shoo-in).

No doubt the "babe factor" has something to do with it: Palin's sex appeal is a frequent topic of right-wing male talkers like Rush Limbaugh, and similar voices in Delaware waxed on about Christine O'Donnell being "easy on the eyes"; one even issued an "Alert" for the "Major Babe." The gambit resembles that of Fox News shows with predominantly male audiences that have featured a bevy of attractive right-wing females, boosting the careers of commentators like Laura Ingraham and Ann Coulter. In Minnesota a Republican district office sparked an outcry in August when it posted a salacious video showing GOP politicians and pundits, including Palin and Coulter, in flattering poses set to "She's a Lady," followed by a montage of stern images of Nancy Pelosi and Hillary Clinton set to "Who Let the Dogs Out?"

More substantively, government-bashing, a favorite pastime of many ultraconservative female candidates, goes over much better with men than with women, who are more likely to support an active government role in the economy, education, health care, and environmental protection. After all, women benefit more from government policies like childcare subsidies and family leave, and they are disproportionately reliant on Social Security to protect them from poverty in old age, so it is only logical that they look askance at politicians of either gender who make careers out of demonizing government.

Michele Bachmann provides a vivid example of how right-wing female politicians divide voters along gender lines. In her quite conservative Minnesota district—as she has emerged as a national Tea Party darling, inveighing against "death panels" and urging Minnesotans to get "armed and dangerous" to "fight back" against cap-and-trade legislation—she has become increasingly dependent on male support. According to political scientist Eric Ostermeier of the University of Minnesota, who blogs at smartpoliticsblog.org, in polling before the 2008 contest Bachmann received support from 49 percent of men and 42 percent of women. In a recent poll, she got the support of 56 percent of men versus just 39 percent of women against her new rival, Democrat Tarryl Clark. What's more, the two women vying in the Democratic primary for a shot to oust Bachmann reaped big donations from female donors, at twice the rate of such contributions to other Congressional candidates, indicating a fierce determination among Democratic women to knock Bachmann out.

"Bachmann's appeal is definitely more to men. People here are really focused on bread-and-butter issues, and women are disproportionately affected when the economy is bad," says Donna Cassutt, associate chair of the Democratic-Farmer-Labor Party. She adds, "Women don't just vote for women. They must be capable, pro-woman, pro-family. Bachmann takes a hard line with the Tea Party against women's issues. And women are starting to say, We don't have jobs; we need more support for public education and health care. And they are looking for an alternative."

In Nevada, where all eyes are on Sharron Angle's Tea Party–infused run against Senate majority leader Harry Reid, the gender gap is similarly pronounced. Angle's unfavorables among women, at 64 percent, surpass even Palin's. (Christie Whitman, apprised of these numbers, quips, "Well, I would hope so, frankly" before hastening to add, "much as I'd love to see Harry Reid go down.") This trend is not lost on Reid's campaign, which has been targeting women with ads featuring Angle's positions on women's issues and others, like Social Security, that are especially important to female voters. Angle has given them a lot to work with, from her statement about how rape victims who become pregnant should avoid abortion and turn "a lemon situation into lemonade"; to her declaration that it is "right" and "acceptable" for women to raise children rather than work outside the home; to her infamous pledges to phase out Social Security and abolish the Education Department; to her vote against a law that, according to Reid's campaign, would prevent Nevada from being a "safe haven" for domestic abusers. In response to these and other attacks, Angle accused Reid of trying to "hit the girl." (In an attempt at damage control, Nevada Republican National Committeewoman Heidi Smith told *Politico*, "We always wondered what would happen with Harry and his nastiness because some people would get upset if he's mean to a woman.")

Even Meg Whitman, an oft-cited role model for moderate women in the party, struggled initially to attract female support in her bid to become governor of California. During the primary, in which she tacked right on issues such as immigration, she had the backing of 40 percent of Republican men, versus 30 percent of women. Now, up against Democrat Jerry Brown, she has been making a concerted effort to appeal to women, forming a campaign group called Mega-Woman, dedicated to attracting female voters and volunteers. And while she still owes much of her strength to her consistent support among white men, she has pulled even with Brown among women, a rare feat for a Republican these days (and something Carly Fiorina, running a more conservative campaign for Senate in the same state, has not achieved). The Whitman campaign is being closely watched by moderate Republican women nationwide, who hope that, if elected, she would broaden the scope of what is permissible in Republican discourse. "Whitman can't afford to talk much about being pro-choice right now. Once she's earned the respect of the right, then she'll have leverage," says Margaret Hoover, a Fox News commentator and self-described conservative Republican who is also an ardent advocate of choice and gay rights.

In the bigger picture, while Republicans crow about their "Year of the Woman" and pander to their base of white men (who prefer them, today, by a whopping margin of 25 points), Democrats see the support of women as a bright spot on an otherwise gloomy horizon. But there are ominous signs of torpor in this ordinarily energetic group. In a Gallup poll taken in September, women were much less likely than men to say they had given much thought to this year's midterms, 31 percent to 45 percent. This is a key indicator of who is likely to turn out at the polls, and it's significantly lower than in previous years, though it is important to remember that women tend to make their decisions later, and they are also more likely to deem themselves uninformed even when they are more informed than male voters. Still, it hints strongly at the much-feared "enthusiasm gap," which may see Tea Partiers flocking to the polls while women—among other core Democratic constituencies like blacks and young people—stay home. "This is what wakes me up at night," says Stephanie Schriock, president of EMILY's List.

Just like the rest of the demoralized progressive base, women had high hopes for Obama but feel let down by his administration. Women, especially those who are not college educated, are economically anxious and frustrated with the jobs situation. And although they might favor some aspects of the health-care reform law, they don't see it as a "lifeline," according to pollster Geoff Garin of Hart Research. They don't feel that the Democrats and the Obama administration have done enough for them. If they had to choose, they'd mostly opt for Democrats; but many don't believe that it makes much difference which party controls Congress.

Schriock contends that when presented with detailed information, women—including those who are swing voters—will head to the polls and pull the lever for Democratic candidates. "What we've seen, in poll after poll, in House and Senate races, is that when you lay out the case clearly about what these Republicans bring to the table, women who are independent or even Republican-leaning come back to the Democratic candidates. That is a really good sign, so that is what we are going to spend our time doing," says Schriock.

EMILY's List launched a "Sarah Doesn't Speak for Me" campaign to challenge Palin's claim to represent ordinary women, and it has received emphatic responses from many women, including Republicans. But it remains to be seen whether the masses of women who are turned off by the Michele Bachmanns and Sharron Angles running for office will turn out to reject them at the polls or will simply tune out the election.

When all is said and done in the 2010 midterms, it's quite possible, even likely, that the ranks of women in Congress will be depleted by ten or more. Given the Democratic advantage in women legislators, even if a few more Republican women are elected, a bad year for Dems will be a bad year for women, as many Democratic women legislators who arrived in 2006 or 2008—like Arizona's Gabrielle Giffords, Colorado's Betsey Markey, and Illinois's Debbie Halvorson—find themselves vulnerable to challenges from Republican men. Such a decline in female representation would be the first in more than thirty years. We may see the faces of some newly elected right-wing female legislators on TV, but moderate and independent women will likely find themselves with an even smaller voice in Washington. The irony is that, in this so-called year of the woman, this result will be, more than anything else, an expression of the preferences and passions of angry white men.

—October, 2010

IS SARAH PALIN PORN?

Jack Hitt

Politics is high school with guns and more money.
—Frank Zappa

The ascension of Sarah Palin beyond the realm of mortal politician occurred sometime after her clumsy resignation as governor of Alaska and before the revelation that a recent speaking contract read like outtakes from *This Is Spinal Tap*, peevishly demanding that if a private jet is available then the "aircraft MUST BE a Lear 60 or larger (as defined by interior cabin space) for West Coast Events," that if cameras are allowed then "the number of clicks as appropriate for length of photo op: 45 min/75 clicks; 60 min/100 clicks and 90 min/125 clicks," and that onstage "Unopened bottled still water (2 bottles) and bendable straws are to be placed in or near the wooden lectern." What, no bowls of green M&Ms?

To the Beltway huzzah of cable shows and newspaper columns, Palin is still understood as someone who might run for president. But she is a surging media phenom whose income since July 2009 is estimated at more than $12 million. Those political followers who dog her with their psychosexually fraught signs ("Palin = G. W. Bush with Lipstick"; "Enter Palin, Exit Obama") are now stage props about as crucial as that small crowd of audience members who awkwardly high-five Jay Leno at the beginning of each show. She no longer has supporters; she has a mass audience for whom she is a soap opera, a Horatio Alger story, trailer trash, a goddess, a lad-mag fantasy, and a glamorous star all in one. To say that Sarah Palin is a politician mistakes a splashy debut for the breathless melodrama that now constantly engulfs her. It's like saying that Paris Hilton is a hotel heiress or that Jon Gosselin is a husband.

The marriage of politics and entertainment has long been the Republican Party's greatest asset, but Palin's rise is different and has changed the old rules. Her climb to celebrity is through politics (not the other way around, as it was for Ronald Reagan and Sonny Bono). She is living proof of David Frum's recent heretical observation that "Republicans originally thought that Fox worked for us, and now we are discovering we work for Fox." And her achievement goes a long way toward explaining why the Democrats can't (and won't) gain political traction even with a popular president, an easily blamed predecessor, and the control of both chambers of Congress.

Modern television politics, we are usually told, begins with the famous 1960 Kennedy-Nixon debates. If you look back to them, what you see is not merely the first presidential candidate to realize that packaged talking points come off convincingly on television but also an obituary for a lost political style. Critics always note that Nixon looked crummy in those debates—the five-o'clock shadow, the sweats, the sideways glances, the tugging at his infamous dewlaps. But those gestures are not what sank Nixon. They were merely symptoms of what Nixon was doing, and he was the last politician ever to do it on live TV: Nixon was thinking.

If Kennedy introduced politics to entertainment, Ronald Reagan merged them. His first memorable outing as a presidential candidate was in February 1980 in Nashua, New Hampshire. During a debate with George H.W. Bush, an angry moderator threatened to turn off Reagan's microphone. "I'm paying for this microphone, Mr. Green!" Reagan seethed. The moderator's name was actually "Breen," but it didn't matter. The crowd roared its approval of such a bully moment, and after that Reagan never looked back. (Others did look back, many years later, to discover a precedent: Spencer Tracy, in the Frank Capra film *State of the Union*, finding himself in similar circumstances, fumed, "I'm paying for this broadcast!")

Sometimes Reagan's fusion of Hollywood and politics was breathtaking. (Both Israeli Prime Minister Yitzhak Shamir and Nazi hunter Simon Wiesenthal independently confirmed that they had heard Reagan tell a moving story about having filmed the death camps, even though he never left the United States during wartime. According to Reagan aide Michael Deaver, just because Reagan may have viewed "footage shipped home by the Signal Corps" and "saw this nightmare on film, not in person," that "did not mean he saw it less.") But those who compare Reagan's stagecraft to Palin's high school senior's gift for snark miss a basic difference. Reagan started his public career as a union president in 1947, was a Democrat and an FDR supporter, and in time made an honest progression to the right. He arrived there with decades of witty lines and conservative pearls. He could quip that "one way to make sure crime doesn't pay would be to let the government run it," or needle the press corps by saying, "Before I refuse to take your questions, I have an opening statement."

In other words, Reagan melded entertainment values with political nuance. Since then, the two parties haven't just had different ideologies; they've pursued them in entirely different political moods—not so much indicative versus subjunctive as triumphal versus tedious. In 1987, for instance, writer P.J. O'Rourke captured the essence of Reagan politics with his book *Republican Party Reptile*. Meanwhile, all the Democrats had to put forward that year was a doorstop called *Man of the House: The Life and Political Memoirs of Speaker Tip O'Neill*. When Republicans do politics, it looks like vicious fun. When Democrats do politics, it feels like conscientious homework. Just after the recent health-care legislation passed Congress, Democrat Anthony Weiner observed that it always feels like Democrats "come into knife fights carrying library books."

The origin of this shift in tone—the first beat of the butterfly's wing that would become the Reagan Revolution—arguably happened during the 1980 congressional election in South Carolina, where I grew up and where this story is told all the time, even by Democrats, and not just because it's so rude. Lee Atwater, then working for the incumbent congressman, Floyd Spence, as well as for my cousin Strom Thurmond, was assigned the task of destroying the rising career of a Democrat who bore the Faulknerian name Tom Turnipseed. People who knew Turnipseed well were aware that he'd once undergone electroshock therapy, and Thomas Eagleton's sudden withdrawal from the 1972 Democratic ticket when his similar history became public was still in people's minds. Turnipseed accused Atwater of dirty tricks (push polling, specifically), but instead of responding to the charges, Atwater winked at reporters and joked that you can't always trust the accusations of a man who's been "hooked up to jumper cables." The reporters laughed, skipped reporting the facts, and a new politics was born.

And yet this is where the Republicans' love of Palin is perilous. Her ease before the cameras happens only when she has a line or two scripted for the character she's decided to play in public. At a recent Tea Party gathering, she leaned over the lectern and sneered, "How's that hopey, changey stuff working out for you?" It was a great bit, but a great written bit.

Here Palin most resembles Reagan, but cut her loose from her speechwriters and she shrivels into Dan Quayle. It would not be fair to make this case if she'd had only a few frozen moments with television interviewers. But without a tight script or notes scrawled on her palm, she quickly becomes confused. Her itinerant syntax is now legendary, what Bill Maher calls her gift for unspooling the "sentence to nowhere." You don't need to be an English teacher correcting an essay to know that the student did not read the assignment and is slipping into classic high school bullshit.

Ronald Reagan spent twenty-five years on the lecture circuit, honing his toastmaster's chops to such burnished perfection that any kid in the 1980s could imitate his amiable head tilts and the

soothing susurrus that bathed his every line. Palin's rhetorical training ground—where she learned to say to Katie Couric that her favorite newspaper is "all of them, any of them," and to Glenn Beck that
her favorite founding father is "all of them"—was the Q & A segment
of the small-town beauty pageant. Off the cuff, she always sounds like
she's standing at three-quarter profile in an ill-fitting evening gown,
struggling to discourse on the judges' moronic request to name her
favorite nation ("All of them!").

Astonishingly, she has continued to resist any media training
since she steadfastly refused the help offered by the McCain campaign back in the fall of 2008. Instead, she bitterly brings up her most
colossal failures like an adolescent trying to explain away an embarrassing mistake—and then can't stop talking about it, convincing no
one but herself.

When Rahm Emanuel referred to liberal activists as "retarded"
in a private conversation, she opportunistically pounced. Typically,
conservatives stay away from the political-correctness angle. But
Palin howled that she was deeply offended. Unfortunately, Rush
Limbaugh shortly thereafter denounced the retards in the White
House. Retard, retard, retard—he said it forty times, with the usual
honking, farting, grandmother-horrifying derision that passes for
humor on radio these days. The day after that, Palin defended Limbaugh, drawing a meandering distinction between Emanuel's comments and Limbaugh's "satire." The very next day, an actual satirist,
Stephen Colbert, made the argument that "we should all come to
her defense and say Sarah Palin is a fucking retard." For once, Palin
shut up.

She pratfalls now as regularly as she pirouettes—and she stumbles
whenever she veers from the playbook. Her resignation as governor
of Alaska is a torturous piece of video; it's impossible not to feel near
Aristotelian catharsis watching such a calamity unfold right in front
of your eyes. But that hideously painful moment—Palin straining
to spin her quitting into an act of resolution—was more than just

a beauty-pageant moment. It's actually what Palin's audiences love about her. They never know what they will get. She can be the petty, mean girl who gets caught using her authority as governor to ruin her hated ex-brother-in-law or using a marker to black out "McCain" on an old campaign sun visor. She can be the deliberately trashy girl who in college favored sassy T-shirts ("I may be broke but I'm not flat busted) and who as a vice-presidential candidate not only wore a pair of harlot-red pumps (sold under the name "Naughty Monkey Double Dare") but then gave them to her niece to sell on eBay for $2,025.

She seethes at the mention of her daughter's old boyfriend, Levi Johnston, cattily characterizing his *Playgirl* photo shoot as "aspiring porn." Her Facebook updates are as bitchy as those of any fourteen-year-old girl. And her treacly tweets are classic examples of what the philosopher Daniel Dennett calls "deepities"—vagaries that can easily pass as profundities ("Kids: be more concerned w/ your character vs reputation bc character is what you are, reputation is merely what others think you are").

She can also do, by her own standard, some "porn." She showed off major leg in a racy spread in *Runner's World*, wearing a pair of tight, short shorts, with an American flag chucked on a chair like a sweat towel. In other pictures, she wears skin-tight leggings and assumes saucy "warm-up" positions. For her fans, it was an issue to keep in that special place where Mom never looks. When *Newsweek* ran the tight-shorts pic as a cover image, Palin swiftly denounced it as "sexist." But she recently showed up at John McCain's side in Arizona and thrilled her followers by wearing a black leather jacket, cut in butch style, with zippered accents defining her breasts. Palin knows her fan base, and she knows what they want: a brief tour of Google reveals dozens of Photoshopped Palin fantasy images—and it's clear that they're not posted by her enemies.

A few days after appearing with McCain, she debuted her television show, *Real American Stories* (the title an apparent reference to her campaign declaration that her followers lived in the "real America"). Fox promised a show in which "three very different guests will speak to Palin," and what they got was another trademark Palin disaster. Two of her guests, LL Cool J (possibly chosen to chill the reputation of Palin's followers as mostly middle-aged and white) and Toby Keith, separately claimed that they hadn't spoken to Palin and that their interviews were repurposed stuff from more than a year ago. The whole "real" show was mostly canned. It did modestly in Fox ratings but has not been regularly scheduled and will appear, network executives say, "periodically."

And so it goes. From time to time, new rumors about Palin's escapades in Alaska surface or a *National Enquirer* headline declares another one of her children a new "Boozy Wild Child" or a gossip rag alleges that Todd is reducing their marriage to a post on hotchickswithdouchebags.com. But then she'll give a great speech or go on Leno to pull off a decent performance. She seems to swing, like clockwork, from disaster to triumph. The comedian Kathy Griffin has called her the "gift that keeps on giving." And that is where both left- and right-wing politicos don't get Palin at all. The Democrats delight in her antics when she executes one of her routine face-plants, while a significant cohort of Republicans get all hot and bothered whenever she appears as the next great conservative savior. She's adept at always keeping her left antagonized and her right bedazzled. She lives in balanced suspension between two states of being, permanently listing forward, a kind of political optical illusion in which, depending on who's gawking, she appears always to be falling or soaring.

Setting aside her political apologists and detractors, and both are comparatively few, her mass-market base follows her because her triumphs and failures, her family, her bitchy tweets and trashy flaws keep her aloft in that mythic state Barbara Walters describes as "fascinating." She inhabits that dimension occupied by tabloid royalty.

She's *Northern Exposure* meets *Jersey Shore*, with less cowbell and more moose. Sarah Palin has her own show all right, and it's not just on Fox. It's on every channel, across all platforms, all the time, and, for now, the world can hardly wait for the next episode.

—June 2010

THE TEA PARTY AND THE NEW RIGHT-WING CHRISTIAN FEMINISM

Ruth Rosen

Most Americans are not quite sure what to make of the sprawling right-wing Tea Party, which gradually emerged in 2009 and became a household name after it held nationwide Tea Party rallies on April 15, 2010, to protest paying taxes. Throwing tea overboard, as you may remember, is an important symbolic image of the colonial anger at Britain's policy of "taxation without representation."

Many liberals and leftists dismissed the Tea Party as a temporary, knee-jerk response to the recession, high unemployment, home fore-closures, bankruptcies, and an African-American president who had saved American capitalism by expanding the government's subsidies to the financial, real estate, and automobile industries. Perhaps it is a temporary political eruption, but as E.J. Dionne, columnist at the *Washington Post* has argued,[1] the movement also threatens the hard-won unity of the Republicans. "The rise of the Tea Party movement," he writes, "is a throwback to an old form of libertarianism that sees most of the domestic policies that government has undertaken since the New Deal as unconstitutional. It typically perceives the most dan-gerous threats to freedom as the design of well-educated elitists out of touch with "American values."

Who are these angry people who express so much resentment against the government, rather than at corporations? Since national polls dramatically contradict each other, I have concluded that the Tea Party movement has energized people across all classes.

One important difference, however, is race. At Tea Party rallies you don't see faces with dark complexions. Another important distinction is that men and women are drawn to this sprawling movement for a variety of overlapping but possibly different reasons. Both men and women seem to embrace an incoherent "ideology" which calls for freedom from government, no taxes, and an inchoate desire to "take back America," which means restoring the nation to some moment when the country was white and "safe."

Men drawn to this movement appear to belong to a broad range of fringe right-wing groups, such as militias, white supremacy groups, pro-gun and -Confederacy "armies." Some of these groups advocate violence, vow to overthrow the government, and have even begun to use Facebook, Twitter, and YouTube to spread their hatred through social media.

Women also play a decisive role in the Tea Party and now make up fifty-five percent of its supporters, according to the latest Quinnipiac poll.[2] Hanna Rosin reports in *Slate* magazine[3] that "of the eight board members of the Tea Party Patriots[4] who serve as national coordinators for the movement, six are women. Fifteen of the 25 state coordinators are women."

Why, I've wondered, does this chaotic movement appeal to so many women? There are many possible reasons. Some of the women in these groups are certainly women who love men who love guns and who hate the government and taxes. Professor Kathleen Blee, who has written widely about right-wing women, suggests that there are probably more religious right-wing women than men in general, that Tea Party rallies may attract more women who are not working and therefore can attend them, and that the Tea Party emphasizes family vulnerability to all kinds of external danger.

Many men and women attracted to the Tea Party also belong to the Christian Identity Movement.[5] They are right-wing Christians who promote fundamentalist views on abortion and homosexuality. But women come to the Tea Party from new and surprising venues, like the Parent-Teacher Association or groups organized specifically to elect women to political office. As *Slate* recently noted, "Much of the leadership and the grassroots energy comes from women. One of the three main sponsors of the Tax Day Tea Party[6] that launched the movement is a group called Smart Girl Politics.[7] The site started out as a mommy blog and has turned into a mobilizing campaign that trains future activists and candidates. Despite its explosive growth over the last year, it is still operated like a feminist cooperative, with three stay-at-home moms taking turns raising babies and answering e-mails and phone calls."

Some of these religious women also have political aspirations and hope to use the Tea Party to gain leadership roles denied by the Republican Party to run for electoral office. To counter EMILY's List,[8] which has supported liberal women in electoral politics, right-wing conservative women created the Susan B. Anthony List,[9] which is successfully supporting right-wing women in their efforts to run for electoral office. To blunt the impact of liberal feminists, Concerned Women for America,[10] a deeply religious group, supports women's efforts to seek leadership positions within the Tea Party. The Women's Independent Forum,[11] a more secular group of right-wing women, seeks to promote traditional values, free markets, limited government, women's equality, and their ability to run for office.

Some of these women are drawing national attention because they have embraced a religious "conservative feminism." Among them are evangelical Christians and, according to a recent cover story[12] in *Newsweek*, they view Sarah Palin—who ran for the vice presidency in 2009, has five children and a supportive husband, describes herself as a feminist, and gave up the governor's office in Alaska to become a celebrity and millionaire—as the leader, if not *prophet* of the Tea Party.

As a result, Palin is mobilizing right-wing religious women across the nation. They like that she wears makeup, still looks like a gorgeous beauty queen, and yet is bold and strong minded. They don't seem to care that she uses "Ms." instead of "Mrs." Nor are they bothered by her crediting Title IX[13] (legislation passed in 1972 that enforced gender equality in education and sports) for her athletic opportunities. On ABC News she told her interviewer, Charles Gibson, "I'm lucky to have been brought up in a family where gender has never been an issue. I'm a product of Title IX, also, where we had equality in schools that was just being ushered in with sports and with equality opportunity for education, all of my life. I'm part of that generation, where that question is kind of irrelevant because it's accepted. Of course you can be the vice president and you can raise a family."

Palin belongs to a group called Feminists for Life[14] whose slogan is "Refuse to Choose." When she described herself as a feminist at the start of her vice-presidential campaign, she explained that she was a member of this group, led by Serrin Foster, who has carved out a successful career on the lecture circuit by trying to convince young women that you can be a feminist by making the *choice* not to have an abortion. When I interviewed Foster several years ago, I asked her how very poor or teenage girls were supposed to take care of these unwanted children. Since she is against taxes and government subsidies for social services, she evaded my question. She said that women should not be alone, that others should help. In the end, the only concrete solution she offered is that adoption is the best solution for these young women.

Just recently, Palin once again dubbed herself a "feminist" and set off an explosive debate about what constitutes feminism in the United States. She describes religious conservative women as "mama grizzlies" and urges them to "rise up" and claim the cause of feminism as their own. Palin encourages her followers to launch a "new, conservative feminist movement" that supports only political candidates who uncompromisingly oppose abortion.

The response to Palin's effort to draw women into the Tea Party varies widely. Her "sisterly speechifying," writes Jessica Valenti in the *Washington Post*,[15] "is just part of a larger conservative bid for the hearts and minds of women by appropriating feminist language."

Writing in the conservative *National Review*,[16] Kathryn Jean Lopez responds, "Palin isn't co-opting feminism. She's reclaiming a movement that was started by Susan B. Anthony and other women who fought for the right to vote—and were staunchly pro-life." This is true; nineteenth century suffragists wanted to protect the status of motherhood and were against abortion. "The 'feminist' label doesn't have to be so polarizing," argues Meghan Daum in the *Los Angeles Times*.[17] Boiled down, feminism just means viewing men and women as equals, and seeing your gender "as neither an obstacle to success nor an excuse for failure." So if Sarah Palin "has the guts to call herself a feminist, then she's entitled to be accepted as one."

Here is a great irony. Since 1980, when the backlash began attacking the women's movement, young secular American women have resisted calling themselves feminists because the religious right wing had so successfully created an unattractive image of a feminist as a hairy, man-hating lesbian who spouted equality, but really wanted to kill babies. Now, Palin is forcing liberal feminists to debate whether these Christian feminists are diluting feminism or legitimizing it by making it possible to say that one is a feminist.

When I read what women write on Christian women's websites, I hear an echo from the late nineteenth century when female reformers sought to protect the family from "worldly dangers." Frances Willard, leader of the Woman's Christian Temperance Union,[18] urged millions of women to enter the public sphere in order to protect their families, to address the decadent consequences and casualties of capitalism, to win suffrage, and to fight for prohibition, all in the name of protecting the purity of their homes and families.

For many contemporary evangelical Christian women, the motivations are similar. They want to enter the public sphere or even run for office to eliminate abortion, protect marriage, contain sexual relations, oppose gay marriage, and clean up the mess made by the sexual revolution. All this is part of a long and recognizable female reform tradition in American history.

At Tea Party rallies, you often see women carrying signs that read "Take back America." Not everyone is sure what that means. At the very least, however, it means taking back America from an expanding government, from taxes, and more symbolically, from the changing racial complexion of American society.

Within a few decades, the nonwhite population will constitute a majority of the citizens in the United States. Many white evangelical Christians feel besieged, and the women, for their part, feel they must publicly protect their families from such rapid and potentially dangerous changes. They feel that some faceless bureaucrats or immigrants or minorities, described as "they," have taken over our nation and threaten the moral purity of American society. What they don't fear is that corporations have taken over the American government and have distorted its democratic institutions.

Washington bureau chief of AlterNet, Adele Stan, who has fifteen years of close scrutiny of the extreme right under her belt, has warned[19] that we should take the Tea Partiers seriously and that we dismiss them at our peril.

The Tea Party panders to fear and resentment. But they are hardly a lonely minority. A recent *USA Today*/Gallup survey[20] found that 37 percent of Americans said they "approved" of the Tea Party movement. It is not a movement that Americans should ignore. History reminds us that the politics of fear and resentment can quickly turn into a dangerous and powerful political force.

But the Tea Party is not only a grassroots movement. Behind the women at the kitchen table, there is money, and plenty of it. Writing in the *The New York Review of Books*, Michael Tomasky[21] reminded readers that "Money is the ultimate lubricant of politics and that the potential money supply for Tea Parties…is virtually limitless."

Tomasky also underscores the fact that the Tea Party is not about short-term electoral victories. It's about the long-term project of resurrecting the power to protect free markets, deregulation, and for the religious right to gain political power.

Men and women may not join the Tea Party for the same reasons, but without its grassroots female supporters, the Tea Party would have far less appeal to voters who are frightened by economic insecurity, threats to moral purity, and the gradual disappearance of a national white Christian culture.

For good or ill, Christian women have moved mountains before in the American past. The abolition of slavery and the prohibition of liquor are just two examples. Now they have helped organize the Tea Party, and their new conservative feminism may just affect American political culture in unpredictable ways. Perhaps they will gain a new self-confidence and political influence by straying from the Republican Party. Or, as in the past, they may disappear into their homes and churches and become a footnote in the history of American politics. For now, it is too soon to tell how the Tea Party, let alone its female members, will fare in the future.

—July 5, 2010

Notes:

1. http://www.truthdig.com/report/item/how_obama_changed_the_right_20100620/

2. http://www.politico.com/news/stories/0310/35094.html

3. http://www.slate.com/id/2253645

4. http://www.teapartypatriots.org/

5. http://www.carm.org/christian-identity-movement

6. http://taxdayteaparty.com/about/

7. http://smartgirlpolitics.ning.com/

8. http://www.emilyslist.org/splash/signup/splash01/index.pl

9. http://www.sba-list.org/site/c.ddJBKJNsFqG/b.4009925/k.BE63/Home.htm

10. http://www.cwfa.org/main.asp

11. http://www.iwf.org/

12. http://www.newsweek.com/2010/06/11/saint-sarah.html

13. http://www.dol.gov/oasam/regs/statutes/titleix.htm

14. http://www.feministsforlife.org/

15. http://www.washingtonpost.com/wp-dyn/content/article/2010/05/28/AR2010052802263.html?sid=ST2010052804193

16. http://article.nationalreview.com/434723/sarah-palin-a-feminist-in-the-pro-life-tradition/kathryn-jean-lopez?page=1

17. http://www.latimes.com/news/opinion/commentary/la-oe-0520-daum-fword-20100520,0,4933552.column

18. http://en.wikipedia.org/wiki/Woman's_Christian_Temperance_Union

19. http://www.alternet.org/news/147307/the_tea_party_is_dangerous:_dispelling_7_myths_that_help_us_avoid_reality_about_the_new_right-wing_politics/

20. http://www.gallup.com/poll/127181/tea-partiers-fairly-mainstream-demographics.aspx#2

21. http://www.nybooks.com/articles/archives/2009/oct/22/something-new-on-the-mall/?page=1

22. http://www.opendemocracy.net/blog/2008/11/04/palinism-taking-advantage-of-feminism-for-personal-gain

23. http://www.opendemocracy.net/godfrey-hodgson/great-american-refusal

LAST COLUMN ABOUT SARAH PALIN—EVER

Katha Pollitt

Going Rogue has been out only a day or two as I write, and I've already read so many blogs and columns and articles and reviews and participated in so many listserv discussions about it, I'm sick to death not only of Sarah Palin but of Palin-related snark, outrage, ruminations, and fact checks. I don't want to follow the timeline of Bristol's pregnancy on *Vanity Fair*'s website. I don't want to delve into how many hockey games this self-described hockey mom actually attended or how many moose she really shot. I don't want to find out the backstory behind her digs at Levi Johnston or the McCain campaign. Fish in a barrel! You know something's gone off the rails when the ferociously smart Linda Hirshman defends Palin's charging her $150,000 campaign wardrobe to the McCain campaign (or possibly, depending on whom you believe, not) at the *Daily Beast* on the grounds that, unlike stylish Michelle Obama, she doesn't have a rich husband to pay for her clothes—and when writers hammer away at this thesis for seventy posts on a listserv. All right, I admit I wrote several of those posts. And, yes, I am writing this column. What is it about this absurd woman that is so fascinating?

As just about every columnist in the world has noted by now, including me more than once, Palin is a bundle of contradictions: a Christian reactionary who has kind words for Title IX and thinks it's fine to have a top government job, five kids, and a lower-earning husband; a seriously underqualified politician chosen by the desperate

John McCain at least partly because of her gender and looks who exploits those assets every chance she gets—but if called on it, accuses her critics of sexism. And you know what? Some of them deserve to be called out! *Newsweek's* cover, for instance, was doubly sexist. The headline *How Do You Solve a Problem like Sarah?* (a cutesy reference to Maria, the madcap novice nun in *The Sound of Music*) would never have been used for a man. (How do you solve a problem like Bart Stupak? Glenn Beck? Hamid Karzai?) The accompanying photo, originally shot for *Runner's World*, showed Palin in running shorts, with a come-hither smile, a beauty-queen curve-accentuating pose, leaning on the flag and holding not one but two BlackBerrys: Ooh, Patriot Barbie is busy! (The inside is worse: a shot-from-behind pic of her shapely calves and shiny black high-heeled shoes, a plastic Palin doll in schoolgirl pornwear. Oh, women of *Newsweek*, have you no influence at all with your frat-boy overlords?) But it also has to be said that *Runner's World* did not tie Palin up and make her pose like that. Any more than the McCain campaign required her to go unprepared to her interview with Katie Couric, or Levi Johnston forces her to talk trash just because he does. For a person who says "common sense" is all we need to solve our most intractable problems, Palin seems to have very little.

It is indeed annoying to have Palin paradoxes thrown in one's feminist face all day. You see, says conventional wisdom, you said women should just vote for women, and look what you got! (Note to CW: Feminists never said women should vote for women just because of their gender. They said women should vote for feminists.) But parsing the feminist semiotics of Sarah Palin is getting as old as all those articles about why teenage girls love vampires. Someday there will be whole women's studies conferences devoted to her, the way there used to be scholarly panels on Madonna. Maybe even endowed chairs of Palin studies. But does feminism really have all that much to do with her apotheosis?

The one thing Palin seems to know how to do is use the media's infatuation with celebrity, hotness, and women's bodies to aggrandize herself. As Bill O'Reilly told her, "You are the biggest threat because you are a star.... There aren't any other Republicans who are media stars but you." Except for her politics, she's the living embodiment of the constantly updated *Huffington Post* cover page, in which Washington reporting and Jon and Kate and assorted pushers of quackery and psychobabble jostle against a constant stream of semi-naked photos of semi-celebs, whose breasts and cosmetic surgeries you are invited to rate. For her fans she may be a goddess of vitality and truth, but for everyone else she's the first political female train wreck, the Paris Hilton or Lindsay Lohan of the Republican Party. We can't stop looking. Maybe she'll confuse Iran and Iraq again! And tell about praying on the phone with Rick Warren while taking a shower! Or write another letter in God's voice about her baby, Trig! Maybe Palin is cosmic payback for all those nasty jokes about Hillary's pantsuits and thick ankles, and for the mighty cry of *borrring!* that goes up all over the media whenever a politician—Al Gore?—displays actual knowledge of a complex subject. You wanted hot and relatable? You got it.

It doesn't have to be this way. Consider Angela Merkel. The press (the foreign press, mostly) went wild when she wore a low-cut gown to the opening of the Oslo opera house last year. If you google her, "Angela Merkel cleavage" is the first suggested search term that comes up—but Merkel herself doesn't engage with media-style hyped-up feminine self-presentation. She dresses in a nondescript way, doesn't wear a lot of makeup—in fact, she looks like she doesn't wear any makeup—and her hair is so ordinary, I can't even remember how she wears it. Her husband is not part of her day-to-day story. She is a middle-aged woman with a PhD in physics, a pleasant, lined face, and a low-key, straightforward manner. Even people who would never vote for her seem to respect her as a human being. So far as I know, there are no Angela Merkel nutcrackers or plastic dolls in slutty costumes for sale on the Internet.

It is so restful, you can't believe it.

—November 24, 2009

THE INEVITABLE RISE AND QUASI LIBERATION OF NIKKI HALEY

Sarah Jaffe

Two thousand ten was looking like a good year for Democrats in South Carolina. Rob Miller managed to turn Joe Wilson's famous shout at President Obama into a fundraising pitch, and then Governor Mark Sanford disgraced himself and the would-be heir apparent, Lieutenant Governor Andre Bauer, made headlines by comparing poor children to stray animals.

Then Sarah Palin got involved.

Mark Sanford's estranged wife, Jenny, had already championed a young, charismatic state representative in the Republican primary race, Nikki Haley, 38, a legislator from Lexington, and an Indian-American.

The story goes that Palin saw a video of Haley at a Tea Party rally and liked what she saw. And with her endorsement, Haley's star began to rise. Suddenly she was up in the polls and the national media was taking notice of the fresh, telegenic face. And then, of course, the mudslinging started. State Senator Jake Knotts, a supporter of Bauer, told an Internet talk show, "We already got one raghead in the White House. We don't need another in the governor's mansion."

Political blogger Will Folks and Larry Marchant, working for Bauer at the time, both came forward with claims that they had had extramarital dalliances with Haley. Unlike her former mentor Sanford, Haley steadfastly denied the accusations, deftly turning them around on her opponent in one debate appearance, calling the accusations "everything that's wrong with the establishment... everything that's wrong with South Carolina politics."

The steady support of Sanford's wife allowed Haley to play the victim while enjoying the free media that the sex scandal brought her, and suddenly the campaign was all about Haley. She had a ten-point lead in the polls when the accusations hit. In the first primary round she was twenty points over her nearest rival, and won the runoff by thirty.

The mainstream news media has gone gaga for Haley. She appeared on the cover of *Newsweek* alongside a fawning profile that called her "earthy, attractive, and articulate," and lovingly described her "stilettos you could impale a small animal with." Like other profiles of the South Carolina contender, *Newsweek*'s piece was long on Haley's looks and comparisons to Palin and notably short on discussions of actual policy.

Newsweek's coverage of Haley is par for the course. Conservative women have become the subject du jour, and ignoring other subjects, many in the money media are taking Palin's bait and acting as though Haley and the rest of the "mama grizzlies" represent something new (rather than acknowledging the extent to which they co-opt traditional feminist rhetoric and couple it with very old-school anti-woman policies). Other exciting, accomplished women running for office in other states get less press—one could count the big national profiles of tradition-busting candidates Linda Chavez-Thompson in Texas or Tarryl Clark in Minnesota, on one thumb—or less than that.

After all, underneath the surface, Haley is no kinder, gentler Republican. Among the bills she's co-sponsored in the immediate run-up to the election are an antiunion "right to secret ballot" bill and a bill that would make it harder for women to obtain an abortion. She's a favorite of the disparate Tea Party groups in the state, and she quotes Barry Goldwater on the campaign trail. She supports Arizona's SB 1070, the anti-immigrant bill recently struck down in part as unconstitutional, and co-sponsored a similar bill for South Carolina.

Haley fits one narrative—the year of the Republican woman— and confuses another. While riding a wave of Tea Party support, the small-government, pro-term-limits Haley is a nonwhite woman. Her ethnic identity allows South Carolina conservatives—some of the same people who cheered Tom Tancredo when he said of Obama, "If his wife says Kenya is his homeland, why don't we just send him back?"—to proudly trumpet their nonracist credentials.

So far, Haley has used her difference as a way to distinguish herself and position herself as a Republican Party outsider—a good place to be in a year when the party insiders have been nothing but a disgrace. She seems quite aware of the double edge of her narrative. A story she likes to tell, of being disqualified from a beauty pageant as a child because she could be neither the black queen or white queen, emphasizes her difference from both (and, of course, her looks, without which it seems hard for Republican women politicians to gain media prominence). She subtly implies with this story that black and white both bore her the same degree of animosity—that perhaps black South Carolinians are just as racist as white, a common refrain in the Tea Party victim storyline.

Samhita Mukhopadhyay of Feministing.com noted that Asian- Americans have often been deemed a "model minority," used by conservatives as "a measuring stick to put other ethnic minorities down." The way Haley uses her own immigrant background is notable in this regard. If her parents could come here legally and assimilate, the implication goes, why can't the rest? Dr. Inderpal Grewal, a professor of women's, gender, and sexuality studies at Yale, notes, "It reemphasizes that the American way of life is superior, that an Asian person chooses it."

Indeed, while she is compared to Palin quite a bit, *New York* magazine asked instead if she might be the Republican Party's Barack Obama. It was her speeches at the aforementioned Tea Party rallies,

after all, that made her fame, and she's shared ethnic slurs and specu-
lation about her religion with the president. She seems like the perfect
cross between Obama and Palin; the internationalist background with
its pretty promises of putting the state's ugly background on racial issues to bed at last, combined with the sex appeal and feisty claims of
a kind of conservative feminism—or at least female solidarity—that
Palin brought. She brings the youth and maverick claims of both.

Like Obama, Haley has also seen her full name used as a weapon
against her on the campaign trail—Nikki is her middle name, Haley
her husband's last name. It's worth considering if Nimrata Randhawa
would be able to win by double digits over white men with the same
ease as Nikki Haley. But Grewal notes that the name change is not
rare for Sikh immigrants in the United States; nor are conservative
values or military service (Haley's brother is in the military, her husband in the reserves). She notes instead, "Most controversial within
the Indian-American community is the conversion."

Grewal points out that Haley's personal narrative suits another
familiar conservative storyline—"the born-again discourse." As the
campaign progressed, Grewal and others have noted, Haley's campaign website changed to emphasize her Christianity. For political
success, Grewal notes, religion is a requirement, especially in South
Carolina, where the state constitution still says that "No person shall
be eligible to the office of Governor who denies the existence of the
Supreme Being."

The pressure Haley is under to prove her Christianity is stronger
because her party, and especially the Tea Party faction, has used difference as a weapon to wound President Obama. Wrote Michael Ros-
ton at True/Slant, "By a thousand cuts big and small, 'you're not like
us' has become a way for conservatives to oppose Obama. And when
their base begins using it to eat one of their own, it's really just their
own chickens coming home to roost."

Yet Haley's ethnicity and gender thus far have worked to her
advantage on the campaign trail. Veteran South Carolina political

watcher Ed Kilgore notes "Self-conscious movement conservatives, so long as you're willing to meet their ideological test, absolutely love diversity." Haley hits all the right talking points, echoing Mark Sanford's opposition to the stimulus bill and positioning herself to the right of her white, male rivals. Kilgore points out, too, that Haley appeals to suburban transplants to the South. "They're right-wing but they really hate the good ol' boys," he says, and see Haley as a step toward "ridding Southern conservatism of the old taint of the Dixiecrats." Andre Bauer and Jake Knotts represent that streak of the party, who became Republicans largely over race.

Sanford, with his grandstanding over stimulus money, was also a Tea Party favorite before his fall, and his battles with the legislature are legendary. Claims of favoring small government are one thing, but what happens when you actually have to govern? Haley's connections to Sanford have lost her the endorsement of the state Chamber of Commerce, which battled Sanford's attempts to refuse stimulus money and sees her as more of the same.

While Haley does enjoy a lead in the polls, the Democrats have an unusually strong candidate this year in Vincent Sheheen, who has the coveted Chamber endorsement and the support of a "Republicans for Sheheen" Facebook group where members share concerns about four more years of Sanford, particularly where education is concerned. Kilgore says, "If he wasn't running against Nikki Haley he might be in the lead."

Mention Haley to a South Carolina Democrat, and you get an angry, impassioned response. Terry Bergeron, a media professional from Hilton Head Island, told me, "I'm angry and frustrated about the way this whole story has unfolded in the national media. Why is Nikki Haley the story? She was the fourth-place candidate plucked out of obscurity by Sarah Palin, a failed vice-presidential candidate who had never even been to South Carolina prior to the endorsement. And all of a sudden Nikki Haley's name and face are everywhere." She continued, "Only once have I heard the national media mention Vincent Sheheen, arguably the best candidate either party has nominated for Governor in my twenty-two years living in this state. Even my own so-called 'liberal media,' like MSNBC and now *The Nation*, have let me down by perpetuating the legend."

Without the support of Jenny Sanford, which Kilgore and Grewal agree was crucial in painting Haley as the victim of an old-boys' network, and then the national media spotlight that came with Palin's endorsement, where would Haley be? Kilgore points out that she was never a great fundraiser, but the attention from the sex scandal brought plenty of free media, and Palin came along at just the right time. From there, the boys never had a chance.

But like Sarah Palin, Haley is polarizing, and the more that many South Carolinians learn about her, the less they seem to like her. Can a conservative ideologue win in a state racked by unemployment and aware of its perennial status at the bottom of education statistics? Can she beat a Democrat with business support and bipartisan appeal? And if she wins, can she translate that to national prominence—or governing success? Or is she destined to be another Sarah Palin, catnip for the media but bad luck at the polls?

—August 2010

ALASKANS HATE QUITTERS

Shannyn Moore

Sarah Palin's Alaska isn't better than the Alaska I grew up in.

I love to travel—especially overseas. People you meet inevitably want to know where you're from. During the Bush years, I managed a brief escape to Italy. I avoided the ugly American stigma by saying I was from Alaska! Somehow back then, people thought of Alaska as its own country. Instead of saying, "don't blame me, I didn't vote for Bush," I wound up having broken conversations about snow, sled dogs, mountains, and fishing.

Those days are gone. It's over.

"Do you know Sarah Palin?"

"Yes. She threatened to sue me once, but quit halfway through."

It's not always easy living here. The elements and weather are wilder than our politics and used to matter more. For a time, it was against the law to pass a hitchhiker. People would pull your car out of a snow bank regardless of your bumper stickers.

Who we are was built by the old guard. Ted Stevens admitted breaking the law to get statehood for Alaska. Vic Fischer, a fierce Democrat, wrote a constitution with huge privacy provisions that legalized marijuana and made it possible to legalize abortion prior to *Roe v. Wade*. Democrat Bob Bartlett, one of our first senators, passed more legislation than any other legislator, including mandating accessibility to public buildings for the disabled. This landmark legislation became known as the Americans with Disabilities

Act. Ernest Gruening, another Democrat, was one of only two votes against the Gulf of Tonkin Resolution. He also introduced a Congressional resolution to establish the nationwide emergency 911 number. Governor Jay Hammond flew his own float plane from town to town. He was known as the "Bush-rat Governor." Hammond was the architect of Alaska's Permanent Fund, which has socked away over $35 billion. That same fund pays a dividend to each and every Alaskan. Many times, those dividend checks are well over a thousand dollars.

Wally Hickel was the only other Alaskan governor to "quit." But he was moving up. His appointment by Nixon as secretary of the interior was protested by environmentalists. Little did they know they were protesting a friend. Hickel imposed stringent cleanup regulations on oil companies and water polluters after an oil rig explosion off the coast of Santa Barbara in 1969. He also fought to save the Everglades from being destroyed by developers and advocated making Earth Day a national holiday.

He was also an unwitting war protester.

Hickel was fired as secretary of the interior by President Nixon when he went public about his opposition to military action in Cambodia and the Kent State massacre. When pressured to quit, he told *60 Minutes* he would only go away "with an arrow in my heart, not a bullet in my back." All Sarah Palin needed to quit was a check.

Always an advocate for Alaskan sovereignty, Hickel never stopped pushing for an all-Alaska gas line. He was convinced Palin had the guts to get it done. She didn't. No one had buyer's remorse more than Wally Hickel. He said so.

Writer Geoffrey Dunn asked Hickel in 2009 for a formal, on-the-record response to Palin's stunted career as governor. Dunn wrote:

> he (Hickel) took a deep pause. "She fell in love with the national spotlight and lost her ethical compass," he said thoughtfully. "That was a sad day for Alaska and America."

After the 2008 election, Hickel's *Anchorage Daily News* article eviscerated Palin's race-baiting on the campaign trail.

"Palin became the spokesperson for the divisive voices in American politics. She dismissed the greatness of our immigrant heritage, indeed of today's Alaska, where in Anchorage alone nearly 100 languages are spoken in the homes of the children in our public schools."

The bottom line of these leaders, and countless others was "Alaska First."

Sarah's bottom line is, and always has been, "Sarah First."

The "Lower 48" is also called "Outside" with a capital O. It implies Alaskans are "Inside." On the Inside we fight, bicker, clash, and crash with each other. What we argue about is what is best for Alaska.

Sarah Palin brought a different partisanship than most places will ever experience. It has never been about Alaska or even the Republican Party. She ran against her party for mayor and governor, ousting first John Stein and then Frank Murkowski.

Sarah loves Sarah.

When Sarah called a press conference on Lake Lucille and abruptly quit, rumors ran rampant. Her excuses and explanations didn't add up. Palin supporters who had walked door to door at 5 degrees were crushed. People who had defended her stamina and "mavericky" credentials were abandoned like a boat caught on the mudflats at low tide.

Alaskans have been spoiled by decades of tough, visionary leadership. In some cases, we admired them more then we agreed with them. No one ever quit unless they were moving on to serve the public in an even greater role.

But Palin quit. Why? It must be something *huge*. Just prior to Palin's ascension, Alaska's state legislature was under investigation by the FBI. Ten percent of our lawmakers were indicted. The government ransacked Ted Stevens's Girdwood home. Under that climate, her resignation seemed ominous. Another teenage pregnancy? Maybe she was ill. I was asked on *Hardball with Chris Matthews* about her abrupt departure. "There are rumors swirling about an iceberg scandal; perhaps she's under federal investigation," I said—or something to that effect. Palin's lawyer promptly threatened to sue—but never followed through.

Alaskans searched for the backstory to Palin's surrender. While we were accustomed to corruption, we weren't accustomed to a sellout quitter.

But time has revealed the truth.

For all the baggage attached to some of Alaska's storied politicians, quitting wasn't part of their DNA. Alaska isn't kind to quitters. If you quit, you will drown; you will freeze; you will starve.

Under Sarah Palin, the progressive legacy of Alaska was boiled down to a bumpit and a "You Betcha." Classic punch-line Palin.

Alaskans don't quit, we adapt and persevere: the Japanese occupation during World War II; the 1964 earthquake; tidal waves; volcanoes; the Exxon Valdez oil spill; floods.

Someday, we'll rise up to the place where our bumper stickers won't matter. We'll start fighting over which brine recipes make the best smoked salmon. And hopefully, whenever we travel, we can once again claim to be from Alaska without wondering whether we'll be asked if we know Sarah Palin.

—August 2010

PART FIVE: TV TEA PARTY

AT LAST A CITIZEN MOVEMENT THE CORPORATE MEDIA CAN LOVE

Peter Hart and Steve Rendall

In the first year of the Obama administration, the corporate media suddenly overcame their general aversion to citizen movements that criticize government policies, granting the staunchly conservative Tea Party activists enormous coverage—a decision that seems likely to impact politics for the foreseeable future.

Citizen movements are hardly ever front-page news, even when they have clearly identifiable political agendas and broad public support. But the Tea Party movement—an amorphous, politically incoherent umbrella designation for various strands of opposition to Obama, much of it beset with racism and backed by less-than-grassroots deep-pocket Beltway lobbying groups—has managed to buck that trend, getting the fervent support of conservative media and wide, often uncritical coverage in the corporate media.

The Tea Party name derives from a rant by CNBC's Rick Santelli (2/19/09), who was furious about the White House's home-loan modification programs. "How many people want to pay for your neighbor's mortgages that has an extra bathroom and can't pay their bills?" Santelli barked, making his case with the kind of logic that would later make Glenn Beck such a success: "You know, Cuba used to have mansions and a relatively decent economy. They moved from the individual to the collective. Now they're driving '54 Chevys. It's time for another tea party."

That clip became an Internet sensation, and—so we're told—a movement was born. Anti-tax protests were organized in numerous cities in mid-April; conservatives complained about the lack of coverage, but the events were in fact well documented (FAIR Blog, 4/16/09).

The contentious town hall meetings of the summer of 2009 were seen as another manifestation of budding domestic unrest. Lawmakers conducting routine sessions in their legislative districts were faced by dozens of angry, sometimes threatening citizens, goaded by talk radio and Internet organizers into denouncing the White House healthcare proposals as a socialist menace. Most of the protests were rather small, but nonetheless were covered across the cable news channels, reframing the debate over health care and putting Democrats on the defensive.

The pinnacle of Tea Party power, as media told it, was Republican Scott Brown's unlikely triumph in the special election for Edward Kennedy's Massachusetts Senate seat. A *Christian Science Monitor* headline (1/19/10) declared Brown "The Tea Party's First Electoral Victory." The *New York Times* reported (1/21/10) that Brown's win was "the coming of age of the Tea Party movement, which won its first major electoral success with a new pragmatism." Though it's not entirely clear what role Tea Party voters played in the election—Kevin Drum argues it was very little (Mother Jones.com, 1/23/10)—journalists seem to have attached an importance and power to the Tea Party movement that is out of proportion with its actual numbers.

Journalists routinely label the Tea Party movement as "populist," but researchers Chip Berlet (*The Progressive*, 2/10) and David Barstow (*New York Times*, 2/16/10) point out that, at least at the grassroots level, the movement harbors activists of a variety of stripes, from Ron Paul supporters to Republican Party officials, from longtime militia movement organizers to newly minted political activists troubled by the economic downturn.

It can be hard to discern a consistent Tea Party philosophy, and the contradictions can be glaring. Even some of the movement's supposedly cherished positions seem up for grabs: Tea Partiers can oppose government spending *and* Medicare cuts; they can denounce TARP bailouts *and* make heroes of the likes of Sarah Palin, Glenn Beck, and Newt Gingrich, all of whom supported Bush's bank-rescue program.

But while journalists have often ignored or downplayed the contradictions, there's one *consistency* they ignore in painting Tea Partiers as wholesome adherents to small government, constitutional principles and so on: the movement's singular and often racialized loathing of Barack Obama.

Indeed, anti-immigrant leader Tom Tancredo, a former Colorado Congress member, was cheered at a Nashville "Tea Party Nation" convention (2/4/10) for declaring that Jim Crow–era voting restrictions would have prevented Obama's election:

> Something really odd happened, mostly because we do not have a civics literacy test before people can vote in this country. People who could not even spell the word "vote" or say it in English put a committed socialist ideologue in the White House. His name is Barack Hussein Obama.

Coupled with the tolerance of racist signs (e.g., "Obama's Plan: White Slavery") and symbols such as Confederate flags at movement events, it makes one wonder why journalists largely avoid the conclusion that racism is a factor in the movement. After all, this would not be the first American movement to channel genuine economic insecurity into racial resentment.

Antipathy toward Obama as a black Democratic president goes some way toward explaining why, if the Tea Partiers are really motivated by opposition to government spending, the movement didn't launch years earlier in response to George W. Bush's skyrocketing budget deficits.

After months of coverage, one striking fact began to emerge from media's public opinion polling: Most people seemed to have almost no idea what the Tea Party movement was. But there have been efforts to improve their public standing, as when NBC tried to give them a leg up in a December 2009 poll.

The December 17 headline on MSNBC's website (echoed in some on-air reporting) read, "Tea Party More Popular Than Dems, GOP." But the poll found that 48 percent of respondents knew "very little" or "nothing at all" about the populist uprising; how could such an obscure movement be more popular than the two major parties? Well, the NBC/*Wall Street Journal* poll gave the group a rather upbeat description in their question to the public: "In this movement, citizens, most of whom are conservatives, participated in demonstrations in Washington, D.C., and other cities, protesting government spending, the economic stimulus package and any type of tax increases."

That a "no tax hike, responsible spending" party you've never heard of is more popular than political parties that have earned public mistrust over several decades is not much of a surprise. But that framing was common. After noting that most people it polled had heard little or nothing about the Tea Party movement, the *New York Times* nonetheless identified their potential base of support (2/12/10): "The level of dissatisfaction with both political parties—and the fact that 56 percent of Americans in the poll want a smaller government— suggests that the Tea Party movement has an opportunity to draw more support."

The *Washington Post* reported (2/11/10) that its own poll found that "nearly two-thirds of those polled say they know just some, very little or nothing about what the Tea Party movement stands for." The *Post* still added that "the lack of information does not erase the appeal: About 45 percent of all Americans say they agree at least somewhat with tea partiers on issues, including majorities of Republicans and independents."

So how does a movement of somewhat murky origins and political goals come to command so much media attention? The idea that right-wing agitators could actually elevate the national discourse—despite much evidence to the contrary—was one strand of media thought. In "How the Tea Party Could Help All of Us" (2/15/10), *Newsweek* editor Jon Meacham explained that the movement was, in part, about getting back to constitutional principles and "the recovery of the spirit of the American Founding."

The political message of the Nashville Tea Party convention (2/4–5/10) was appealing to many in the press; *Washington Post* columnist David Ignatius's "Europe Could Use Its Own Tea Party" (2/11/10) gave token mention to troubling aspects of the movement he was recommending to Europe for its populist "fiscal conservatism."

The Nashville gathering was heavily covered by the corporate media—an unusual decision given its size (about 600 attendees) and the fact that it was disowned by many Tea Party activists. CNN, nonetheless, reportedly sent a crew of eleven to report on the festivities (*Politico*, 2/12/10), apparently because Sarah Palin would be making an appearance as keynote speaker.

Palin's support seems to have cemented corporate media's interest in the Tea Party. While right-wingers complain of an anti-Palin media bias, *Politico*'s Jim VandeHei and Jonathan Martin wrote: "The reality is exactly the opposite: We love Palin. For the media, Palin is great at the box office."

But there seems to be more to it than that; many in the press seem to think that Palin's supposed popularity is emblematic of a conservative movement that the media aren't granting enough time. The *New York Times*' David Carr wrote (4/5/10) that if the press doesn't appreciate Palin's allegedly wide appeal, "maybe we deserve the 'lamestream media' label she likes to give us." David Broder (*Washington Post*, 2/11/10) applauded Palin's Nashville speech for its "pitch-perfect populism."

And that may be the real point: The Tea Party's right-wing populism is the perfect kind for corporate news outlets at a time when the wealthy elites who own and support them feel threatened by more authentic populist impulses. And for that reason, with or without Palin's supposed star power, the Tea Party movement is likely to remain a focus of media attention.

On March 12, *Politico* media reporter Michael Calderone (3/12/10) noted that the *Washington Post* would assign a reporter to "make sure the movement's covered fully in its pages." That's a level of attention few progressive citizen groups will ever receive from the corporate press.

—*May 2010*

GLENN BECK AND LEFT-RIGHT CONFUSION

Glenn Greenwald

Last night during his CBS interview with Katie Couric, Glenn Beck said he might have voted for Hillary Clinton and that "John McCain would have been worse for the country than Barack Obama." This comment predictably spawned confusion among some liberals and anger among some conservatives. But even prior to that, there had been a palpable increase in the right-wing attacks on Beck—some motivated by professional competition for the incredibly lucrative industry of right-wing opinion-making, some due to understandable discomfort with his crazed and irresponsible rhetoric, but much of it the result of Beck's growing deviation from GOP (and neoconservative) dogma. Increasingly, there is great difficulty in understanding not only Beck's political orientation but, even more so, the movement that has sprung up around him. Within that confusion lies several important observations about our political culture, particularly the inability to process anything that does not fall comfortably into the conventional "left-right" dichotomy through which everything is understood.

Some of this confusion is attributable to the fact that Beck himself doesn't really appear to have any actual, identifiable political beliefs; he just mutates into whatever is likely to draw the most attention for himself and whatever satisfies his emotional cravings of the moment. Although he now parades around under a rhetorical banner of small-government liberty, anti-imperialism, and opposition to the merger of corporations and government (as exemplified by the Bush-sponsored Wall Street bailout), it wasn't all that long ago that he was advocating exactly the opposite: paying homage to the Patriot Act, defending the Wall Street bailout and arguing it should have been larger, and spouting standard neoconservative cartoon propaganda about The Global Islamo-Nazi Jihadists and all that it justifies. Even the quasi-demented desire for a return to 9/12—as though the country should be stuck permanently in a state of terrorism-induced trauma and righteous, nationalistic fury over an allegedly existential Enemy—is the precise antithesis of the war-opposing, neocon-hating views held by many libertarian and paleoconservative factions with which Beck has now associated himself. Still other aspects of his ranting are obviously grounded in highly familiar right-wing paranoia.

So it's not surprising that confusion has arisen over someone who transformed overnight from a fairly typical *Weekly Standard/ Wall Street Journal* editorial page/Bush-following polemicist into some sort of trans-partisan populist libertarian. All of that, in turn, is colored by the powerful influences on him from the profoundly strange conspiratorial Mormonism pioneered by Cleon Skousen, as documented by the superb *Salon* series authored by Alexander Zaitchik. Ultimately, Beck himself is just a histrionic intellectual mess: willing to latch onto any hysterical accusations and conspiracy theories that provide some momentary benefit, no matter how contradictory they might be from one moment to the next. His fears, resentments, and religious principles seem fixed, but not his political beliefs. Like the establishment leadership of both political parties, he has no core political principles or fixed, identifiable ideology. His description of himself as a "rodeo clown" might be the most perceptive thing he's ever said. Attempts to classify him on the conventional political spectrum are destined to fail, and attempts to demonize him as some sort of standard Republican bogeyman will inevitably be so oversimplified as to be false. Such efforts assume far more coherence than he possesses.

Far more interesting than Beck himself is the increasingly futile effort to classify the protest movement to which he has connected himself. Here, too, confusion reigns. In part, this is due to the fact that these "Tea Party" and "9/12" protests are composed of factions with wildly divergent views about most everything. From paleoconservatives to Ron-Paul-libertarians to LaRouchians to Confederacy-loving, race-driven Southerners to Christianist social conservatives to single-issue fanatics (abortion, guns, gays) to standard Limbaugh-following, Bush-loving Republicans, these protests are an incoherent mishmash without any cohesive view other than "Barack Obama is bad." There are unquestionably some highly noxious elements in these groups, but they are far from homogeneous. Many of these people despised the Bush-led GOP and many of them loved it.

Add to all of that the fact that this anti-Obama sentiment is being exploited by run-of-the-mill GOP operatives who have no objective other than to undermine Democrats and return the Republicans to power—manifestly *not* the goal of many of the protesters—and it's impossible to define what this movement is or what is driving it. In many ways, its leadership (both organizationally and in the media) is fundamentally at odds with the participants. How can people who cheered on the Bush/Cheney administration and who want to reinstall GOP leaders in power (i.e., Fox News, Limbaugh, the right-wing blogosphere, GOP House members) possibly make common cause in any coherent way with those who are in favor of limited federal government power, reduced debt, privacy, and constitutional protections—all the things on which the GOP relentlessly waged war for years? In one important sense, the Tea Party movement is similar to the Obama campaign for "change": It stays sufficiently vague and unspecific to enable everyone to read into it what they want, so that people with fundamentally irreconcilable views believe they're part of the same movement.

But all that said, there are some identifiable—and plainly valid—underlying causes to these protests that are neither Republican nor

Democratic, or even left or right. That's when conventional political language ceases to be useful.

Is opposition to the Wall Street bailout (supported by both parties' establishments) left or right? How about the view that Washington is inherently corrupt and beholden to the richest corporate interests and banks, which, through lobbyist influence and vast financial contributions, own and control our political system? Is hostility toward Beltway elites liberal or conservative? Is opposition to the Surveillance State and endless expansions of federal police powers a view of liberals (who vehemently opposed such measures during the Bush era but now sometimes support or at least tolerate them) or conservatives (some of whom—the Ron Paul faction—objected just as vigorously, and naturally oppose such things regardless of who is in power as transgressions of the proper limits of government)? Liberals during the Bush era continuously complained about the doubling of the national debt, a central concern of many of these Tea Party protesters. Is the belief that Washington politicians are destroying the economic security of the middle class, while the rich grow richer, a liberal or conservative view? Opposition to endless wars and bankruptcy-inducing imperial policy generally finds as much expression among certain quarters on the right as it does on the left.

Some central political debates do break down along standard left-right lines (health care and tax policy). But there are many political issues that defy the conventional left-right political drama in which cable news traffics and which serves as the prism—often the distorting and distracting prism—for virtually all of our political discourse. Much of the citizen rage manifesting itself in the form of these protests doesn't actually fit comfortably on the left-right spectrum. As Frank Rich accurately observed in the *New York Times* this weekend:

> "Wall Street owns our government," Beck declared in one rant this July. "Our government and these gigantic corporations have merged." He drew a chart to dramatize the revolving

door between Washington and Goldman Sachs in both the Hank Paulson and Timothy Geithner Treasury departments. A couple of weeks later, Beck mockingly replaced the stars on the American flag with the logos of corporate giants like G.E., General Motors, Wal-Mart and Citigroup (as well as the right's usual nemesis, the Service Employees International Union). Little of it would be out of place in a Matt Taibbi article in *Rolling Stone*. Or, we can assume, in Michael Moore's coming film, *Capitalism: A Love Story*, which reportedly takes on Goldman and the Obama economic team along with conservative targets.

Are the views expressed in that paragraph liberal or conservative ones? They're neither. Instead, they're the by-product of a completely different dichotomy that is growing in importance: between system insiders and their admirers (those who believe our national political establishment and its elites are basically sound and good) and system outsiders (those whose anger is confined not to one of the two political parties but who instead believe that the political culture itself is fundamentally corrupted and destructive). There are people typically identified as members of either the conventional right or left who are, in fact, more accurately described as being in this latter group: those disenchanted with the political culture itself. Anger over the Wall Street bailout and corporate excesses was one example where that trans-partisan disenchantment was evident. The railing by Beck quoted in Rich's paragraph reflects the same thing. And that trans-partisan rage is clearly playing an important role in driving these protest movements.

But crucially, it is the Republican Party and its various appendages—the same people who presided over massive expansions of debt and federal government power—that are exploiting this citizen activism, and they're harnessing it for their own petty, partisan ends. There's a reason why Glenn Beck is on Fox News, which is nothing more than a media outlet for the Republican Party, Wall Street, and neoconservatism, yet which is also the driving media force behind these protests: It's because, with Democrats in power, the same Republicans who wildly expanded government power when they controlled it now, out of power, suddenly love antigovernment sentiment. Currently, opposition to "the government" is easily translated into "opposition to Democrats," and these protests are thus exploited and distorted as partisan Republican tools even though many of the individual protesters are as anti-GOP as they are anti-Democrat. Add to that the Democratic Party's general distaste for citizen activism (especially street protests) as well as its servitude to Wall Street and corporate interests, and Democrats are straitjacketed into ceding this protest movement to GOP operatives, who are cynically exploiting it to promote goals that have nothing to do with—are even at odds with—the goals of many of the protesters themselves.

It's true that some of the protesters believe in nothing more than Republican resurgence, and that this movement has become a tool of Fox and the GOP. But much of the citizen anger that is driving these protests and that Glenn Beck is channeling is more complex than that. It has far more to do with deep economic anxieties and anger toward the political establishment and its elites than it does allegiance to one of the two parties or standard left-right debates. It's an overstatement to claim that "there's not a dime's worth of difference between the parties" (see here for yet another example of that), but on many critical issues, the relevant breakdown has little or nothing to do with Republican versus Democrat or even left versus right. As the confusion around Glenn Beck and these protests reflect, those distinctions serve far more to obfuscate and distract than they do to explain and clarify.

—September 22, 2009

GLENN BECK'S GOLDEN FLEECE:
THE RIGHT WING'S PARANOID PITCH FOR
OVERPRICED GOLD

Stephanie Mencimer

Tune in to Glenn Beck's Fox News show or his syndicated radio program, and you'll soon learn about the precarious state of the U.S. dollar, a currency on the verge of collapse due to runaway government spending, a ballooning national debt, and imminent Zimbabwe-style hyperinflation. To defend yourself against the coming financial holocaust, Beck explained on his radio show last November, you need to "think like a German Jew in 1934, maybe 1931." And that means thinking about buying some gold.

Conveniently, Beck made that suggestion as he was in the midst of interviewing his own "gold guy," Mark Albarian,[1] the president and CEO of Goldline International,[2] a Santa Monica, California–based precious metals company that is a major sponsor of Beck's radio and cable shows. In a seamless intertwining of anxiety and entrepreneurship, the two amicably debated whether we've already hit "peak gold" or whether the price of gold, then at $1,100 an ounce, might yet hit the inflation-adjusted high of $2,200 it saw back in 1980. Beck speculated that gold could go as high as $2,500 an ounce: "I think people are running out of options on what, you know, could be worth something at all."

For more than a century, gold has held a special allure for conservatives. Amid economic downswings and social upheaval, the precious metal has come to be seen as a moral and political statement as much as an investment. Ever since the late nineteenth century, when the gold standard became the center of a ferocious debate about the country's financial future, gold has been mythologized as a bulwark against inflation, federal meddling, and the corrosive effects of progressivism. In the late 1970s, South African Krugerrands became a refuge from soaring interest rates and oil prices. In the '90s, militia groups fearful of big banks and the Federal Reserve hoarded gold.

And now, with the economy limping along and a black Democrat in the White House, gold mania has gone mainstream. Gold prices hit a recent high last December and remained strong as the European debt crisis unfolded this spring. John Paulson, the hedge-fund giant who made billions bundling and betting against Goldman Sachs subprime mortgage securities, has invested heavily in gold, even starting a new fund devoted solely to it. A recent *New York Times* poll[3] found that 1 in 20 self-identified Tea Party members had bought gold in the past year.

Cashing in on all this is a raft of entrepreneurs who have tapped into financial insecurity and fever dreams of impending tyranny. Nearly every major conservative radio host, including Rush Limbaugh, Sean Hannity, Michael Savage, and Dr. Laura Schlessinger, has advertised gold. But none has done more to cheer on the new gold rush than Glenn Beck.

Beck, whose various media enterprises brought in $32 million last year, according to *Forbes*, has a particular interest in plugging gold. Since 2008, Goldline has been one of his most reliable sponsors. Last year, after Beck called President Obama a racist[4] and advertisers bailed on his cable show,[5] Goldline stuck by him. And its loyalty appears to have paid off. In an e-mail, Goldline's executive vice president Scott Carter says that while its Beck sponsorship doesn't bring in the majority of its customers, it "has improved sales," which exceed $500 million a year.

In turn, Beck has stood by Goldline. Last year, he made a promo video[6] in which he stated, "This is a top-notch organization"—a quote featured prominently on Goldline's website. After the liberal watch-dog Media Matters complained about Beck and Goldline's partner-ship, Beck posted a video on his site[7] in which he unapologetically noted that he'd started buying from Goldline long before it was his sponsor, back when gold was $300 an ounce.

Such coziness between spokesman and sponsor is not uncommon on talk radio, where hosts can be paid to personally recommend just about any product. In fact, liberal hosts such as Ed Schultz and Thom Hartmann have advertised gold. However, their pitches generally have lacked Beck's tone of apocalyptic urgency.

The feedback loop between Beck and Goldline is unusually pow-erful even for talk radio, and even more so by cable standards. When he's not talking up Goldline, Beck still hypes gold as a way to weather the coming end of the world as we know it. Last December, he stood in front of his famous chalkboard, where he'd written "Gold, God, Guns," and admonished viewers, "The smart money is saying, 'Hun-ker down!'" The more worked up Beck gets, the more Goldline can employ his fears in pitching its products to his audience.

Yet in putting his seal of approval on Goldline, "the people that I trust," Beck has gone beyond simply endorsing an advertiser. He's rec-ommending a company that promotes financial security but operates in a largely unregulated no-man's land, generating a pile of consumer complaints about misleading advertising, aggressive telemarketing, and overpriced products. As this story went to press, Representative Anthony Weiner (D-N.Y.) asked the Federal Trade Commission and the Securities and Exchange Commission to investigate Goldline for its "predatory policies" and accused the company and conservative pundits of working "hand in hand to cheat consumers."[8] Beck and other on-air personalities "who are shilling for Goldline," he said, "are either the worst financial advisers around or knowingly lying to their loyal viewers."

James Richardson heard about Goldline on Beck's radio show late last year. A disabled former trucker who lives in Tennessee, Richardson called the company with the intention of buying one-ounce gold bullion coins. The purity of American bullion is guaranteed by the Treasury and its prices are transparent, because they're closely linked to the spot price of gold. But when Richardson got on the phone with Goldline, he says, a sales rep pressured him into buying something entirely different: $10,000 worth of tiny, 20-franc Swiss gold coins.

"I paid them on a credit card the same day, didn't have no brochures on them or nothing," he says. "They make it sound really good, like you can't lose on them."

Richardson regretted the purchase almost as soon as he hung up. "I'm not a coin collector," he says ruefully. The $10,000 represented one-fifth of his entire savings, and after some research he realized that he had vastly overpaid for the francs. The thirty-four coins he'd ordered from Goldline were 90 percent gold, amounting to about 6.3 ounces of gold, which was then selling at around $950 an ounce. He'd paid the equivalent of around $1,600 an ounce, meaning it could be years before he recouped his investment—if ever. "It was just a lose-lose situation," he says.

Goldline's marketing and disclosure materials explain that customers buying coins "for investment purposes" may not be able to recoup their costs. They also say that first-time customers can cancel an order within seven days of purchase. But Richardson says that when he tried to get his money back within that time period, salespeople gave him the runaround and insisted he should keep the coins because the price of gold was going to double. He filed a complaint with the Los Angeles–area Better Business Bureau (BBB), of which Goldline is a member, and eventually he got a refund.

Richardson suspects he's not the only Goldline customer who didn't know what he was getting into. "I ain't got no college degree or nothing, but some of these older people think they're investing in gold, but you're not. You're investing in coins," he says. The price of gold increased 133 percent between early 2006 and this May, yet many Goldline customers say they have lost money on their purchases after discovering—as Richardson did—that they had badly overpaid. Richardson is one of forty-four people across the country who have filed complaints against Goldline with the Los Angeles BBB in the past three years; customers have also have griped about their dealings with the company on message boards such as Ripoff Report and the Pissed Off Consumer. Regulators in Missouri have sanctioned the company for pressuring an elderly couple to liquidate their other investments to buy overpriced coins.

The Federal Trade Commission (FTC) received seventeen individual complaints about Goldline's sales tactics between early 2006 and this May, according to information obtained through the Freedom of Information Act. Many of those stories mirror Richardson's. One customer, whose name was redacted, filed a complaint in February, writing, "Not knowing anything about buying gold, I called Goldline International, Inc. because of their advertisement on Fox News and the fact that Glenn Beck endorses them." Like Richardson, this customer originally wanted bullion, but the sales rep "absolutely insisted" on 20-franc coins, and the customer relented. Unable to get a refund, the customer reported paying $369 apiece for coins that could be bought elsewhere for as low as $208.

A Washington State couple nearing retirement told the FTC they'd invested $31,812 in foreign coins after calling to inquire about gold bullion "as a hedge against the falling dollar." Once they realized they'd overpaid, they were too late for a refund. Another customer complained that a sales rep "insisted" on selling coins, in this case French francs: "He would not relent. He told me lies." A quadriplegic Californian described being persuaded to pay $5,000 for $3,000 worth of gold coins after disclosing a recent inheritance to a Goldline rep.

I wanted to ask Glenn Beck about these complaints. He never responded, but after I sent his publicist some questions, I received a call from David Cosgrove, a former Missouri securities commissioner and lawyer who represents Goldline. He explained that Goldline is a large operation with 200 salespeople. A few problems, he said, are inevitable, but Goldline works hard to avoid them through compliance monitoring and other safeguards.

Undoubtedly, Beck fans who take his financial advice bear responsibility for not reading the fine print. But their trust in the pitchman is an essential part of the symbiotic relationship between host and sponsor that is common on talk radio, where "direct response" advertisers carefully tailor their spots to complement the programming. Toll-free numbers provide instant feedback on how well promotions are faring and allow companies to fine-tune their ad copy on a week-to-week basis. If, for instance, an advertiser sees a surge in calls during a Beck segment focusing on currency collapse, it can play off of his program's message in an upcoming round of ads.

Take the Survival Seed Bank, another loyal Beck radio and TV advertiser, whose promotions echo both his and the gold companies' doomsaying. A spot that ran on Beck's Fox show earlier this year warned[9] that "the politicians and the bankers are going to bring the whole thing crashing down," making its vegetable seeds "more valuable than even silver and gold."

The line between content and commercial is further blurred by guest appearances like the one Goldline CEO Albarian did with Beck last year. Goldline says it does not require such appearances on the shows it sponsors; a spokeswoman for Premier Radio Networks, which syndicates Beck's radio show, likewise says the host has invited Albarian on "because he wants to. It's not a contractual obligation."

Bob Leonard is the head of business development at Strategic Media, a firm that specializes in radio advertising. He says talk radio is a great venue for direct-response advertising because its listeners are especially engaged with what they're hearing. It's not a stretch for them to pick up the phone and dial a company like Goldline because, "If you have someone like Glenn Beck saying, 'You gotta call these guys,' they're gonna call."

Beck often says that when he buys gold, he sticks with collectors'

coins instead of bullion because the government is less likely to con-
fiscate them. Like many Americans, you are probably unaware that
the Obama administration is plotting to raid your safe-deposit box
and melt down your bullion. But Beck insists that we must be on
guard against such a scenario, citing a Depression-era executive order
that made all gold federal property.

In his Goldline promo video, Beck explains, "Back in 1933, FDR
said, 'Okay, we're going to take all your gold, and [slipping into a
Muppet voice] gee, it's worth—$8 an ounce.'" Beck suggests that some
folks "got smart" and claimed their antique coins couldn't be melted
down because they were, well, antiques, and presto! They got to keep
their gold. It's a message Beck has hammered home[10] in other Goldline spots—that in the face of an "out of control" government, collector coins are a safer deal than other kinds of gold.

Of course, this is revisionist history. With Congressional autho-
rization, Roosevelt did indeed sign a 1933 executive order that made
most private gold ownership illegal, but G-men didn't go door to
door seizing bullion. Instead, the government offered gold owners
almost $21 an ounce—the market rate (and not $8, as Beck claims)
to turn in their gold voluntarily. Antique and foreign coins were ex-
empt. The move was intended to combat deflation by getting people
to stop hoarding wealth that could instead circulate in the economy.
The government also temporarily suspended the gold standard so it
could adjust the value of the dollar, stabilizing prices, helping debtors,
and encouraging more production. Georgetown University history
professor Michael Kazin says FDR's gold policy, which was championed by populists, boosted the economy and in turn contributed to
his landslide reelection in 1936.

Goldline has not let the facts get in the way of using the confisca-
tion myth for marketing. As early as 2002, its website (which then
featured an endorsement from Charlton Heston[11]) trumpeted[12] how
"the events of the 1930s...prove how important owning scarce and de-
sirable gold coins really is!" Its current website and "investor kit" both

provide a copy of FDR's 1933 order,[13] noting that in its wake, gold's value increased nearly 75 percent—all the more reason to buy coins and hope for the worst. The pitch seems to be working: Its website reports that European gold coins are "the most popular choice among Goldline clients."

What Goldline doesn't say in its promotional materials is that for its own bottom line, collector coins are a lot more lucrative than mere bullion. Profits in the coin business are based on "spread," the difference between the price at which a coin is sold and the price at which the dealer will buy it back. Most coin dealers, including Goldline, will sell a one-ounce bullion coin for about 5 percent more than they'll buy it back for, a figure that closely tracks the price of an ounce of gold on the commodities markets. That 5 percent spread doesn't leave a lot of room for profits, much less running dozens of ads a week on national radio and cable programs, with endorsements by everyone from Beck to Mike Huckabee, Fred Thompson,[14] and Dennis Miller.[15] So, Goldline rewards its salespeople for persuading would-be bullion buyers to purchase something with a bigger markup.

Twenty-franc Swiss coins are a little smaller than a nickel and contain a little less than two-tenths of an ounce of gold. The coins are about sixty to 110 years old and not especially hard to find (though Goldline describes them as "rare"). They are not fully considered collectors' items or commodities, making their value more subjective than bullion's. Goldline sets a 30 to 35 percent "spread" on the coins, meaning that it will pay $375 to buy back coins it's currently selling for $500. At that rate, gold prices would have to jump by a third just for customers to recoup their investment, never mind making a profit. Investing in Goldline's 20-franc coins would be like buying a blue-chip stock that lost a third of its value the minute it was purchased. It's difficult to think of any other investment that loses so much value almost instantly. So what persuades people to buy anyway?

Beck has assured fans that Goldline's sales reps are "not going to pressure you." I called to find out. I dialed the company's toll-free number from my office to request one of its free "investor kits." When I mentioned that I'd heard about Goldline from Glenn Beck, the salesman informed me right away that Beck was one of the company's best clients. "We're the only company he buys from," he told me. After learning that I had never invested in gold before, he plugged "investment grade" coins by assuring me, "That's what Glenn buys."

He also cited FDR's gold order. It "all has to do with the devaluation of the dollar," he said, warning, "It's very similar to 1933 today." He quickly ran through some disclaimers, like the spread and how the company recommends holding on to the coins for at least three to five years—preferably ten. But in the end, he told me, gold is just a great investment. "Are you ready to get started today?" he asked. "Nobody can take it away from you. You can't print more of it. There is a finite amount of gold."

About two weeks later, after I'd received my investor kit, the same sales rep called me at work, even though I'd never given him my phone number. Just to double check that Goldline was indeed using caller ID to track potential customers, I called one of its 800 numbers on my cell phone and asked about putting gold into an IRA. I didn't offer my name or number, but the same sales rep called me back not five minutes after I hung up.

Goldline's assertive tactics also extend to its efforts to protect its image. In response to the disgruntled consumers who have congregated on Ripoff Report, it has joined the site's "Corporate Advocacy Business Remediation and Customer Satisfaction Program," which has allowed it to bury the negative comments. Its own customer review site, goldlinereviews.com,[16] features only positive feedback. "I am writing to you about my account manager," writes Y.L.C. from California. "He is the very definition of a caring and polite professional, he is in fact the main reason I chose Goldline (and Glenn Beck)."

Goldline has also tried to keep unhappy customers from making their stories public. Take John Quirindongo,[17] a 77-year-old former New York City postal supervisor. Quirindongo has spent nearly four years trying to get compensation for the money he believes he lost trying to buy platinum bullion from Goldline. When I visited him in Fort Lauderdale, Florida, he was reclining on a sofa, laptop open. A box with two rolls of gold coins sat on a table. His much younger Russian wife flitted around, pouring syrup on a blintz for me before darting off to her job at a children's clothes store. Quirindongo's vision is mostly gone. He relies on a walker to get around and a nebulizer to breathe. His hearing is going, he's missing a couple of bottom teeth, and he gets a little confused sometimes. But when it comes to Goldline, he's lucid—and very angry.

Quirindongo's saga started in 2006, when a mortgage broker talked him into taking out a $100,000 subprime loan on his condo, which he owned outright. After paying off his car and some bills, Quirindongo decided to invest $70,000 in platinum. He called Goldline and ordered fifty-four one-ounce platinum American Eagle bullion coins. After the company received his wire transfer but before the sale was confirmed, a salesman called, telling him he needed to "diversify" his portfolio and pushing him to transfer $34,000 into Swiss 20-franc gold coins.

Even though Goldline's disclosure materials do mention that its sales reps may call to "discuss other products which carry a higher spread such as the European gold francs" before an order is finalized, Quirindongo was caught off guard. He says he argued that platinum was a better investment, but eventually caved and bought the francs.

Looking on eBay, Quirindongo found similar-looking coins selling for far less. He says he called to complain every day for a week, but the Goldline rep insisted he should let his coins gain value for eighteen months. Quirindongo missed the weeklong window for a refund and then spent the next year and a half letting his order appreciate. But he was still mad, and in May 2007, he sold the platinum part of his order back to Goldline, making about $219, all of which was eaten up in commissions and storage fees. The real shock came a few months later, when he tried to sell back his gold coins and discovered the buy-back price would leave him more than $10,000 in the hole.

After Quirindongo complained to the American Numismatic Association, of which Goldline is a member, the company offered a partial refund, so long as he signed an agreement promising not to speak publicly or contact any consumer or government agencies. Quirindongo refused. After he rejected a full refund, Goldline tried to close the matter by sending him his gold coins, which now sit partly unwrapped in his apartment.

Still bitter that he was talked out of his original platinum order, which would have appreciated significantly, Quirindongo has continued to bash Goldline. He has posted long online tirades and is currently pursuing a RICO case (an earlier federal suit he'd filed on his own was tossed out). Posting on Ripoff Report, a Goldline representative accused Quirindongo of trying to "extort" money from the company. Quirindongo says he is fighting mainly for his wife Irina's sake: His monthly postal-service pension will die with him, and her earnings won't cover his mortgage and metals misadventures. He worries she'll end up on the street. "I feel like a real chump now," he says. "The last few years have been absolute torture for me."

Quirindongo wasn't the only person I came across who'd been offered a deal in exchange for keeping quiet. California residents Peter Kim and Kyoung Park-Kim bought about $35,000 in 20-franc coins from Goldline in 2007 after listening to the company's radio show, *The American Advisor*, which airs on more than 100 stations. They complained about overpaying, and Goldline offered to refund most of their money if they'd sign an agreement like the one offered to Quirindongo. The couple refused and sold the coins on their own, losing between $1,000 and $2,000. "At least we're young, so we can recoup some time and make money," says Kim. "But senior citizens, they don't have that luxury of recouping their investment." (At press time, Goldline had not responded to a request for comment on Kim's and other individual consumers' complaints.)

Goldline's unhappy customers have few options. They can't take the company to court, due to a mandatory arbitration clause in its contracts. And even as it plays up fears of big government, Goldline neatly slips between the regulatory cracks. While it describes its coins as investments, it's not licensed as an investment company. Its salespeople are not licensed as securities brokers or investment advisers and therefore are beyond the reach of state or federal agencies charged with keeping brokers honest. When Quirindongo complained to the FTC, Florida securities regulators, and the Department of Justice, he says, he got the same response: "Everybody said, 'That's gold.' It's like stamp collecting. It's unregulated."

"Trading in coins has been an area that's very, very difficult for regulators to wrap their arms around," confirms Maine securities administrator Judith Shaw. As the economy turned sour in 2008, Shaw's office saw a large uptick in the aggressive telemarketing of gold, prompting her to issue a consumer advisory about "potential scams and pitfalls" being perpetrated by "numerous shady companies operating on the margins of this industry."

There has been one successful state action against Goldline. In 2006, the children of an octogenarian Missouri woman complained to the state securities commissioner that Goldline had persuaded their mother to invest about $230,000 in gold coins and antique paper currency worth half as much. The state determined that a Goldline salesperson had acted as an unlicensed investment advisor when he encouraged her to liquidate an annuity to buy coins. Goldline agreed to refund $217,000 to the woman.

Cosgrove, who represented Goldline in the Missouri case, cautioned me not to see it as representative of the company as a whole. He said the salesperson who prompted the complaints had already left the company by the time Goldline learned about the problem.

Beck has never acknowledged any of the complaints against Goldline, just as he's shrugged off concerns about his cozy relationship with the company. If anything, his endorsement of Goldline has taken on a new edge of defiance. Responding to Representative Weiner's accusations in May,[18] Beck accused him of McCarthyism and asked his fans to send in images of the congressman "with a wiener nose." As he railed against the "assault on my advertisers and me" on his radio program, he still managed to sneak in a plug, noting that he had 15 or 20 percent of his investments in gold—"From Goldline. Now, you tell me. If I'm such a scam artist, why would I be scamming myself?"

—May 19, 2010

Notes:

1. http://www.glennbeck.com/content/articles/article/196/33029/

2. http://www.goldline.com/

3. http://www.nytimes.com/2010/04/15/us/politics/15poll.html

4. http://colorofchange.org/beck/

5. http://motherjones.com/get-free-access

6. http://www.youtube.com/user/goldlineint#p/u/4/dJtr91OuyF0

7. http://www.glennbeck.com/content/videos/?uri=channels/338017/727555

8. http://www.youtube.com/watch?v=3GDts0Q1dK8

9. http://mediamatters.org/blog/201005050058

10. http://www.glennbeck.com/content/videos/?uri=channels/338017/690018

11. http://web.archive.org/web/20020206052145/http://goldline.com/newsletter5.htm#happened

12. http://web.archive.org/web/20020201001737/http://goldline.com/index.html

13. http://www.goldline.com/government-gold-confiscation

14. http://www.youtube.com/user/goldlineint#p/u/7/OrCev-YivXs

15. http://www.youtube.com/user/goldlineint#p/u/5/2vkFIKOWNzk

16. http://www.goldlinereviews.com/

17. http://www.youtube.com/watch?v=0dsh-_QQMzg&feature=related

18. http://www.glennbeck.com/content/articles/article/198/40834/

FALLING FOR THE ACORN HOAX: THE STRANGE 'JOURNALISM' OF JAMES O'KEEFE

Veronica Cassidy

When conservative activist James O'Keefe was arrested on January 25 for attempting to interfere with the phone lines of Democratic Senator Mary Landrieu from Louisiana (*Washington Examiner*, 1/26/10), outrage in the media was hard to come by.

O'Keefe secretly filmed two accomplices as they impersonated telephone company employees in the senator's office; he claimed he had "decided to investigate" why constituents couldn't get through to the senator's office (Big Journalism, 1/29/09) after the senator said in December that her phone lines had been "jammed for weeks" with calls about health-care reform (*Advocate*, 12/23/09).

After O'Keefe's arrest, commentators cautiously distanced themselves from his newest scheme, framing it as the misguided efforts of a well-intended young "journalist." Conservative blogger Michelle Malkin (1/26/10) advised: "For now, let it be a lesson to aspiring young conservatives interested in investigative journalism: Know your limits. Know the law. Don't get carried away. And don't become what you are targeting."

But it would have been difficult for pundits to be too hard on O'Keefe—without some embarrassing backpedaling from the media's earlier praise for the provocateur. Last fall, O'Keefe was widely lauded for a string of undercover videos he and colleague Hannah Giles produced that allegedly exposed lax ethical standards at the community-organizing group ACORN. "You guys ought to be getting, you know, a journalism award for this," Fox News's Sean Hannity (9/20/09) told the duo.

This celebration of O'Keefe's earlier video activism required pundits—on both the right and center—to withhold even the most casual scrutiny of O'Keefe's peculiarities. The ACORN videos promoted the false premise that he and Giles had entered those offices posing as a pimp and prostitute and gotten advice on how to conceal their illegal activities. O'Keefe appeared on *Fox & Friends* (9/7/09; Media Matters, 2/17/10) in what the host described as "exactly in the same outfit that he wore to these ACORN offices"—a ridiculous costume reminiscent of '70s blaxploitation films, complete with giant sunglasses, cane, and a chinchilla coat incongruously draped over an otherwise demure blazer and khakis.

Countless outlets made the same assumption about O'Keefe's getup. "Mr. O'Keefe…was dressed so outlandishly that he might have been playing in a risque high school play," wrote Scott Shane in the *New York Times* (9/16/09). A *Dallas Morning News* editorial (9/17/09) reported that O'Keefe "dressed up as a cartoon version of a pimp. Hannah Giles, 20, barely dressed as a stereotypical hooker…. They stashed their camera and walked into ACORN offices from coast to coast."

Yet the videos O'Keefe and Giles released never actually show him dressed as a pimp inside ACORN offices, and ACORN employees contended he entered in business casual attire. Despite repeated claims to the contrary by both O'Keefe and Andrew Breitbart, the conservative media producer whose Big Government website featured the videos (Stage Right Show, 2/16/10; *Washington Times*, 9/21/09), Giles herself admitted (*Washington Independent*, 2/19/10) that footage of O'Keefe in pimp costume was "purely B-roll," and disingenuously asserted that "we never claimed that he went in with a pimp costume."

An ACORN-commissioned review of the incident by former

Massachusetts Attorney General Scott Harshbarger (Independent Governance Assessment of ACORN, 12/7/09) had much earlier found that not only did O'Keefe enter ACORN offices dressed as "a college student," but actually introduced himself as a student trying to help Giles escape an abusive pimp. But corporate media continued to push the pimp angle (AP, 1/26/10, 1/27/10; *New York Times*, 1/27/10, 3/2/10). After one of blogger Brad Friedman's readers asked *New York Times* senior editor for standards Greg Brock for a correction of the erroneous claims, Brock responded (Brad Blog, 2/8/10):

> Our article included that description because Mr. O'Keefe himself explained how he was dressed—and appeared on a live Fox show wearing what HE said was the same exact costume he wore to ACORN's offices.... If you feel the ACORN videos have been doctored, then perhaps you will want to contact Fox news and ask them how and why they doctored his image.

In other words, the *New York Times* position is, "Fox reports—you decide."

Mainstream media further reported (e.g., CNN, 9/11/09; *Los Angeles Times*, 9/23/09) that videos caught "low-level employees in five cities sounding eager to assist with tax evasion, human smuggling and child prostitution" (*New York Times*, 9/19/09). Yet corporate media never saw the full tapes nor demanded their release, despite profound discrepancies between the filmmakers' transcripts and videos—and O'Keefe's having been accused of selective editing in the past (*New York Times*, 9/19/09).

In his report, Harshbarger, who was himself denied full viewing of the tapes, concluded:

> The videos that have been released appear to have been edited, in some cases substantially, including the insertion of a

substitute voiceover for significant portions of Mr. O'Keefe's and Ms. Giles's comments, which makes it difficult to determine the questions to which ACORN employees are responding. A comparison of the publicly available transcripts to the released videos confirms that large portions of the original video have been omitted from the released versions.

The *Washington Post* (9/18/09) failed to muster any skepticism, though, when it reported that O'Keefe "dismissed" allegations that the videos were doctored, failing to point out editing tricks that are obvious in even a quick viewing of the released portions of the tapes. CNN's Bill Tucker (*Lou Dobbs Tonight*, 9/11/09) qualified his report by explaining that the video in question was in part blacked out, yet reported the video exactly as O'Keefe presented it.

To many in the corporate media, O'Keefe simply wasn't to be questioned: In an NBC report (9/23/09), host Mara Schiavocampo left unchallenged O'Keefe's false assertions that he was never rebuffed by an ACORN office and that he was an "absolutely independent" journalist, despite being on Breitbart's payroll (Hugh Hewitt, 1/26/10).

Los Angeles Times media critic James Rainey (9/23/09) chided Fox for offering "little context and less proportion in recycling the ACORN story" and called on media to subject the activists' material to "serious scrutiny," but continued: "No mitigating factors can explain away the behavior of pathetically accommodating ACORN workers.... Here's how to conceal your prostitution income!... Not pretty"—parroting O'Keefe and Giles's false claim that ACORN employees advised them how to evade taxes, a claim later discredited by the filmmakers' own transcripts.

The *Washington Post*'s media critic, Howard Kurtz, similarly called for "skepticism" (9/25/09) over O'Keefe and Giles's "ideologically driven reporting," while in the same paragraph lambasting ACORN employees' "nutty" behavior: "Who offers advice about pimping out

13-year-old girls? What planet were these people living on?" Kurtz, too, overlooked the filmmakers' transcripts, which showed ACORN workers advising Giles on how to protect 13-year-old girls from an allegedly abusive pimp.

Even as evidence poured in that the right's newest criticisms of ACORN were unfounded, corporate media continued to look the other way. The *New York Times* failed to once mention Harshbarger's report, although when the Congressional Research Service (12/22/09) released a report that similarly found ACORN innocent of any legal wrongdoing, the paper did cover it—in a 434-word story on page A15 of Christmas Eve's late edition.

A Nexis search found only five other mentions of the CRS report in major newspapers (*Boston Globe*, 12/24/09; *Detroit Free Press*, 12/27/09; *Kansas City Star*, 12/27/09; *Los Angeles Times*, 1/13/10; *USA Today*, 12/24/09). As recently as January 27, the *New York Times*, reporting O'Keefe's recent arrest, stated, "Mr. O'Keefe's ACORN videos won credit from several quarters for drawing attention to long-held conservative suspicions about the group," while quoting two conservative thinkers and no progressives other than ACORN's Bertha Lewis—and never mentioning that ACORN had been cleared of any criminal activity or that the videos were found to have been substantially doctored.

Hardball's Chris Matthews (MSNBC, 9/17/09), while not prepared to absolve ACORN for its alleged illicit behavior, rightly called out the network of conservative activists and media that initially created the story, lamenting, "The right wing and its allies on talk radio and on Fox TV have claimed another victim."

Yet many media critics gave Fox News credit with breaking a legitimate story that other media were slow to pick up on, suggesting that the news channel should be taken still more seriously. "ACORN got caught on candid camera, and they got caught good," declared the *Columbia Journalism Review* (9/18/09). *New York Times* public editor

Clark Hoyt (9/27/09), stating that "a video sting had caught ACORN workers counseling a bogus prostitute and pimp on how to set up a brothel staffed by underage girls," called it an "intriguing story" of the sort that "a newspaper like the *Times* needs to be alert to…or wind up looking clueless or, worse, partisan itself." *Slate* media critic Jack Shafer (9/23/09) asserted that even "critics of Breitbart and the filmmakers don't really dispute the basic information unearthed by the videos."

Meanwhile, Howard Kurtz (*Washington Post*, 10/7/09) used it all to defend the "influence wielded by Beck and Hannity and Limbaugh (or by liberal commentators on the other side)," claiming that "if they peddle misinformation and exaggerations, that can be neutralized by others in the media marketplace." In the next breath, Kurtz pronounced that "the ACORN videos [Beck] and Hannity trumpeted on Fox proved to be a legitimate story." When the media marketplace is policed by these kinds of critics, misinformation and exaggeration have little to fear.

ADDENDUM: ACORN IN THE CROSSHAIRS

The right wing has long targeted ACORN for its work registering voters in low-income communities where Democrats predominate, and corporate media have seemed happy to serve as their handmaidens. During the 2008 presidential campaign, journalists often repeated conservative attacks on ACORN for supposed voter fraud (e.g., CNN, 9/16/09) after eleven of its employees were arrested for registering false voters—although ACORN itself turned in those employees (*Extra! Update*, 12/08).

As a result of the media blitz, the Justice Department removed ACORN from its work on the 2010 Census, and Congress voted to defund ACORN, which had received $53 million since 1994 (*Washington Examiner*, 5/5/09). Following ACORN's lawsuit against the government, however, a U.S. district judge ruled (12/11/09) that the vote was likely an unconstitutional bill of attainder, in which the legislature punishes an individual or organization without trial, and barred the government from enforcing the congressional vote while the lawsuit works its way through the courts.

—V.C.

—*April, 2010*

APOLOGIES TO THE BECKSTER

W. Kamau Bell

Dear Glenn Beck,

I am sorry. I know you don't know me, but I owe you an apology.

For years—or at least ever since I first heard of you—I thought you were evil. I even named a track of my latest comedy CD, *Face Full of Flour*, "Glenn Beck Is Evil!" (available on iTunes and from Amazon).

But I have to apologize because I had never even watched one entire episode of your show, *The Glenn Beck Program*. I had only seen a couple clips online, like the one where you said of Obama he has "a deep-seated hatred for white people or the white culture. I'm not saying he doesn't like white people. I'm saying he has a problem. This guy is, I believe, a racist."

WOW! A racist? Seriously? A racist? Look, Glenn, Obama may be a lot of things, but he's not a racist. He's way more Tiger Woods than Malcolm X. (Of course I am referring to the old Tiger Woods, who wanted us all to believe that he was Jesus, not the new Tiger, who wants us to believe that he's Wilt Chamberlain.) Obama is not "by any means necessary." He's "by all reasonable means necessary as long as everyone is on the same page and no one feels left out." That's not a racist. In fact, Glenn, I have a secret for you. For the most part, black people wish he was more racist. We kind of wanted the first black president to be a dick. We wanted the first black president to—how do I put this?—we wanted the first black president to WANT REVENGE!

But Barack is not racist. Even Brian Kilmeade, the Fox News co-host of the children's show sounding *Fox and Friends*, challenged you on this point.

Which brings up an interesting question... How screwed up do you have to be that you say something on Fox News and someone on Fox News says, "Slow down! That's too far even for Fox." Careful, you are entering Geraldo Rivera Self-Parody Territory.

But I was wrong to take your statement seriously. Once I watched your show, it became clear that you don't want to be taken seriously. You are an entertainer. And a very, very good one. You admit that you are an entertainer all the time. You did so in *Forbes* and the *New York Times*. On the few episodes of your show that I watched, you regularly asked people not to listen to you. You even admitted that maybe YOU are the crazy one. Usually this occurred after one of your Howard-Beale-from-Network style rants or after one of your Jimmy Swaggart evangelical style teary entreaties to America.

And look, Glenn, there's nothing wrong with being an entertainer. Full disclosure: I happen to be one myself. Some of my best entertainers are friends. The problem is that your audience doesn't know that you're an entertainer. I now understand that isn't your fault.

There is historical precedent for this kind of entertainer to audience relationship. For years professional wrestling claimed that it was a sport just like any other sport. They claimed that their participants were in straight-up competition with each other. Nothing was rigged. The fix was never in. It just so happened that while one wrestler hit the other wrestler in the back with a folding chair, the ref got distracted EVERY TIME. Well, then at some point in the '80's, Congress said, "OK, then. If you are a sport then you probably need some federal regulation." (Not a direct quote.) And then professional wrestling said, "Ummm... Did we forget to mention that we're totally fake. Completely and utterly fake. No sports here." (Also not an actual quote.)

Well Glenn, you are the Fox News equivalent of professional wrestling. And just like we can't accuse one professional wrestler of doing a bad job of pretending to hit another professional wrestler, we can't accuse you of being dumb... or racist... or xenophobic... or chauvinistic... or, well you get the point. If you go before Congress and admit you're just pretending to be that thick, then you get to spout whatever comes to your head, AND your audience won't be tempted to take you seriously, AND because you will no longer be a role model for the children, you can be free to take any performance-enhancing drugs that you want. And whenever Rupert Murdoch's not looking, you can hit people in the back of the head with folding chairs. I'd start with Geraldo.

And if you do this, Glenn, I promise to get my friends to stop calling you names and insulting your intelligence. And calling you stupid will be reduced to a distant past time. It will be as interesting a critique as people who think it makes them smart to say they don't like *Larry the Cable Guy* or *Two and a Half Men*.

So again, I'm sorry that me and my friends took you seriously. You are clearly much closer to Andy Kaufman than Walter Cronkite. Although, as a fellow entertainer, I'd recommend that you work on that Obama chunk. It could use a few more punch lines.

Kamau Bell

P.S. Maybe the problem is that you are on Fox News. Some people think of that as a news channel. Maybe if we moved your show to Comedy Central then people would know you were just being an entertainer. Look how well it has worked for Stephen Colbert.

—August 2010

PART SIX: TOMORROW FOR TEA?

TEA PARTY IN THE SONORA: FOR THE FUTURE OF GOP GOVERNANCE, LOOK TO ARIZONA

Ken Silverstein

In 1897, when the Territory of Arizona was seeking to demonstrate its fitness for statehood, the legislature solicited bids to design a new capitol building and grounds in Phoenix. The winning entry was that of James Riely Gordon, the architect behind a number of well-regarded public buildings in Texas and Maryland. He drew up ambitious plans: an expansive dome, a grand rotunda, stately wings for each house. But funding fell short, and so the legislative wings were scrapped, and a diminutive lead-alloy top was chosen in lieu of Gordon's more elaborate dome. Worse, in the building's interior, a mosaic of the state seal was bungled by the contractor, who forgot to include the images of cattle and citrus, two of Arizona's "five C's" (the others being climate, copper, and cotton).

Despite much talk over the years of an upgrade—including a proposal from none other than Frank Lloyd Wright, who envisioned the addition of fountains, gardens, and reflecting pools—all plans were rejected as too expensive. In the 1960s, two new buildings were finally erected on either side of the capitol, one for the house and one for the senate; but these structures, which resemble Soviet apartment blocks, only made matters worse. Nowadays, the capitol's dingy, unshaded plaza is bare save for a few small rosebushes and some patches of dry grass. The buildings themselves have been plagued by plumbing problems and leaks, making the complex "wholly inadequate" to

Arizona's future needs, according to a task force charged with studying the matter.

The general unsightliness of the capitol makes it a fitting home for today's Arizona legislature, which is composed almost entirely of dimwits, racists, and cranks. Collectively they have bankrupted the state through a combination of ideological fanaticism on the Republican right and acquiescence and timidity on the part of GOP moderates and Democrats. Although dozens of states are facing budget crises, the situation in Arizona is arguably the nation's worst, graver even than in California. A horrific budget deficit has been papered over with massive borrowing and accounting gimmickry, and the state may yet have to issue IOUs to employees and vendors. All-day kindergarten has been eliminated statewide, and some districts have adopted a four-day school week. Arizona's state parks, despite bringing in 2 million visitors and $266 million annually, have lost 80 percent of their budget, with up to two-thirds of the parks now in danger of closure. The legislature slashed the budget for the Department of Revenue, which required the agency to fire hundreds of state auditors and tax collectors; lawmakers boasted that these measures saved $25 million, but a top official in the department estimated that the state would miss out on $174 million in tax collections as a result.

Any way out of Arizona's crisis will require raising taxes, a move that is tantamount to heresy for most lawmakers. For nearly a year, the legislature refused to approve the emergency sales-tax increase (of just one cent per dollar) proposed by Governor Jan Brewer, a Republican who had been elected as secretary of state but assumed the top job in 2009 when Janet Napolitano joined the Obama administration. Eventually, lawmakers passed the buck to voters by authorizing a May 18 statewide ballot on the sales tax—which passed, after a $2.2 million marketing effort by education and business groups—but before doing so they enacted tax cuts that over four years will deprive the state of more money than the sales-tax increase is estimated to bring in.

Instead, to raise cash, the legislature has pursued a series of wild sell-offs and budget cuts. It privatized the capitol building and leased it back from its new owner, an arrangement that brought in substantial revenue but over time will cost Arizona far more. The legislature has sold off numerous other state properties at bargain prices, and has put up future lottery revenues as collateral on a $450 million loan. Meanwhile, Arizona removed more than 300,000 adults from state health coverage and terminated one health-care program for 47,000 poor children. Funding was slashed at the agency that deals with reports of child abuse and neglect, and also at Children's Rehabilitative Services, so that parents of children with cystic fibrosis, cerebral palsy, and a number of other conditions are now required to pay 100 percent of treatment costs.

All totaled, the cuts amounted to roughly $1 billion, which came on top of a similar amount that had been slashed the previous year. These cuts, in combination with the sale of state assets (which raised more than $700 million) and the securitization of the lottery, plugged a massive hole in next year's budget. But the deficit for 2011 is already projected to be at least $1 billion and possibly double that, on a total budget of only $9 billion. The situation will only worsen from there, as federal stimulus money dries up and the state runs out of short-term sources of cash. "Could we cut our way out of it mathematically?" Dennis Hoffman, an economist who has forecast revenue for Arizona governors since 1983, mused when I asked him about the crisis. "Anything is possible on paper, but for practical purposes it can't be done, unless you want to start releasing prisoners, shutting down universities, and eliminating extracurricular activities in the schools. We've already had a $2 billion haircut over the past two years. Try another $2 billion and see what the state looks like."

Arizona lawmakers have shown little enthusiasm for dealing seriously with the state's insolvency. They have instead preferred to focus on matters that have little to do with the crisis. Lawmakers have turned racial profiling into official policy, through a new law that requires police to stop suspected illegal immigrants and demand to see their papers; anyone not carrying acceptable proof of citizenship can be arrested for trespassing and thrown in jail for up to six months. But this is just one bill in what has been a season of provocative legislating. Another new law bans the funding of any ethnic-studies programs in the public schools, while a third prohibits "intentionally or knowingly creating a human-animal hybrid." Lawmakers declared February 8 the "Boy Scout Holiday," took time out to discount fishing-license fees for Eagle Scouts, and approved a constitutional right to hunt.

In January, Senator Jack Harper, an immaculately combed zealot who speaks in the patter of an infomercial voiceover, submitted a bill that would allow faculty members to carry guns on university campuses, saying it was "one very small step in trying to eliminate gun-free zones, where there's absolutely no one who could defend themselves if a terrorist incident happened." The house passed a measure that would force President Barack Obama to show his birth certificate to state officials if he runs for reelection, as well as a bill that bars Arizona from entering into any program to regulate greenhouse gases without approval from the legislature. "There are only two ways to vote on this," said Representative Ray Barnes of the latter initiative. "Yes, or face the east in the morning and worship the EPA because they own you."

As the national midterm elections approach in November, the Tea Party movement is supplying the Republican Party with most of its momentum. But this movement, and the strain of aggrieved libertarianism it espouses, cannot claim much representation in elected office. This disparity has led many on the left to dismiss Tea Partiers as a media phenomenon, and to speculate that their ideas could not possibly "stand up to the test" of real governance. But there is, in fact, one place where the results of Tea Party governance has already been tested: Arizona, where the Tea Party is arguably the ruling party. Less driven by issues of national security, on the one hand, or moral values on the other, Arizonan conservatives are largely obsessed with taxes and immigration—also the twin fixations of Tea Partiers, who, like Arizonans, are disproportionately white and older. So it comes as little surprise that top Republican elected officials in Arizona eagerly seek the Tea Party's support and make time to speak at the group's rallies. Should the Republicans succeed in retaking power nationwide over the next four years, the country might start to resemble the right-wing desert that Arizona has become.

Arizonans are generally moderate. In-migration has brought a flood of independents and Democrats, who in 2008 won five of the state's eight U.S. House seats. Although registered Republicans outnumber Democrats by 36 percent to 33 percent, independents now stand at 30 percent and are rapidly gaining ground at the expense of both parties. And yet Arizona politics are disproportionately controlled by ultraconservatives. Only a handful of the state's house districts are genuinely competitive between Democrats and Republicans, with the latter holding thirty-five of the sixty seats. Being a member of the legislature is not considered a prestige job—the office pays only $24,000 annually—and many lawmakers are small businessmen. The Republican primaries are dominated by hard-core conservatives who spurn moderates and back ideologues.

Antigovernment sentiment here is longstanding, and can be traced in part to the influence of the Church of Jesus Christ of Latter-day Saints. Mormons make up only around 6 percent of the state population, but they are enormously influential in Republican politics—and they don't approve of borrowing money, whether it's an individual or a state that's doing the borrowing. Mormons tend to believe that the role of government is to let people fend for themselves. After the church created a nationwide Welfare Services Department, back in 1936, its Arizona branch displaced the government among church members as the provider of many social services, offering everything from job training to family counseling to educational programs.

Since the days of Barry Goldwater, an axiom of Arizona politics, particularly among Republicans, has been that tax cuts generate economic growth in all circumstances. Hence total state taxation has declined during fifteen of the past seventeen years; the individual income tax has taken the biggest hit, but sales, property, and corporate-income taxes have also come down substantially. The legislature has created tax exemptions for everything from country-club memberships to pedicures to food purchases by airlines (the latter at the behest of local airline lobbyists). None of this has produced the hoped-for effect. Although tax cuts "have lowered government revenues," they "have not had any perceptible effect on the state's economic growth," concluded an Arizona State University business-school study, published last November, that examined the past three decades of fiscal policy.

Yet even as the state has teetered toward bankruptcy, political leaders have remained unwilling to acknowledge that taxes in Arizona are too low. Indeed, thirty-eight of Arizona's ninety lawmakers, together with Governor Brewer, have signed the "Taxpayer Protection Pledge" of Grover Norquist's group Americans for Tax Reform, a pledge that they will never vote for a tax increase. Democrats have played the game as well: In 2007, then-Governor Napolitano approved a 10 percent reduction in the income tax, which cost the state about $500 million. The combination of historic tax cuts with the recession has reduced government revenues from $9.5 billion in 2007 to $6.4 billion this year. That latter figure is roughly equal to the amount of money the state took in six years ago, even as the population—and the need for government spending on health care, education, and prisons, for example—has continued its rapid growth.

The antigovernment attitude in Arizona is now reflexive, especially because of its entanglement with the issue of immigration. As one local resident, who didn't want to be identified because she has a government job, told me: "People who have swimming pools don't need state parks. If you buy your books at Borders you don't need libraries. If your kids are in private school, you don't need K–12. The people here, or at least those who vote, don't see the need for government.

Since a lot of the population are not citizens, the message is that government exists to help the undeserving, so we shouldn't have it at all. People think it's OK to cut spending, because ESL is about people who refuse to assimilate and health care pays for illegals."

This confluence of nativism and antigovernment sentiment makes Arizona fertile ground for an especially showy brand of symbolic politics. One day in February I sat in the audience during a session of the Senate Appropriations Committee, which meets in a wood-paneled room with a stained carpet, on the ground floor of the senate building. During the meeting, committee chairman Senator Russell Pearce—sponsor of the anti-immigrant bill and one of the most powerful politicians in the state—called on the federal government to put the National Guard on the border and "have rifles with bullets in 'em." Apropos of nothing, the balding, red-faced Senator Al Melvin brought up his pet topic of inmate labor, which he views as a solution to the state's budget crisis. Jailbirds, burbled Melvin, should fill potholes, keep golf courses open, and refurbish public buildings.

Soon the committee began to debate whether to post the Ten Commandments at the entrance to the old state capitol. A six-foot granite version located a few hundred feet away did not, it seemed, sufficiently convey the state's piety. "George Washington, our first recognized president of this republic, said you cannot properly govern without the Bible and God, and I couldn't agree more. And John Adams once made the statement that this republic is designed wholly for a moral and religious people and will survive under none other," Pearce, the measure's sponsor, told his colleagues. After a few minutes' more debate, the measure passed, and the committee, having done the people's business, adjourned for the day.

Besides its aging mining industry and its few remaining aerospace plants, Arizona doesn't manufacture or even sell much of anything. Phoenix is a branch-office town, not a headquarters town, and much of the population works low-paying jobs at call centers and assembly plants. Yet over the past half-century, the population of Arizona has grown faster than that of any other state besides Nevada. Between 1950 and 2009, Phoenix swelled from 105,000 people to 1.5 million, making it the fifth largest city in the United States. The climate—one of those "five C's"—has been a major attraction, especially for senior citizens. So have low taxes, weak business regulation, and (for a long time) cheap housing, especially when compared with neighboring California. The engine of economic growth in Arizona was growth itself—real estate in particular, but also a host of related industries: construction, hauling, landscaping, roofing, painting, remodeling, swimming-pool maintenance, architecture, plumbing, and on and on.

Real estate prices rose wildly in Arizona during the past decade, pushed, as elsewhere in the country, by low interest rates, ARMs, and the reckless practices of such companies as Countrywide Financial and Goldman Sachs. When the market went bust, Arizona—along with Florida, Nevada, and California—crashed particularly hard. Last spring, Phoenix became the first major American city where home prices had fallen by half from their mid-decade market peak. Recent figures show that 61.5 percent of Phoenix mortgages are "underwater," with commercial real estate in even worse shape. It is unlikely that a major office building will be erected in Phoenix in the next five years. Since its peak in 2006, the state's construction industry has lost roughly 113,000 jobs, a drop of almost 50 percent. The official unemployment rate is above 9 percent, but that figure nearly doubles when people who can't find full-time work and people who have given up are factored in. The Arizona Department of Health Services estimates that as many as 260,000 Hispanics have left the state since late 2007, partly because of anti-immigrant laws and sentiment and partly because jobs dried up.

"Texas has oil and gas, and Nevada has gambling, so they generate money even during a recession—but Arizona needs growth to grow," Grady Gammage Jr., a lawyer and real estate developer, told me at his office in Tempe, thirteen miles from downtown Phoenix. "We're also not a low-problem state like Vermont. We're a big border state with only a few private institutions to take care of social problems. We need government."

Gammage walked me out to a balcony that faces Arizona State University's Sun Devil Stadium. He pointed off to the left, toward two unfinished towers, barely visible in the distance. They had been started with financing from a company headed by Scott Coles, a leading local businessman; as the project was unraveling last year, Coles's wife left him and he committed suicide. "Investors put $130 million into it," Gammage said. "The penthouses had private pools and they were talking about selling them for between $5 million and $10 million apiece. Now they'll be lucky to get $30 million for both buildings, and it would cost another $20 million to finish them. But the market's gone and no one knows what to do. There's talk of turning it into a hotel or student dormitories."

Drive around Greater Phoenix, and one sees a procession of commercial real estate projects in bankruptcy and for-rent signs plastered across strip mall windows. But to take in the full scale of the damage—and to understand why the state government is bankrupt—requires heading out to communities at the edge of recent development, communities that were growing at a breakneck pace up until the crash.

Few spots are worse off than Maricopa, forty-five minutes southwest of Phoenix by car, a town that sprang from desert scrub in 2003 and within five years had a population of 45,000. On a sunny Sunday morning, John Guthrie, a thirty-five-year-old real estate agent, met me at the Carl's Jr. in the town's main shopping mall, off the John Wayne Parkway. He moved here from Orange County, California, in 2004, just as the real estate boom was gathering force, before there was a mall or nearly anything else in Maricopa. But by the end of that year, the real estate market in Maricopa was in a frenzy. Lotteries became normal in the most popular new developments; would-be buyers had to put up a deposit of $20,000 or more just for the right to bid. "Developers said we'd be getting a Home Depot and movie theaters and restaurants," the soft-spoken Guthrie recalled. "Over twenty-five years they were saying there would be amusement parks and resorts."

Guthrie crumpled up his sandwich wrapper, grabbed his soda, and ushered me to his car in the parking lot. In 2007, the market stalled out, and by early the following year it collapsed, he explained as we pulled out onto the road. "You could see it hit street by street," he said. "One house would go into foreclosure and then it would just move down the street, and then hit the next block and then the next. There were a bunch of families who came out here who didn't have assets, and when they started going upside-down by $150,000 there wasn't much to do but walk away."

Guthrie handed me several documents as he drove. One showed that in Maricopa the "Distress Index"—the percentage of sales in which the property is bank-owned or in pre-foreclosure—was 76.8 percent. Guthrie looked increasingly shell-shocked as he laid all this out, and soon I found out why: He was upside-down on a home of his own by about $100,000.

In a neighborhood called Maricopa Meadows, we drove past numerous empty lots—builders as well as homeowners had gone under during the crash—and many "short sale" signs in front of houses. Soon we rolled past a block of McMansions, all but a handful of which had gone into foreclosure. "These houses have about 4,000 square feet and swimming pools," he said. "They topped out at $600,000. Now you can get one for about $250,000. You've got people doubling up in houses so they can split utilities. During the summer the air conditioning bill can be $500 a month. The story is the same from here to Queen Creek to Buckeye, in all these places that people scattered out to before the crash."

Politically, there was almost no fallout from the economic crisis. In the GOP primary of 2008, when the impending disaster was already apparent, a number of Republican state legislators who opposed further tax cuts lost to fire-breathers on their right, all but eliminating the party's "moderate" wing. In the state senate, Russell Pearce—who as a house member had already sponsored a number of anti-immigrant bills, including an employer-sanctions law—trounced his Republican opponent, an attorney who had handled immigration cases and who was backed by the Chamber of Commerce (which is highly conservative on most issues but splits on immigration because its members like cheap immigrant labor). Steve Pierce, a right-wing rancher, ousted Senator Tom O'Halleran, a pro-environment moderate who had helped broker a budget deal with Governor Napolitano. Al Melvin, who had never before held public office, won his primary race against Pete Hershberger, whom he tarred as not sufficiently "loyal" to the GOP on issues of taxes, gun rights, and gay marriage.

Then there was Sylvia Allen, a real estate broker from the town of Snowflake, who, in 2008, was appointed by the local Republican Party to finish the term of a respected conservative who had died in office. Allen, who retained her seat in an election that fall, has since gained minor notoriety after calling for more uranium mining, saying in a speech that "this earth has been here 6,000 years, long before anybody had environmental laws, and somehow it hasn't been done away with." She also has complained that trees are "stealing Arizona's water supply" and sponsored a new law that allows carriers of concealed weapons to forgo safety training and the indignity of background checks.

A similar crew was elected to the house, including Frank Antenori. "I despise expansion of government into people's lives," he said on the campaign trail. "K–12 is meant to prepare kids to enter the world.... We need to spend less time teaching how to put condoms on cucumbers and more time on balancing a checkbook."

In 2010, the same paradoxical process seems to be at work: Despite the disastrous policies of the right in Arizona, the state's Republicans are threatening to move rightward still. This slide was clearly visible at the February campaign kickoff for J.D. Hayworth, who is hoping to beat Senator John McCain in the August GOP primary. A former sports anchor and radio talk-show host, Hayworth served in Congress from 1995 to 2007, where he was best known for his cornball jokes—from the House floor he cracked that Democrats should "hire Freddy Krueger as the new liberal Democratic spokesman" and "set up a new political-action committee, the 'Whine Producers.'" He also was embroiled in the scandal around the lobbyist Jack Abramoff: In 1997, Hayworth helped stop a proposal to tax Indian casinos and five years later helped prevent a change in the law that would have capped campaign contributions by Indian tribes. Between 1998 and 2005, Hayworth received $150,000 from Indian tribes and other groups connected to Abramoff.

Conservatives have always been suspicious of McCain's support for campaign-finance reform and his opposition (before he flip-flopped on the presidential campaign trail) to torture and to George W. Bush's tax cuts. But what truly sank McCain's standing in Arizona was his long-standing support for comprehensive immigration reform, a position he has now desperately abandoned as well—he came out in support of the state immigration bill during an interview with Bill O'Reilly, saying that "illegals...are intentionally causing accidents on the freeway"—though this switch has been of no avail in placating the Arizona right.

At Hayworth's campaign kickoff, held in front of his new campaign headquarters in a Phoenix strip mall, a series of local conservatives stood beneath a banner proclaiming Hayworth the "Consistent Conservative," thrilling the crowd with stories of Hayworth's devotion to conservative causes and McCain's betrayal of same. One of the most warmly received speakers was right-wing Senator Ron Gould. A big guy with a flattop haircut and a shit-kicker's mustache, Gould prefaced his endorsement of Hayworth by calling himself "probably the most conservative legislator in the state," and he closed with the words, "God bless America and may America bless God." The crowd, mostly white retirees, picked up doughnut holes and coffee from a table draped with a yellow banner that featured a coiled rattlesnake and the words "Don't tread on me." (That design dates to the Continental Congress in 1775 and has been widely adapted by Tea Party activists.) Vendors sold green buttons supporting the Tea Party; red buttons bearing the slogan "Proud member of the angry mob"; and pink buttons that said, simply, "Sarahcuda." From speakers blared a soundtrack that included "Hound Dog," "Wake Up Little Susie," and the theme from *Hawaii Five-O*.

"Sheriff Joe is here!" a woman next to me exclaimed. She was referring to longtime Maricopa County Sheriff Joe Arpaio, known for housing prisoners in tents and making them wear pink underwear, and for having his officers raid Latino neighborhoods to round up suspected illegal immigrants. Wearing a dark jacket, maroon shirt, and a tie pin shaped like a gold pistol, Arpaio took the stage to declare that McCain had been in Washington too long. "We have to give McCain a map to help him find his way back to Arizona," he said to a big cheer.

"Give him a map to Mexico," someone shouted from the audience.

Now Hayworth took the microphone, and scanned the crowd. He was taller and tanner than anyone else on stage. "Like Ronald Reagan, I believe that government is not the solution to our problems, but too often it is part of the problem," he said.

"If they do anything more for the poor I'm gonna be one of them," yelled a well-dressed man from the audience.

Backed into an ideological corner on taxes, Arizona continues to cut indiscriminately. The three state universities have scrapped whole degree programs and may soon have to shutter entire campuses. Funding for GED programs and adult-education courses has been reduced to zero. Arizona has furloughed more than 15,000 state employees and has closed thirteen of eighteen highway rest stops. (This latter move provoked an outcry, especially among truckers; state authorities responded by asking roadside businesses to allow motorists to use bathrooms free of charge.) The budget for the Department of

Water Resources—an important agency in the desert—has been cut from $23 million to $7 million during the past two years. "Demand for water exceeds supply, and we share what there is with six states," Herb Guenther, the agency's director, told me. "We have to protect what we have collectively while looking for new supplies, but everyone is fighting for resources. There's a cliff coming, and we haven't figured out how to fly. 'No government' is not the answer when it comes to water."

Lawmakers have siphoned off state funds allocated for specific purposes, pouring the money into the state's general fund. The legislature seized $160,000 in voluntary contributions and mandatory fees from the agriculture industry that were supposed to be used for research and marketing. It swiped another $7 million from the Arizona Early Childhood Development and Health Board, whose revenue comes from a voter-approved tobacco tax. (Arizona's supreme court ruled that the legislature had acted illegally and forced the return of the tobacco money; the state may eventually be ordered to give back tens of millions of dollars more from other "sweeps.")

In addition to selling the state capitol, the legislature has examined auctioning off dozens of other properties—among them the house and senate buildings, the offices of the secretary of state and the treasurer, and most of the state's prisons, including maximum-security units and death row. One of the major proponents of privatization is Representative John Kavanagh, an amiable oddball originally from Queens and a former Port Authority Police Department detective. "We haven't cut taxes that much," he told me during an interview at his legislative office, which is decorated with a variety of GOP-related knickknacks, including a large pink plush elephant on a bookshelf. "Here's the problem: We grew government during good times far beyond responsible levels, and instead of cutting, we've been relying on tricks and massive borrowing to sustain it. Now we've reached the end of the line. It's going to require major cuts; you're talking about government super-light."

Kavanagh blithely opined that the benefits of all-day kindergarten "dissipate by third grade for all but poverty level" and that the state should offer Medicaid only to people at one-third of poverty-level income—which works out to less than $7,500 for a family of four—as opposed to the current practice of offering it to everyone at poverty level and below. "We can't afford to be that generous anymore," he said.

Despite passage of the sales tax in May, no one believes that Arizona's financial crisis is over. But the state's electoral system, which rewards extreme right-wing rhetoric, has allowed the political class to be as irresponsible and reckless as it likes. State residents seem content to cheer on the legislature for lowering their taxes—even as massive budget cuts pack their children into classrooms with more and more students, or force them to stand in line for a day to renew driver's licenses at the gutted Department of Motor Vehicles. Arizonans will complain about their legislature—one recent poll showed that just 15 percent thought state lawmakers' performance was "good"—but keep sending ever more radical Republicans to office. It is much like the Tea Party nationwide, which will, quite sensibly, demand political reform and protest the bank bailout, even as it backs hacks like Hayworth who represent the most corrupt wing of the GOP.

Russell Pearce, basking in the triumph of his immigration-law victory, is hoping to become senate leader, and he likely will win that post. Representative Antenori—who distinguished himself in the house by opposing federal light-bulb efficiency standards (which he dismissed as "touchy-feely legislation") and by proposing that welfare recipients be required to sign an affidavit swearing they do not smoke, drink, use drugs, or have more than basic cable—was recently appointed to a vacant senate seat. And as for Senator Sylvia Allen, the senator who once complained that trees were "stealing Arizona's water supply," she stands for reelection this year and, by all accounts, is almost certain to prevail.

—July 2010

DEMOCRATS: REMEMBER THE LADIES!

Rebecca Traister

Funny how, even in these days of female CEO candidates and maverick "mama grizzlies," many Democratic women still relate to Abigail Adams's 234-year-old wry (and slightly pissy) plea to her husband, John, and his nation-building buddies to "remember the ladies and be more generous and favorable to them than your ancestors." Some of us find ourselves wondering why our party still shuns a public celebration of its female power and why it still appears hesitant to boost its strong female candidates.

Left-leaning lady trouble is ironic, since by many measures women are the Democratic Party—or at least 57 percent of it in the 2008 election. Moreover, the party has long been tagged as feminine: focused on purportedly soft concerns like health care, reproductive rights, social programs, and the economy, as opposed to the more testicular national security obsessions of Republicans. Twenty-five of the thirty-eight female senators in history have been Democrats, and sixty-nine of the ninety Congressional seats currently held by women belong to Democrats. As Stephanie Schriock, head of EMILY's List, says, "I think the Democratic Party strives to be a party of fairness and equal opportunity; that can be seen in the Democratic structure itself. You have a chair and vice chair, and in every state one has to be a man and one has to be a woman."

The gender quotas, (usually) female-friendly policy priorities, and slowly but steadily improving stats are all terrific. So why are we not hearing the party own its commitment to women's progress by lending full-throated support to its female candidates? Democrats were recently forced to cough up the baleful statistic that only three of thirteen members of Red to Blue, its battleground district support network, are female. At around the same time, the Democratic Congressional Campaign Committee backed the male candidate, Representative Ed Case, in a special election for a Hawaii House seat, attempting to push his female opponent, Colleen Hanabusa—endorsed by EMILY's List, labor unions, and both of Hawaii's senators—out of the race. Although gifted Texan orators Barbara Jordan and Ann Richards have given star-making keynote addresses at the party's national conventions, Democrats have not put a woman on that particular podium since 1992. And in the six cycles since the history-making nomination of Geraldine Ferraro for the vice presidency, in 1984, not one other woman has been named to the top ticket.

A reluctance to advertise the centrality of women within the Democratic Party has been explained away for years as tactical necessity. Labeled the Mommy Party since the gender gap first yawned open (and understanding this not to be a compliment), Democratic leaders have made a series of strategic moves to masculinize—and thus legitimize—their brand, including bargaining away reproductive rights to secure majorities on legislation. It's a process that has not been exclusive to politics. "In any profession, philanthropy or business or anything that becomes majority women, that [female reputation] gets to be a problem, and men get put in power to compensate," says Marie Wilson, head of the White House Project, which aims to advance women's leadership.

This aversion to any hint of femininity is likely why we rarely hear about the pro-woman legislation Democrats have pushed through. The first bill President Obama signed was the foot-stomping, beret-tossing Lilly Ledbetter Fair Pay Act, about which we don't hear a peep these days, even as the purportedly women-driven Tea Party barks about the ways women have been economically injured by this administration. And while Nancy Pelosi crowed in March about how, thanks to health-care reform, being a woman no longer counts as a preexisting medical condition, she was among the few Democrats to whoop it up on this score. And why are so many Congressional Democrats distancing themselves from the first female speaker of the House—arguably one of the most efficient, effective, and dynamic ones in recent history—and apparently siding with the GOP attack featuring Pelosi as the Wicked Witch of the West?

The party's reluctance to capitalize on its feminist successes makes it look scared and, well, weak. It has also allowed Sarah Palin and her brood of appallingly conservative female candidates to step into the void, attempting to rebrand their female-unfriendly ideology as the estrogen-driven arbiter of gender equality. Of course, that's strategic too. As Schriock notes, the current Republican vogue for the language but not the mechanisms of women's empowerment "is a political tactic to decrease the gender gap [to benefit Republicans]...and there's no policy behind it that [benefits] American women."

Fair enough. But Palin's explosive success in attracting an impassioned female following offers evidence that some entrenched attitudes about women and power are beginning to shift in ways that Democrats would be wise to pay attention to. As false as Palin's claims to feminism ring, we can't forget that they are coming just two years after 18 million Democrats voted for a woman with a real-life commitment to socially progressive policy and an actual stake in the feminist legacy. It should be increasingly clear that an appetite for dynamic female leadership, perhaps long suppressed, has been whetted, and that either party might benefit by rising to satisfy it.

Yet in this election cycle, we see no Democratic equivalent to the "mama grizzlies," no energetic retort to Republicans' anemic claims that they are the party of women. Why are Democrats reluctant to take this moment to assert their association with the legacy of women's liberation as a point of pride? Why has there been no attempt to promote national stars or to capitalize on the argument that empowering gifted women—especially those whose policy aims actually benefit other women—is a noble, progressive goal to which we should all proudly commit ourselves?

"They come to you every four years and say, We need your vote, but never ask for voices and visions," says Wilson. "If you don't give people opportunity and power within a system, they don't stick with you.... It's time for the party to stop just asking us to vote and say, We want you at the table of power."

Indeed, the argument that not enough women put themselves forward to run for office is growing increasingly feeble. The year after Hillary Clinton's candidacy, enrollment in the White House Project's leadership training programs mushroomed, Wilson says, noting that she recently returned from training 100 women, a third of them Native American, in Minnesota's north country. Two hundred and ninety-eight women from both parties filed to run for either the House or Senate during this cycle, an all-time high.

"I've traveled all over the country for the past two years, and everyone knows this is the time," says Wilson. "It's also a time when the Democrats could call on their women's base, go out there and recruit like mad on its women's base. Health care and education are at the top of the nation's agenda now. Women are the ones out there creating jobs, pioneering micro-enterprise, doing small businesses." Referring to Democrats as "a party full of grizzlies all over the country," Wilson urges, "You really want to get the party moving again? Be the party that declares they are going for parity in political leadership in our country. That would be such a message."

Democratic leaders must recognize that the nation's views on women and power are changing. They might also consider it a moral and social imperative for the party that relies on women, and to which women's progress has been historically tied, to treat its women as a fundamental asset rather than a vaguely irritating embarrassment.

"We need to be louder about how we're the party that's supported and empowered women in this country," says Schriock, adding that of late, "there is more conversation and dialogue about feminism and women's empowerment." The opportunity to capitalize on the re-emerging engagement with gender issues, she concedes, might be one "that Sarah Palin has allowed us to take, because we've got truth on our side." Among the truths Schriock says she and her organization will set about publicizing as soon as the midterms are over are that "we are the party that kept women from being a preexisting condition in health care, who fought for Lilly Ledbetter."

Democrats must hammer home their woman-friendly bona fides, and they must also be fundamentally more woman-friendly. They must reaffirm a commitment to reproductive rights as a cardinal component of a progressive mission—not simply a pesky single issue but crucial to the social, economic, and political equality of half the population. They must seek out the future female faces of the party. Yes, recruit more women, but take advantage of the ones already in office, the Amy Klobuchars and Debbie Wasserman-Schultzes. Give them the spotlit berths and career-making speeches. And the next time there is a female Democratic candidate for president (which, nota bene, might not be so far in the future), for God's sake, take time to celebrate—or at least note—the remarkable, historic strides she's made.

If Democrats are to stay relevant and persuasively assert them-selves as the party of progressive America, they must man up by ad-mitting—and more than that, proudly promising—that their future will rest in part in the hands of women.

—*September 30, 2010*

THIS COUNTRY NEEDS A FEW GOOD COMMUNISTS

Chris Hedges

The witch hunts against communists in the United States were used to silence socialists, anarchists, pacifists, and all those who defied the abuses of capitalism. Those "anti-Red" actions were devastating blows to the political health of the country. The communists spoke the language of class war. They understood that Wall Street, along with corporations such as British Petroleum, is the enemy. They offered a broad social vision that allowed even the non-communist left to employ a vocabulary that made sense of the destructive impulses of capitalism. But once the Communist Party, along with other radical movements, was eradicated as a social and political force, once the liberal class took government-imposed loyalty oaths and collaborated in the witch hunts for phantom communist agents, we were robbed of the ability to make sense of our struggle. We became fearful, timid, and ineffectual. We lost our voice and became part of the corporate structure we should have been dismantling.

Hope in this age of bankrupt capitalism will come with the return of the language of class conflict. It does not mean we have to agree with Karl Marx, who advocated violence and whose worship of the state as a utopian mechanism led to another form of enslavement of the working class, but we have to speak in the vocabulary Marx employed. We have to grasp, as Marx did, that corporations are not concerned with the common good. They exploit, pollute, impoverish, repress, kill, and lie to make money. They throw poor families out of homes, let the uninsured die, wage useless wars to make profits, poison and pollute the ecosystem, slash social assistance programs, gut public education, trash the global economy, loot the U.S. Treasury, and crush all popular movements that seek justice for working men and women. They worship only money and power. And, as Marx knew, unfettered capitalism is a revolutionary force that consumes greater and greater numbers of human lives until it finally consumes itself. The nightmare in the Gulf of Mexico is the perfect metaphor for the corporate state. It is the same nightmare seen in postindustrial pockets from the old mill towns in New England to the abandoned steel mills in Ohio. It is a nightmare that Iraqis, Pakistanis, and Afghans, mourning their dead, live each day.

Capitalism was once viewed in America as a system that had to be fought. But capitalism is no longer challenged. And so, even as Wall Street steals billions of taxpayer dollars and the Gulf of Mexico is turned into a toxic swamp, we do not know what to do or say. We decry the excesses of capitalism without demanding a dismantling of the corporate state. The liberal class has a misguided loyalty, illustrated by environmental groups that have refused to excoriate the Obama White House over the ecological catastrophe in the Gulf of Mexico. Liberals bow before a Democratic Party that ignores them and does the bidding of corporations. The reflexive deference to the Democrats by the liberal class is the result of cowardice and fear. It is also the result of an infantile understanding of the mechanisms of power. The divide is not between Republican and Democrat. It is a divide between the corporate state and the citizen. It is a divide between capitalists and workers. And, for all the failings of the communists, they got it.

Unions, organizations formerly steeped in the doctrine of class warfare and filled with those who sought broad social and political rights for the working class, have been transformed into domesticated partners of the capitalist class. They have been reduced to simple bartering tools. The social demands of unions early in the twentieth century that gave the working class weekends off, the right to strike, the eight-hour day, and Social Security have been abandoned. Universities, especially in political science and economics departments, parrot the discredited ideology of unregulated capitalism and have no new ideas. Artistic expression, along with most religious worship, is largely self-absorbed narcissism. The Democratic Party and the press have become corporate servants. The loss of radicals within the labor movement, the Democratic Party, the arts, the church, and the universities has obliterated one of the most important counterweights to the corporate state. And the purging of those radicals has left us unable to make sense of what is happening to us.

The fear of communism, like the fear of Islamic terrorism, has resulted in the steady suspension of civil liberties, including freedom of speech, habeas corpus, and the right to organize, values the liberal class claims to support. It was the orchestration of fear that permitted the capitalist class to ram through the Taft-Hartley Act in 1948 in the name of anticommunism, the most destructive legislative blow to the working class until the North American Free Trade Agreement (NAFTA). It was fear that created the Patriot Act, extraordinary rendition, offshore penal colonies where we torture, and the endless wars in the Middle East. And it was fear that was used to see us fleeced by Wall Street. If we do not stop being afraid and name our enemy we will continue toward a state of neofeudalism.

The robber barons of the late nineteenth century used goons and thugs to beat up workers and retain control. The corporations, employing the science of public relations, have used actors, artists, writers, scholars, and filmmakers to manipulate and shape public opinion. Corporations employ the college-educated, liberal elite to saturate the culture with lies. The liberal class should have defied the emasculation of radical organizations, including the Communist Party. Instead, it was lured into the corporate embrace. It became a class of collaborators. National cohesion, because our intellectual life has become so impoverished, revolves around the empty pursuits of mass culture, brands, consumption, status, and the bland uniformity of opinions disseminated by corporate-friendly courtiers. We speak and think in the empty slogans and clichés we are given. And they are given to us by the liberal class.

The "idea of the intellectual vocation," as Irving Howe pointed out in his essay "The Age of Conformity," "the idea of a life dedicated to values that cannot possibly be realized by a commercial civilization—has gradually lost its allure. And, it is this, rather than the abandonment of a particular program, which constitutes our rout." The belief that capitalism is the unassailable engine of human progress, Howe added, "is trumpeted through every medium of communication: official propaganda, institutional advertising and scholarly writings of people who, until a few years ago, were its major opponents."

"The truly powerless people are those intellectuals—the new realists—who attach themselves to the seats of power, where they surrender their freedom of expression without gaining any significance as political figures," Howe wrote. "For it is crucial to the history of the American intellectuals in the past few decades—as well as to the relationship between 'wealth' and 'intellect'—that whenever they become absorbed into the accredited institutions of society they not only lose their traditional rebelliousness but to one extent or another *they cease to function as intellectuals.* The institutional world needs intellectuals *because* they are intellectuals but it does not want them *as* intellectuals. It beckons to them because of what they are but it will not allow them, at least within its sphere of articulation, either to remain or entirely cease being what they are. It needs them for their knowledge, their talent, their inclinations and passions; it insists that they retain a measure of these endowments, which it means to employ for its own ends, and without which the intellectuals would be of no use to it whatever. A simplified but useful equation suggests itself: the relation of the institutional world to the intellectuals is as the relation of middlebrow culture to serious culture, the one battens on the other, absorbs and raids it with increasing frequency and skill, subsidizes and encourages it enough to make further raids possible—at times the parasite will support its victim. Surely this relationship must be one reason for the high incidence of neurosis that is supposed to prevail among intellectuals. A total estrangement from the sources of power and prestige, even a blind unreasoning rejection of every aspect of our culture, would be far healthier if only because it would permit a free discharge of aggression."

The liberal class prefers comfort to confrontation. It will not challenge the decaying structures of the corporate state. It is intolerant within its ranks of those who do. It clings pathetically to the carcass of the Obama presidency. It has been exposed as a dead force in American politics. We must find our way back to the old radicals, to the discredited Marxists, socialists, and anarchists, including Dwight Macdonald and Dorothy Day. Language is our first step toward salvation. We cannot fight what we cannot describe.

—May 31, 2010

OBAMA, THE FALLEN MESSIAH

Max Blumenthal

Obama's messianization invited his demonization and created false expectations among his most zealous supporters on the left.

During a time of economic decline, persistent cultural strife, deepening American involvement in far-off military conflicts, and rapid environmental deterioration, is there any wonder that some have turned to apocalyptic salvation narratives promising both a transcendent, everlasting future and violent retribution against perceived evildoers? A 2002 CNN poll found that 59 percent of Americans believe that the prophecies in the Book of Revelation will come true. The startling number reflected the still-fresh trauma of the 9/11 attacks, but I suspect that it has held steady, if not risen. Indeed, mainstream American culture is permeated by apocalypticism; the blockbuster movie hit *2012* is but one recent example.

I spend several chapters in my book following the Christian right's ascent to the mountaintop with George W. Bush's reelection, detailing how the movement shrouded science and reason in the shadow of the cross, then observing as it swiftly imploded during the Terri Schiavo charade. Because I completed my book days after Barack Obama's inauguration, I was only able to foreshadow the right's plan to undermine the new president. Having watched the right attempt to delegitimize and literally overthrow Bill Clinton for eight years, I did not harbor any illusions about Obama transcending partisan division by becoming the "liberal Reagan who can reunite America," as many argued.

What I did not include in my book was any sense of where the Democratic left was going, or how this movement had developed its own salvation narrative during the Bush era. Only a presidency as destructive and radical as Bush's could have produced such deep levels of anxiety and desperation among progressives. When the Democratic primary began, some progressives seemed to ache for a secular messiah to descend from the political heavens, reverse Bush's disastrous legacy, and save the country from itself.

In their quest for a savior, progressives discovered Barack Obama. "I serve as a blank screen on which people of vastly different political stripes project their own views," Obama proclaimed in his book *The Audacity of Hope*. As Obama's primary battle against Hillary Clinton intensified, his rhetoric and the language of his supporters grew increasingly messianic. At a rally in South Carolina, Oprah Winfrey referred to Obama as "The One," a fusion of Jesus and Neo from *The Matrix*. When Obama defeated Clinton in Iowa, he quoted from a Hopi Indian end-times prophecy that had become popular among New Agers: "We are the ones we've been waiting for." Moved to the point of ecstasy by Obama's victory speech, Ezra Klein declared the candidate "not the Word made flesh, but the triumph of the word over flesh.... Obama is, at his best, able to call us back to our higher selves."

Though he is not a progressive by even the wildest stretch of the imagination, it is worth noting that Louis Farrakhan, who had consistently ordered his followers to boycott elections and who attacked black politicians from Harold Washington to Jesse Jackson as tools of the white power structure, declared in no uncertain terms that Obama was the messiah.

Now that some of Obama's most zealous supporters are beginning to express grave doubts about his ability to deliver the transcendent change he promised, I think it is time for them to consider their role in contributing to the problems Obama faces with both his Democratic base and his opponents on the right. They embraced a secular salvation narrative that Obama cleverly channeled to excite them and distract from his lack of progressive accomplishments. In the end, Obama's messianization created false expectations while establishing political space for the right to undermine and delegitimize him.

To be sure, Obama's salvation narrative was dramatically different than the dualistic, malignant version that prevails on the Christian right. Obama never, to my knowledge, played to his supporters' dark sides by promising them holy retribution against their perceived enemies. In fact, part of his appeal stemmed from his repudiation of partisan rancor—there were no red states where people reject science, demonize gays, and attack minority rights. Until he was inaugurated, Obama behaved like a secular messiah in a world without a devil.

In my book, I detail a series of experiments by a group of political psychologists seeking to provide evidence that the fear of death inspires extreme conservative beliefs—including apocalypticism. Their study was inspired by a theory of cultural anthropologist Ernest Becker: "The idea of death, the fear of it, haunts the human animal like nothing else; it is a mainspring of human activity—designed largely to avoid the fatality of death, to overcome it by denying in some way that it is the final destiny of man." The professors discovered that time and again, their study subjects would register more conservative responses to questions if they were first reminded of their own deaths. (See John Judis's excellent article on the studies for more.)

The use of mortality reminders came in to play as soon as Obama was inaugurated. Almost immediately, the right attempted to delegitimize him by reversing the phenomenon he relied on to win: While he attempted to serve as a blank screen for Americans to project their aspirations upon, they projected their most fearsome inner demons onto him. During the October McCain-Palin rallies, Sarah Palin and far-right surrogates like Joe the Plumber attacked Obama as an Other, a strange outsider who did not share mainstream American values. Their intention was to make him as unfamiliar and frightening as possible, and in doing so, to scare off wavering independent voters. By this time, it was too late in the campaign for the tactic to take effect, so it extended into this year and peaked during the Fall tea-bagger rallies and town hall disruptions.

Tea-bagger activists transposed images of Stalin *and* Hitler onto Obama's face. (Their propaganda bore a disturbing resemblance to the signs waved by right-wing Jewish settlers during rallies against Yitzhak Rabin that depicted the soon-to-be-assassinated Israeli PM in Nazi S.S. garb *and* as the collaborator Marshall Petain, two seemingly incongruous images.) Obama was a Muslim; Obama was a commie; Obama was a cosmopolitan globalist; Obama was a black nationalist. It did not matter who Obama really was. The right simply wanted to convince America he was the Other. As cynical as their tactic is, it has damaged Obama in large part because he offered himself up as "a blank screen," defining himself as he thought different audiences wished to see him, and ultimately not establishing a very clear identity at all.

The right has complemented its anti-Obama propaganda with false rumors designed to inject the language of death into the health-care debate. The single most damaging rumor, adopted from the cult of Lyndon LaRouche, refined by health-care-industry lobbyist Betsy McCaughey, and popularized by Sarah Palin, was that Obama's health-care reform proposal included a plan to implement "death panels." While the president pleaded for compromise and reason, the right repeated the baseless charge over and over that he planned to pull the plug on grandma, euthanize the severely handicapped, and kill the sick. Obama has not yet recovered from the damage the right's mortality reminders did to his political standing.

Since Obama announced his plan to escalate the war in Afghanistan, and with the White House apparently poised to scrap the public option and Medicare buy-in proposals to mollify Senator Joseph Lieberman, the progressive left is going into contortions. Turn on MSNBC or read any major progressive blog and you will see former

Obama zealots proclaim, "Kill the bill!" while assailing the president as an empty suit.

The liberal left has become so disgruntled that a leading conservative talk-radio host asked me recently if progressives were considering a primary challenge to Obama. I laughed and stated my belief that despite his troubles, Obama would win a second term. Whether or not that happens, those former Obama fanatics experiencing a crisis in faith should look in the mirror. They demanded a secular salvation narrative and participated in the near-deification of the politician who so eloquently delivered it to them. They now know that Obama is just a politician. What they have refused to acknowledge is that he would not have fallen so hard had they not lifted him so high.

—*December 18, 2009*

DOWNHILL FROM GREENSBORO:
THE LEFT, 1960–2010

Alexander Cockburn

Half a century ago, a new decade ushered in the rebirth of the American left and of those forces for radical change grievously wounded by the savage cold war pogroms of the '50s. If you want to draw a line to indicate when history took a great leap forward, it could be February 1, 1960, when four black students from Agricultural and Technical College of North Carolina, sat down at a segregated lunch counter in Woolworth's department store in Greensboro, North Carolina. The chairs were for whites. Blacks had to stand and eat. A day later they returned, with twenty-five more students. On February 4 four white women joined them from a local college. By February 7, there were fifty-four sit-ins throughout the South in fifteen cities in nine states. By July 25 the store, part of a huge national chain, and plagued by $200,000 in lost business, threw in the towel and officially desegregated the lunch counter.

Three months later, the city of Raleigh, North Carolina, eighty miles east of Greensboro, saw the founding of the Student Nonviolent Coordinating Committee (SNCC), seeking to widen the lunch-counter demonstrations into a broad, militant movement. SNCC's first field director was Bob Moses, who said that he was drawn by the "sullen, angry and determined look" of the protesters, qualitatively different from the "defensive, cringing" expression common to most photos of protesters in the South.

That same spring of 1960 saw the founding conference of Students for a Democratic Society (SDS) in Ann Arbor, Michigan, the organization that later played a leading role in organizing the college-based component of the antiwar movement. In May the House Un-American Activities Committee was scheduled to hold red-baiting hearings in San Francisco. Students from the University of California at Berkeley crossed the bay to jeer the hearings. They got blasted off the steps of City Hall by cops with power hoses, but the ridicule helped demolish the decade-long power of HUAC.

Within four short years the civil rights movement pushed Lyndon Johnson into signing the Civil Rights Act of 1964. By 1965 the first big demonstrations against the war were rolling into Washington. By the decade's end there had been a convulsion in American life: a new reading of America's past, an unsparing scrutiny of the ideology of "national security" and of empire. The secret, shameful histories of the FBI and CIA were dragged into the light of day; the role of the universities in servicing imperial wars exposed; mutinies of soldiers in Vietnam a daily occurrence; consumer capitalism under daily duress from critics like Ralph Nader. By 1975 the gay and women's movements were powerful social forces; President Nixon had been forced to resign. The left seem poised for an assertive role in American politics for the next quarter-century.

Of course a new radical world did not spring fully formed from the void, on January 1, 1960. Already, in 1958 a black boycott of lunch counters in Oklahoma City, suggested by the eight-year-old daughter of NAACP Youth Council leader Clara Luper, a local high school teacher, had forced change in that city. Luper was greatly influenced by Rosa Parks, who famously refused to surrender her bus seat to a white man in Montgomery, Alabama, in 1955, starting the bus boycott that launched Martin Luther King Jr.'s public career.

Parks was a trained organizer who, like King, attended sessions at the Highlander Folk School, founded by Christian Socialists, close to the Communist Party, one of whom, Don West, began his career as a high-school agitator organizing demonstrations in 1915 outside cinemas featuring Griffith's *Birth of a Nation*, a violently racist movie praising the Ku Klux Klan for protecting whites from black violence after the Civil War.

So there are political genealogies that must be honored, but this is not to occlude disasters endured by the left in the 1940s and '50s—disasters whose consequences reverberate to this day. The first was the historic bargain struck by Roosevelt with organized labor from the late 1930s on, by which unions got automatic deduction of members' dues for their treasuries sanctioned by the federal government, in return for witch-hunting the Trotskyite and later communist left out of the labor movement.

Hugely important was Roosevelt's ouster of the great progressive, Henry Wallace, from the vice presidential slot in 1944, substituting the appalling machine-Democrat Harry Truman who stepped into the Oval Office on Roosevelt's death in 1945, and promptly dropped atom bombs on Hiroshima and Nagasaki, then presided over the birth of the cold war and the rise of a permanently militarized U.S. economy. Wallace headed the Progressive Party ticket in 1948 in a four-way race, which, with Truman's victory, inscribed the unvarying Democratic-Republican either/or on the American political landscape.

By the end of the 1940s there was no powerful independent left political formation, an absence which continues to this day. By the mid-1950s the labor unions, the academies, all government establishments had been purged in the witch hunts—a bipartisan auto-da-fé whose most diligent red-baiters included not only Senator Joe McCarthy but Robert Kennedy. The surviving left was mostly in the peace movement, notably the Quakers. A prime issue was atmospheric nuclear testing, dooming thousands of Americans to premature deaths from cancer.

In terms of organized politics the explosion of radical energy in the 1960s culminated in the peace candidacy of George McGovern, nominated by the Democrats in Miami in 1972. The response of the labor unions financing the party, and of the party bosses, was simply to abandon McGovern and ensure the victory of Nixon. Since that day the party has remained immune to radical challenge. Jimmy Carter, the Southern Democrat installed in the White House in 1977, embraced neoliberalism, and easily beat off a challenge by the left's supposed champion, the late Ted Kennedy. The antiwar movement that cheered America's defeat in Vietnam mostly sat on its hands as Carter and his national security aide Zbigniev Brzezinski ramped up military spending and led America into "the new cold war," fought in Afghanistan and Central America.

Demure under the Democrat Carter, the left did organize substantial resistance to Reagan's wars in Central America in the 1980s. It also rallied to the radical candidacy of Jesse Jackson, the first serious challenge of a black man for the presidency, a Baptist minister, and political organizer who had been in Memphis with Martin Luther King Jr. when the latter was assassinated in 1968. With his "Rainbow Coalition" Jackson ran for the Democratic nomination in 1984 and in 1988, with a platform that represented an anthology of progressive ideas from the 1960s. He attracted a large number of supporters, many of them from the white working class. Each time the Democratic Party shrugged him aside and elected feeble white liberals—Mondale and Dukakis—who plummeted to defeat by Reagan and George Bush Sr.

The left's rout was consummated in the '90s by Bill Clinton, who managed to retain fairly solid left support during his two terms, despite signing two trade treaties devastating to labor, in the forms of the North America Free Trade Agreement (NAFTA) and the WTO; despite the lethal embargo against Iraq and NATO's war on Yugoslavia; despite successful onslaughts on welfare programs for the poor and on constitutional freedoms.

Two important reminders about political phenomena peculiar to America: the first is the financial clout of the "nonprofit" foundations, tax-exempt bodies formed by rich people to dispense their wealth according to political taste. Jeffrey St. Clair and I wrote several pieces about this in our *CounterPunch* newsletter in the mid-'90s. Much of the "progressive sector" in America owes its financial survival—salaries, office accommodation, etc.—to the annual disbursements of these foundations, which cease abruptly at the first manifestation of radical heterodoxy. In other words, most of the progressive sector is an extrusion of the dominant corporate world, just are the academies, similarly dependent on corporate endowments.

The big liberal foundations were perfectly happy with Clinton's brand of neoliberalism and took swift action to tame any unwelcome radical tendencies in both the environmental and the women's movements. Clinton's drive to ratify the "free trade" treaty with Mexico and Canada provoked a potentially threatening alliance of labor unions and environmental groups. Eventually the big liberal foundations exerted some muscle, and major enviro groups came out for the treaty. It was John Adams of the Natural Resources Defense Council who crowed, "We broke the back of the environmental resistance to NAFTA." The major funders of these latter groups included the Pew Charitable Trusts, a foundation set up in the 1940s by heirs to the Sun Oil company. By the mid-1990s Pew was giving the environmental movement about $20 million a year. Two other foundations, both derived from oil companies, gave another $20 million. The Howard Heinz Endowment and the Heinz Family Philanthropies, run by Teresa Heinz, Senator John Heinz's widow (now John Kerry's wife) have played a major role in funding a neoliberal environmental agenda. Also influential is the Rockefeller Family Fund, which oversees the Environmental Grantmakers Association, pivotal in allocating the swag, hence controlling the agenda. By the end of the '90s the green movement—aside from small, radical, underfunded grassroots groups—had become a wholly owned subsidiary of the Democratic Party, hence of corporate America.

For its part, the women's movement steadily devolved into a single-issue affair, focused almost entirely on defending women's right to abortions, under assault from the right. Women's groups, many of them getting big money from liberal Hollywood (which devotedly supported Clinton), swerved away from larger issues of social justice and kept silent as Clinton destroyed safety nets for poor women. The gay movement, radical in the 1970s and 1980s, steadily retreated into campaigns for gay marriage and "hate crime laws," the first being a profoundly conservative acquiescence in state-sanctioned relationships, and the second being an assault on free speech.

A second important reminder concerns the steady collapse of the organized Leninist or Trotskyite left, which used to provide a training ground for young people who could learn the rudiments of political economy and organizational discipline, find suitable mates, and play their role in reproducing the left, red diaper upon red diaper, tomorrow's radicals, nourished on the Marxist classics. Somewhere in the late '80s and early '90s, coinciding with collapses farther east—presumptively but not substantively a great victory for the Trotskyite or Maoist critiques—this genetic strain shriveled into insignificance. An adolescent soul not inoculated by sectarian debate, not enriched by *The Eighteenth Brumaire* and study groups of *Capital*, is open to any infection, such as 9/11 conspiracism and junk-science climate catastrophism substituting for analysis of political economy at the national or global level.

Thus the Bush years saw near extinction of the left's capacity for realistic political analysis. Hysteria about the consummate evil of Bush and Cheney led to a vehement insistence that any Democrat would be qualitatively better, whether it be Hillary Clinton, carrying all the neoliberal baggage of the '90s, or Barack Obama, whose prime money source was Wall Street. Of course black America—historically the most radical of all the Democratic Party's constituencies, was almost unanimously behind Obama and will remain loyal to the end. Having easily beguiled the left in the important primary campaigns of 2008, essentially by dint of skin tone and uplift, Obama stepped into the Oval Office confident that the left would present no danger as he methodically pursues roughly the same agenda as Bush, catering to the requirements of the banks, the arms companies, and the national security establishment in Washington, most notably the Israel lobby.

As Obama ramps up troop presence in Afghanistan, there is still no antiwar movement, such as there was in 2002–04 during Bush's attack on Iraq. The labor unions have been shrinking relentlessly in numbers and clout. Labor's last major victory was the UPS strike in 1997. Its foot soldiers and its money are still vital for Democratic candidates—but corporate America holds the decisive purse strings, from which a U.S. Supreme Court decision on January 21 has now removed almost all restraints.

Labor has seen its most cherished goal in recent years vanish down the plug. This was Employee Free Choice Act (EFCA) amendments to the National Labor Relations Act that would help boost organizing and bargaining in the private sector. The statistics from the Department of Labor regularly show why EFCA is necessary, if not entirely sufficient, for a union revival. Organized labor in private industry lost 10 percent of its membership in 2009 mainly in manufacturing and construction—the worst annual decline in the last quarter-century. Obama was explicit, even in the campaign, in telling labor leaders that as president he would not press labor law reform.

For the rest of his term Obama, can press forward with the neo-liberal agenda that has now flourished through six presidencies. He and the Democratic Party display insouciance toward the left's anger. Rightly so. What have they to fear?

—February 2010 (Petrolia, California)

THE U.S. SOCIAL FORUM:
THE ANTI-TEA PARTY EXPERIENCE

Bill Fletcher Jr.

It was unlike any political experience I have had. The extent of the racial/ethnic diversity; the preponderance of people under thirty-five; the gender balance; the international guests; the broad range of progressive social and political organizations; this and much more were in evidence for all to see at the phenomenal US Social Forum (USSF). The gathering, from June 22–26 in Detroit was the second such gathering in the USA, inspired by the World Social Forum movement that commenced in Brazil in 2001 (the first US Social Forum was held in Atlanta in June 2007). I forgot to mention, there were somewhere between 15,000 and 20,000 attendees! The US Social Forum was the product of an immense amount of work on the part of a planning committee that drew from a variety of organizations and movements, with one particular network, Grassroots Global Justice, playing a very central role in moving the process. One of the striking features of the USSF was that the political diversity did not result in sectarian behavior. People who, outside of the USSF context, are often at odds, found a safe meeting place, and actually more than that: a place where fruitful exchanges could take place. Yet in walking through the conference—which in many ways was multiple conferences, given the hundreds of workshops and plenaries—what struck me the most was that this was the antithesis of the Tea Party movement. Instead of the fear, ignorance, and hatred emanating from the Tea Party crowd, there was a sense of optimism—yes, optimism—from the gathering, mixed with an urgency to defend and change planet Earth before it is too late. This was remarkable given that the gathering was, as mentioned, so diverse and there was no consensus as to what is the specific, progressive alternative to the madness of global capitalism. That said, the slogan of the conference, "Another World is Possible," truly defined the nature of this assembly. It did so in some very fundamental ways, most especially, the recognition that actually existing capitalism is in the process of destroying the planet, what with environmental degradation and the exploitation of working people in order to achieve grand profits. It was also an accurate slogan in that there are social movements and some countries around the world that are taking the lead in experimenting with everything from alternative economies to revolutionary approaches toward the environment. Actually existing capitalism, then, is not the only possible reality; it is the reality to which most of us have become accustomed. The diversity of the USSF, at the same time, presents certain challenges. Though the USSF and its multiple constituencies represent a clear alternative to the evil represented by the Tea Party movement, what it does not contain is a coherent direction in order to contest for power. This is where the Tea Party movement has an advantage. More than anything else, the core of the Tea Party movement appreciates the necessity to gain the reins of power. Though they are themselves quite diverse, they have a set of principles, myths, and fears that unite them, along with an unquenchable thirst to gain political power in order to implement their twisted dreams. The USSF represents a wonderful safe space for exchanges. It was something of an oasis in a political desert. But as with many an oasis, the caravans arriving and sharing the space are not necessarily going in the same direction when they depart. In that sense, the USSF does not replace the need for an alternative political project that can advance many of the visions that were proposed in Detroit, but advance them with the intent that they become the guiding views of a truly civilized, post-capitalist society. The organizers of the USSF are to be congratulated for their work and the thousands of participants are to be applauded for their constructive interactions. Let us hope that the USSF becomes more than a gathering transpiring every three-plus years. Let us hope that it becomes a process through which new and progressive ideas can be generated and that those who wish to move in the same direction join the same caravan as they depart the oasis.

—July 1, 2010

POPULISM IS NOT ABOUT MOBS, ANTIGOVERNMENT RANTS, OR OPINION POLLS: TO PUT THE PROGRESS BACK IN 'PROGRESSIVE,' WE NEED A REAL POPULIST MOVEMENT

Jim Hightower

If a political pollster came to my door and asked whether I consider myself a conservative or a liberal, I'd answer, "No."

Not to be cute—I have a bit of both in me—but because, like most Americans, my beliefs can't be squeezed into either of the tidy little boxes that the establishment provides.

Also, most of the big issues that our country faces defy right-left categorization. Take conservatism. It's a doctrine that classically embodies caution and... well, conservation. Yet the gushing and spreading Gulf Coast oil disaster was caused by people who proudly identify themselves as conservatives—including top executives of BP, Halliburton, and Transocean, as well as the top regulatory officials involved. However, they're not conservatives, they're anything-goes corporatists. Likewise, the five Supreme Court justices who recently enthroned corporate money over democracy are routinely labeled by the media as "conservative"—but their reckless rulings destroy our democratic values, rather than conserve them. Again, corporatists all.

As I've rambled through life, I've observed that the true political spectrum in our society does not range from right to left, but from top to bottom. This is how America's economic and political systems really shake out, with each of us located somewhere up or down that spectrum, mostly down. Right to left is political theory; top to bottom is the reality we actually experience in our lives every day—and the vast majority of Americans know that they're not even within shouting distance of the moneyed powers that rule from the top of both systems, whether those elites call themselves conservatives or liberals.

For me, the "ism" that best encompasses and addresses this reality is populism. What is it? Essentially, it's the continuation of America's democratic revolution. It encompasses and extends the creation of a government that is us. Instead of a "trickle down" approach to public policy, populism is solidly grounded in a "percolate up" philosophy that springs directly from America's founding principle of the Common Good.

Few people today call themselves populists, but I think most are. I'm not talking about the recent political outbursts by confused, used, and abused tea-bag ranters who've been organized by corporate front groups to spread a hatred of government. Rather, I mean the millions of ordinary Americans in every state who're battling the real power that's running roughshod over us: out-of-control corporations. With their oceans of money and their hired armies of lobbyists, lawyers, economists, consultants, and PR agents, these self-serving, autocratic entities operate from faraway executive suites and Washington backrooms to rig the economic and governmental rules so that they capture more and more of America's money and power.

The superwealthy speculators and executives who own and run these far-flung, private empires don't live in our zip codes, but their power reaches into all of our lives. During the past thirty years or so, they have quietly succeeded in untethering their ilk from our country's quaint notion that we're all in this together. They've elevated their private interests above the public interest and entrenched themselves as the preeminent decision makers over our economy, environment, and media—and our government. They pull the strings.

You can shout yourself red-faced at Congress critters you don't like and demand a government so small it'd fit in the back room of Billy Bob's Bait Shop & Sushi Stand—but you won't be touching the corporate and financial powers behind the throne. In fact, weak government is the political wet dream of corporate chieftains, which is why they're so ecstatic to have the Tea Party out front for them. But the real issue isn't small government; it's good government. (Can I get an *amen* from Gulf Coast fishing families on that!?)

This is where populists come in. You wouldn't know it from the corporate media, but in just about every town or city in our land you can find some groups or coalitions that, instead of merely shouting at politicians, have come together to find their way around, over, or through the blockage that big money has put in the way of their democratic aspirations. Also, in the process of organizing, strategizing, and mobilizing, these groups are building relationships and community, creating something positive from a negative.

This is the historic, truly democratic, grassroots populism of workaday folks who strive (and, more often than not, succeed) to empower themselves to take charge economically as well as politically.

With the rebellious spirit and sense of hope that have defined America from the start, these populists are directly challenging the plutocratic order that reigns over us. This populism is unabashedly a class movement—one that seeks not merely to break the iron grip that centralized corporate power has on our country, but also to build cooperative democratic structures so that ordinary people—not moneyed interests—define and control our country's economic and political possibilities.

RECLAIM POPULISM

It's necessary to restate the solid principles of populism and reassert its true spirit, because both are now being subverted and severely perverted by corporate manipulators and a careless media establishment.

To these debasers of the language, any politicos or pundits who tap into any level of popular anger (toward Obama, liberals, the IRS, poor people, unions, gays, immigrants, Hollywood, community organizers, environmentalists, et al.) get a peel-off "populist" label slapped onto their lapels—even when their populist pose is funded by and operates as a front for one or another corporate interest. That's not populism; it's rank hucksterism, disguising plutocrats as champions of the people.

Witness Sarah Palin, whose political flowering was induced by the rich stimulant of corporate money and who has now been turned into an overnight multimillionaire by agreeing to serve as the political face and voice for such corporate barons as Rupert Murdoch. Palin's chief function is to rally the tea-bag faithful (who are less than 20 percent of the public) into a cacophonous, furious, and ludicrous defense of the domineering power of—guess who?—corporate barons.

Yet, few in the media peek behind her facade. After hearing Palin loyally denounce the unmitigated evil of government at a recent Tea Party convention, for example, *Washington Post* columnist David Broder, the eminent establishmentarian, gushed about her "pitch-perfect populism."

Even worse than the media's misapplication of the label is its desperate determination to marginalize what is actually a venerable and historic movement as nothing more than assorted gaggles of grumps and quacks. George Will, the effete conservative commentator, sniffed in a February column that populism is "a celebration of intellectual ordinariness." Then he dismissed its political importance with a sweeping declaration that populism "always wanes because it never seems serious as a solution."

Perhaps George had his signature bow tie too tightly tied that day, cutting off the flow of blood to his memory cells. Otherwise, someone of his intellectual extraordinariness would have recalled that the populists of the 1880s were the ones who formed the first U.S. political party to propose and push such serious solutions as women's suffrage; wage protections and an eight-hour day for labor; direct election of U.S. senators by the people; elimination of poll taxes and literacy tests for voting; corralling the power of lobbyists; civil-service laws; pensions for veterans; a graduated income tax; elimination of all subsidies to private corporations; outlawing the Pinkterton system of corporate mercenaries to bust unions; and preserving America's natural resources from being monopolized for speculative purposes.

It's important to reclaim populism from dissemblers and hijackers because populism is a legitimate, positive, uniting political expression with a rich history (though largely untaught), a genuine appeal to today's disaffected majority, and a huge potential for making real democratic progress against corporate rule. There is serious power in the concept, which is precisely why corporatists are out to hide its long and proud history and to squeeze its meaning down to something as vacuous as "popular," allowing them to capture it for their own use.

Now is the time for progressives to reassert their populist beliefs and bona fides, for we're living in a teachable moment in which it's possible to reach most Americans with an aggressive and positive approach to achieving a higher level of economic and political democracy. There is a spreading and deepening recognition within today's broad middle class that they've been abandoned to a plutocracy that feels free to knock them down and leave them there. The disdain that the power elites have for the rest of us is glaringly and gallingly apparent:

- **Wall Street billionaires** crash our economy but are bailed out at our expense to continue their banksterism against us.
- **We're told to accept a "jobless recovery"** and to sit still for a "new normal" of perpetually low wages, continuing losses of American jobs, and steady erosion of union and consumer power.

- **We're presented with two flagrant examples** of murderous corporate greed—first at Massey Energy's deadly coal mine, then at BP's deadly offshore oil well—yet no corporate executive has even been arrested.

Do the Powers That Be (whether liberal or conservative) really imagine that the great majority of Americans don't see or don't care about this rank classism, this in-your-face stiffing of the middle class? Not only do regular folks see and care, but there has been a corresponding rise in populist attitudes and activism each time the government shows itself to be in cahoots with the stiffers. Following Bush, Obama brought "the audacity of hope" to Washington, and most of us cheered. But people have since seen too many times when he and other top Democrats posed as reformers, only to back off when push came to shove, ending up coddling the corporate plutocracy.

Take that January Supreme Court ruling that literally allows corporations to buy our elections. Arcane issues of campaign financing don't usually move the bubble in opinion polls, but the Great Unwashed instantly grasped that this was raw corporate usurpation of the people's democratic authority, and they howled. With polls showing that 83 percent of Americans (including 73 percent of Republicans) are demanding immediate action to overturn this outrage, Obama himself pledged to jump right on it.

Months passed. No action. Finally, Democrats introduced what they called "a sweeping reform." Big Whoopie. Rather than boldly leading the charge for a constitutional amendment to reverse this corporate coup, the bill caves in to the Court's disastrous ruling, meekly proposing nothing more than some new campaign-finance disclosure rules. It actually gives legal cover for Exxon Mobil, Goldman Sachs, Walmart, and the rest to steal our government—they just have to wear name tags while doing it. Harsh, huh?

This kind of stuff is why there's a yearning for—as we say in Texas—politics with hair on it. On April 30, I was interviewed by Bill

Moyers for a special edition of his PBS television show. It was the final broadcast of his long-running, excellent, and important *Journal*, and he chose to close with his own testament to what he sees as the promising rise of modern-day populism:

"Plutocracy and democracy don't mix.... The fate and character of our country are up for grabs. So along with Jim Hightower and many of you, I am biased: Democracy only works when we claim it as our own."

Following the broadcast, hundreds of e-mails and letters poured into my office, with many more going to Bill—practically all of them positive. Populism clearly struck a chord with folks, and I was encouraged by the many who accepted our interview as a call to action. Here's a sampling from around the country:

- **Plattsburgh, New York**: "A couple of my friends and I are most inspired by the populist message and would like to meet other like-minded people. You speak my language and have inspired me to get more involved."
- **North Carolina**: "Always thought I was a frustrated Southern Democrat, but I'm thinking I may be a populist now. I would love to find out where I can get involved here in North Carolina."
- **Western Massachusetts**: "I was very cynical about grassroots movements, especially the Tea Party. Your remarks were clarifying. Any advice on how I can help?"
- **Hillsboro, Oregon**: "I have the energy to help drive these changes but am unsure as to how I can most effectively help. I know just being involved is a huge step, and so I want to get involved."
- **Nebraska**: "I would just like to get a dialogue going [and] to make my website one that would be useful in getting people aware and aroused to put the government back to work for the people, not just the rich folks."

- **Wisconsin:** "To know that there are people that are not just lying down to be trampled on and stepped over, brings me some comfort."
- **Washington State:** "I just watched Moyers's show and found out I'm a populist; where do I sign up?"

A MOVEMENT

We have a populist majority in America right now. Look at nearly any poll or talk with people at the local Chat & Chew Café, and you'll find—contrary to tea-bag hype, the contrived "wisdom" of major media outlets, and the political weenieness of too many Democratic "leaders"—that most folks are already with us on practically all of the big issues related to the corporatization of America (jobs, Wall Street, pollution, money in politics, a green economy, health care, media, unions, affordable housing, pensions, K-Street lobbyists, local businesses, infrastructure investment, progressive taxation, you name it).

Moreover, there is huge support for our fundamental populist values (economic fairness, social justice, and equal opportunity for ALL) and for our guiding principle of the Common Good. People believe in these ideals and hold them deep in their hearts, even though our corporate rulers don't want them discussed, much less implemented.

From coast to coast, in nearly every community, you'll find people who are implementing these principles in their work, businesses, schools, families, organizations, religions, neighborhoods, and every other area of their lives. Millions of Americans are deliberately defying the corporate order to create new structures, groups, systems, and relationships based on richer values than the stilted corporate ethic.

Cooperatives, for example, are one bright populist path to structural economic change. You can join with others in your community to own, control, manage, profit from, and enjoy the places where you work, live, produce, play, buy, eat, bank, get health care, etc. These are democratic entities in which decisions are not handed down from the top, but made by the members. As opposed to aloof, absentee, autocratic corporate owners who extract wealth from communities, co-ops are of, by, and for the community, creating good jobs and distributing both wealth and power locally.

The cooperative idea is big and growing rapidly in every state. About 72,000 are up and running, involving 120 million members. It's a valid, large-scale alternative for building democratic values directly into America's economic structure, so turn your imagination loose. For instance, here in my town of Austin, a bunch of enterprising folks have launched Black Star, America's first cooperatively owned and run microbrewery and pub! Needless to say, I'm in.

Big changes require big ideas rooted in big ideals—combined with strategic thinking, lots of grunt-level organizing, a broad willingness to cooperate, and the tenacity to stick with it. In other words, a movement. It's not something that can be created by one presidential campaign, and it has to be more than an uncoordinated collection of issue groups.

The populist movement of the late nineteenth century, for example, was not a helter-skelter organization thrown together on the whim of some angry, inept know-nothings. It was built by smart, knowledgeable big thinkers, strategists, and organizers.

They created a nationwide network of cooperative enterprises to provide capital, supplies, and marketing mechanisms for movement members. They formed their own integrated media network of newspapers, magazines, books, and speakers, allowing the movement to communicate and educate constantly. They trained thousands to be leaders. They ran their own members for public office, electing hundreds all across the country. They taught literacy classes, put on cultural events, provided lecturers, formed bands and singing groups, held festivals, and otherwise linked members into fun, self-improvement, and a shared social experience.

That's what a movement looks like.

LET'S GET MOVING

Progressive forces today already have nearly all of the components of an effective movement at work around the country, but there's little connection among the components, no uniting theme to our many issues, no long-term focus, and no common strategy. Because of this, we're not actually a movement—and we're not really moving much.

To make the whole of our efforts greater than the sum of our diverse, dispersed parts, we urgently need to be more unified. I don't mean anything grandiose like one big happy organization, but modest steps forward. It could begin simply by having some serious conversations among our groups, media sources, organizers, funders, and other resources about how we can produce a bit more cooperation and slightly more coordination.

It seems to me that the rallying point is a focus on the populist possibilities presented by the corporate arrogance and avarice that is crushing our country's potential. With that, we might actually become a movement that moves.

—June 2010

FIGHT THE RIGHT: LOOKING FORWARD, LOOKING BACK

Suzanne Pharr, Eric Ward, Tarso Ramos, Rachel Carroll,
Marcy Westerling, and Scot Nakagawa
(Transcribed by Isabel Braverman & Anna Lekas Miller)

Suzanne Pharr: It was eighteen years ago that Scot Nakagawa invited me to come to Oregon to work against the Oregon Citizens Alliance (OCA). That began my journey of beginning to understand that what the right was doing was an attack against democracy as well as against the LGBT (lesbian, gay, bisexual, and transgendered) community, with huge roots in race, and that much of what was going on then was preparing us for the anti-immigration effort that would come afterward. What we came to understand during that time was the OCA didn't just spring out of anywhere. It had roots that went back to Goldwater, to George Wallace, to the Eagle Forum; it went back to the resentment against the civil rights movement.

For emotional context, it had always chosen to have a hidden language about race and it had always chosen to play on people's emotions. It did it then and it's doing it today. Right now, I believe we have had a perfect storm for right-wing organizing. [The right had already done a lot of work before September 11, but] if you want to pick up a place to play on people's fear that is a great place to begin. We had the USA Patriot Act, and the stronger move to what I think is a police state. You have the demographic change in this country. (People are beginning to understand for the first time that it's not going to be demographically majority white, it's going to be majority people of color.) Then you have a left and progressive movement that has not developed its base. A left and progressive movement that is somewhat trapped, in fact terrifically trapped, in the nonprofit sector. Then you have the crash of the economy; you have two wars; and you have the election of a black president. That is a perfect storm I believe for this kind of organizing.

What I want to do is just to help people to keep in mind that what we're facing today is actually the playing out of the Reagan agenda. You don't hear people talk about it enough: tax cuts, the whole anti-taxation movement [brought us to the place] where now you have impoverished states and a government in terrific debt, and the states all crying out "We have no money left," because they have no tax base.

We have attacks on working people, resulting in weak unions. People coming out of high school, if they don't have the privilege of going to college (and it is now a privilege), face either low-wage jobs, the military, or an underground economy, which can put them in prison. We have the whole move to globalization with outsourcing and downsizing. We have the free market economy with the stock-market economy, where the bottom line becomes the most important thing, not the worker [having] any kind of means. The separation of the rich and the poor becomes greater. The racialization of issues in order to take down the social contract by making people feel that to pay taxes is to give money to those who don't deserve it. [This is at the heart of today's anti-immigrant debate.] Deregulation has had an incredible effect on everything, just think of the environment. The media takeover during that time, in which the media outlets were bought by the right.... And then, the systematic move more and more toward a police state.... I guess the question was, after you take everything away from folks, then how do you control them?

We already had the exponential growth of prisons. September 11 gives more reasons to create more police and policing situations.... We get distracted from the fact that that's happening because it comes bit by bit by bit. It was in the [George W.] Bush period in which that all that really became mainstreamed. Many people stopped talking about the right; they started talking about "conservatives" and the "red states" and the "blue states," and about Republicans and Democrats and Independents. And then also, more people wrote about the right. When we were doing work in the '90s in Oregon there weren't many of us. Now there are a lot more people who are at least writing about it but not necessarily researching it and being careful about it. We have now moved into a very us-and-them setting. And it has not led to us making significant change in the country. What is missing is the genuine conversation with people that are the ordinary people like ourselves.... We have to do political education like we have never done it before. Not talking down but talking with and we have to organize like we've never organized before.

Eric Ward: When I reflect on 1992, today I think one of the most important lessons I want to talk about first is that we really can do it, if we choose. [The right's] vision of the world is not one we need to compromise with, unless we're willing to look at the people at the table around us and are willing to give some of them up.

We assumed in 1992 that the right was actually innocent and it was growing. What we hadn't understood is that the right had actually won. It had set the stage and the infrastructure to take over the Republican Party—to make space for the most extreme elements of the right. With that, I'm talking about everything from white supremacists, who were willing to firebomb the homes of gays and lesbians; to the "wise use" movement, which was willing to try to take over covert functions and threaten environmentalists; to the Christian Coalition, which was willing to mobilize tax structures and to harass and intimidate the gay and lesbian community; to attacks on the idea of government itself.

We made a mistake of not understanding that the right wasn't in ascendance; the right had actually already won. That said, some incredible things came out of fighting. [We learned] that we could build infrastructure and movement to defend democracy and the idea of a future multiracial, pluralistic society. [But] we spent much of our time in those early days fighting the right as a social movement: We took on infrastructure, government policies, or institutional racism. What we didn't understand was that this was a battle over principles. [We have to understand that there are many strands. Some] segments of this movement are backward looking, such as segments of the Tea Party movement, and some are forward looking such as the white nationalist movement. Some, such as elements of the corporate right, the neoliberals, are willing to dispense with the idea of race all together if it will drive new profits. What's important to understand is that the right is not monolithic, there are many different tendencies, but what brings them together is that their tendencies lead toward antidemocratic principles and an antidemocratic society.

Tarso Ramos: I want to start with a few myths that I think are really common [even on shows I enjoy like Rachel Maddow's and others]. One is [the idea that] this right-wing backlash that we're in right now [comprises] socially maladjusted people who are on the wrong side of history but may be just outright crazy. [The myth is] they don't have any staying power, nor have the capacity to fundamentally transform our society, culture, or politics. Maybe all these folks are just corporate shills; what's behind all this is just the profit motive. [This myth suggests that] to the extent that this kind of backlash can do damage, it's kind of a faction fight on the right. The Tea Party folks are going after conservative Republicans, and that's great [for progressives and Democrats] because maybe they'll fight with each other.

I would say there's a grain of truth in all that, but not much more than a grain. [And it] reinforces a complacency that is easy to see when we look at the level of national de-mobilization among progressives and the left. Frankly, it's a de-mobilization that's been encouraged by the current administration to its own peril.

These kinds of messages about the right are not only wrong; they are also dangerous. [I look] at this as one of the largest historical moments of right-wing populism in the history of this country. (And there have been a lot of others, whether it's the period of backlash against the end of slavery and Reconstruction; the surging Klan organizing of the 1920s; the backlash that we saw under the McCarthy period, [or] the Reagan revolution.) These are all periods that profoundly changed the culture and politics and fortunes of people in the United States. We're in a moment like that now.

About 15 percent of the U.S. electorate identifies as members of the Tea Party. Fifteen percent is pretty substantial. If you believe the polling, something like 40 percent of the electorate sympathize with the Tea Party. You have a lot of higher income folks who support that, but it's really this traditional base of right-wing populism.

This is a highly fluid political moment that really favors the bold. [Consider:] Most of us were inclined to snicker when that initial Tea Party rallies on tax day in 2009 [were called] when the Obama administration put through the largest middle-class tax cut in history. [But the right were] carving out the turf to claim an economic populism for themselves. They were betting on the idea that the economy was not going turn around. [If] they couldn't pin the economy on the Obama administration, they could mobilize racial resentment combined with economic fear, [in order to] mobilize.

As preposterous as that idea sounded, look where we are now. Does the left control the debate around the economy and economic populism? Far from it. Audacity has favored the right in a moment when there's nothing but timidity from liberals and progressives at the national level. This is the moment to talk about what we really want and really believe, and to compete for the 60 percent of working class voters who voted for Scott Brown. We can compete.

Rachel Carroll: Two years ago in the Bitterroot Valley in western Montana, two folks who believed the Republican Party in the valley was not conservative enough formed [an organization called] Celebrating Conservatism under the guise of economic conservatism (much like the Tea Party movement), but their actions have been not primarily economic. While this group has a few new players who aren't part of our research history, they have tapped into an existing and historical enclave of right-wing heroes for their advice and guidance. These include "county supremacy" activists, like former Arizona sheriff Richard Mack, the right-wing conspiracy theorist Jack McLamb, tax-protesting anti-Semite M.J. "Red" Beckman, and Montana Militia communications director Paul Stramer. This is who they're going to for advice. These are their speakers. This is who they are taking their ideology from.

They've also utilized players from the political right, from the more Christian theocratic advocates of the Constitution Party, including the presidential candidate Chuck Baldwin and Montana's former [state assemblyman and] Constitution Party member Rick Jore. Also Gary Marbut of the Montana Shooting Sports Association—someone that what we use as an example of what we call moving from the margins to the mainstream, someone who was active and spoke at militia meetings of the '90s and whose base comes from the idea of county supremacy but has managed to legitimize himself in the political mainstream.

Everyone, of course, is looking to take a piece of this energy, from the John Birch Society and our state Republican Party (who gave a day and an event for Celebrating Conservatism and the Tea Party movement, in Montana at their party convention). The advice that they're getting from these groups has taken them to some not unpredictable places. They are running a slate of five libertarian candidates for our state legislature and Democrats in the area think, All right, this is our opportunity because they are going to split the vote for us, not seeing the reality of where they're pushing that valley. (They're advocating for issues and forming committees to deny women the right to choose, fighting against health reform, fighting against immigration rights, and fighting against wilderness.) This isn't that economic guise that they started under two years ago. They are trying to…gain legitimacy, and at the same time their message is getting more radical and more worrisome. There are very serious risks on the ground in Montana from Celebrating Conservatism, and those risks include a risk of violence. They're advocating forming a militia in Ravalli County.… They openly advocate carrying weapons and guns in public meetings. Just six months ago in a rural area of Montana , they turned out 500 people at their events.

We responded in Montana by using the history that the Human Rights Network has brought to the issue. The Bitterroot Human Rights Alliance has existed in that valley for quite a while and has fought fiercely for human rights and against the right wing. In response, our local members and other members of the community formed the Bitterroot Democracy Project; they are working to give another option to people. [While the right is bringing in people from the early '90s to talk about the Constitution, the Project] brought an event to the valley recently and said, "Let's tell you our perspective on the Constitution"— and they're talking about democracy and values that unite us, not divide us. We're also working with our government (not against it) to use the processes that are there for us to challenge dangerous activity and to make sure that law enforcement doesn't let these folks off the hook.

So where is Celebrating Conservatism today? Well they're not gone, and they're not going anywhere quickly. I can tell you a little over a month ago they held an event at the University of Montana's Adams Center, a facility that holds almost 5,000 people. They brought a litany of speakers from across the country, spent $30,000, planned on packing the place, and they turned out at most 300 people. They blamed it on us.

Marcy Westerling: While I have been a paid organizer in recent decades, what I think has sharpened my game has been my after-hours community work in Columbia County. It started in the late '80s where I was a young chick and I was running the only crisis line. I knew I wasn't always in the most friendly place. I would come out (as a lesbian) and there would be pornography on my windshield and the rotary would have bets on my sexual orientation.

It was a lovely, small-town, rural community, majority white, not too different from our entire region twenty years ago. And yet progressive organizing at that time was actually done out of a couple of zip codes that were traceable back to the Portland area. The folks in my community weren't very hip and cool and it's not because we didn't have that potential—we were kind of forgotten. When the Oregon Citizens Alliance started up and said, "You've got to be scared of these gay people," those of us that were around in the '90s can probably remember—they told very effective stories. Right before the infamous Ballot Measure 9 (writing discrimination into the state constitution against gays and lesbians) under the cloak of darkness [the Alliance] went door to door and dropped this massive drop of literature that told the story of little Bobby and Frankie—twelve-year-olds…. Bobby took little Frankie out and things were never the same. It was so memorable when you showed up the next day at work, they said, Did you know about little Bobby and Frankie, and how are you voting?

They had a very great advantage of taking things in particularly smaller towns people didn't have familiarity with and running with them. We called that the culture wars.

One of the things that I think is really important is—as we document and research the right at the macro level and look at the money behind the curtains and who's benefiting from these deals—that we don't get [that] confused with the folks on the ground who are our neighbors. Or if they're not our neighbors, how sharp can our political analysis be if we are living in ideological segregation from a big swath of our country? It's really critical that we understand that the big folks in D.C. masterminding things are not my neighbor.

I remember in March of '91, a creationism debate that took place in our community where there was no progressive community in Colombia County. We all realized there was going to be a school board meeting to decide whether or not creationism was going to be the law of the land. We showed up and what we saw was a standing-room-only crowd. We were there till past midnight. Half of the room was really organized, they looked good, they knew what they were doing. The rest of us had no plan, didn't know each other and were pretty under-impressive.

One by-product of the early '90s is we trained up a lot of smart, motivated people that have the capacity to talk to their neighbors. But if we don't have that in every zip code, we will continue to see ourselves as the three people on the sidelines while the Tea Party folks have 2,500 people showing up.

These are really confusing times, really chaotic times, economically downturned times, [in which] people are not necessarily able to figure out how to keep their families going. Our role as leaders is to get a leadership team that is not working night and day on every task that needs to happen, but instead is orchestrating a team and...really being our best selves, ...looks at the nuggets of what we really hold in common with our neighbors.

[In August 2009] we had twenty-eight town halls in small-town Oregon. In '92 we had two groupings showing up: the people in their suits, and ourselves, the straggly people who didn't have a game plan. When the town halls happened, there were the Tea Party folks (however you want to describe them) that were really new to showing up; the health-care-no-matter-what folks, who were coming in from out of town; and an inside team, the Human Dignity Group, who had a plan, because we had eighteen years to work on having a plan before you show up. The inside team made sure that not only would health care get good discussion at these town halls, but that we would give equal space to talking about the critical issue of immigration, talking about it in the context of the economy, health care, and all of the rest of it.

Scot Nakagawa: Once upon a time, a long, long time ago, I was in the middle of this fight, here in Oregon, first through an organization, based here in Portland, called the Coalition for Human Dignity, starting in the late '80s. Later, through a couple of political campaigns and the National Gay and Lesbian Task Force, we created a project called "Fight the Right," that went around to states and LGBT communities faced with anti-LGBT ballot initiatives. During those years I did quite a bit of study of the right and tried to understand what it was that I was looking at. I had recently come from Hawaii, where I had been a social worker and a teacher, and one of the things that came as a big surprise to me as someone who had been from Hawaii was how incredibly, deeply, widespread racism there was [on the mainland]. It's not like there was no racism in Hawaii, but this was a whole new thing. [The right] seemed to rely on this idea that was really easy for people to pick up—that race and nationality in the United States were the same thing. What it meant to be an American was to be white, and to be male, and to be Christian, and to be heterosexual. People who live within that identity seem to accept it, and on the basis of that ready acceptance, think they are entitled to certain kinds of privileges.

The right organized people around that sense of privilege and said that people of color were taking over and demanding special rights. Gay people were a threat to the nuclear family. Feminists would erode the nuclear family and traditional gender roles, and that would cause a moral collapse in America. *Morality* and *Christianity* in America are co-words for the same thing. So, anyone who was not a Christian was a threat. Anybody who did not comply with this notion of rigid, patriarchal gender roles; anybody who was not straight; and anybody who was not white was a problem. This idea of America that they put out there and that people responded to I found frightening, so I got involved in organizing. I started to see what I could do about decoding all of this stuff, teasing it out, and making it apparent to people that this isn't about just one given issue, but about a whole idea about what it means to be an American...that with this strategy they could win. And one of the things I experienced once Clinton got elected and things had started to turn around, is that the right had lost momentum and that we were starting to win!

Then the year 2000 came around, and I thought to myself—I thought we had won. I was just shocked by it all. That experience led me to the belief that we can't stop talking about this. We can't stop doing this work. It's way too easy to get complacent. It's too hard for us to accept that people can get this mean, that people will actually act against their own self-interest in such an incredible way. Yet they do. They do it all the time. People keep telling me it's the re-rise of the right—it's kind of like the second rising of the dough—that they're back. But, I don't really think they've ever gone away.

Way back then I had all these ideas about what we should do to out-organize the right that involved very complicated political formations.... I thought people needed to form these really complicated coalitions in order to defeat these right-wing initiatives. What we found out instead was what really worked was people who were affected by these initiatives, going out into the community and talking to people and saying, "Hey look, I'm gay. This affects me. You shouldn't vote for it." It's an oversimplification, but that's what it came down to. What they rely on to be successful is a big lie, about you, about me, about all of us. They demonize us, they tell stories about us, and those stories are just not true. In the end, though they seem to have so much on their side, what we have that they don't have is the truth about us.

—July 30, 2010

CONTRIBUTORS

W. Kamau Bell is a San Francisco–based comedian, author of the comedy albums *Face Full of Flour* and *One Night Only*. He recently ended a run of his one-man show, *The W. Kamau Bell Curve: Ending Racism in about an Hour*.

Max Blumenthal is an award-winning journalist and bestselling author whose articles and video documentaries have appeared in the *New York Times*, the *Los Angeles Times*, the *Daily Beast*, *The Nation*, the *Huffington Post*, *Salon*, Al Jazeera English, and many other publications. He is a writing fellow for the Nation Institute. His book, *Republican Gomorrah: Inside the Movement that Shattered the Party*, is a *New York Times* and *Los Angeles Times* bestseller.

Eric Boehlert is the author of *Lapdogs: How the Press Rolled Over for Bush* (Free Press, 2006) and *Bloggers on the Bus: How the Internet Changed Politics and the Press* (Free Press, 2009). He worked for five years as a senior writer for *Salon*, where he wrote extensively about media and politics. Prior to that, he worked as a contributing editor for *Rolling Stone*. Boehlert has a bachelor's degree in Near Eastern studies from the University of Massachusetts and is a senior fellow at Media Matters for America.

Joanna Brooks grew up in a conservative Mormon home in the orange groves of Orange County, California. Now she's an award-winning American religion scholar and writer.

Rachel Carroll is a researcher at the Montana Human Rights Network.

Veronica Cassidy is a Brooklyn-based freelance writer.

Alexander Cockburn is co-editor of *CounterPunch* and a columnist for *The*

Nation, First Post, and the *Anderson Valley Advertiser.* He has written many books, including *Corruptions of Empire* and *The Golden Age Is in Us.*

Lisa Duggan is professor of American studies and gender and sexuality studies in the Department of Social and Cultural Analysis at New York University, and co-editor of *Our Monica, Ourselves: The Clinton Affair and the National Interest.*

Barry Eisler is a novelist, blogger, former CIA officer, and author most recently of *Inside Out* from Ballantine Books (June 29, 2010).

Laura Flanders is a former Air America Radio host and now hosts GRITtv, the nationally syndicated daily talk show which she founded. Flanders is the author of the *New York Times* best-seller, *BUSHWOMEN: Tales of a Cynical Species* (Verso, 2004) and *Blue GRIT: True Democrats Take Back Politics from the Politicians* (Penguin Press, 2007.) She is also the editor of *The W Effect, Sexual Politics in the Age of Bush,* (The Feminist Press, 2004.) A regular contributor to MSNBC, Flanders has appeared on TV shows from Real Time with Bill Maher to the O'Reilly Factor. She contributes regularly to *The Nation* and the *Huffington Post.*

Bill Fletcher Jr, is a BlackCommentator.com editorial board member and a senior scholar with the Institute for Policy Studies, the immediate past president of TransAfrica Forum and co-author of *Solidarity Divided: The Crisis in Organized Labor and a New Path toward Social Justice* (University of California Press).

Greg Grandin teaches history at New York University. His most recent book, *Fordlandia,* now out in paperback (Picador), was a finalist for the Pulitzer Prize in history.

Arun Gupta is a founding editor of *The Indypendent* newspaper. He is writing a book on the decline of American Empire for Haymarket Books.

Peter Hart is the Organizing Director at FAIR and author of *The Oh Really? Factor: Unspinning Fox News Channel's Bill O'Reilly* (Seven Stories Press, 2003).

Melissa Harris-Lacewell, an associate professor of politics and African-American studies at Princeton University, is completing her latest book,

Sister Citizen: A Text for Colored Girls Who've Considered Politics When Being Strong Isn't Enough. She is a contributor to MSNBC.

Chris Hedges, a Pulitzer Prize–winning reporter, is a senior fellow at the Nation Institute. He writes a regular column for TruthDig every Monday. His latest book is *Empire of Illusion: The End of Literacy and the Triumph of Spectacle.*

Jim Hightower is a national radio commentator, writer, public speaker, and author of the book, *Swim against the Current: Even a Dead Fish Can Go with the Flow.* He was was twice elected Texas agriculture commissioner.

Jack Hitt is a contributing editor of *Harper's Magazine* and the author of the forthcoming book *Bunch of Amateurs: A Search for the American Character* (Crown).

Julie Ingersoll is associate professor of religious studies at the University of North Florida. She is the author of *Evangelical Christian Women: War Stories in the Gender Battles* and is currently writing a book on the influence of Christian Reconstructionism.

Sarah Jaffe is the web director of GRITtv and the deputy editor of Global Comment.

Richard Kim is the managing editor of *The Nation* magazine and co-editor, with Betsy Reed, of the *New York Times* bestseller *Going Rouge: Sarah Palin—An American Nightmare* (OR Books, November 2009).

Sally Kohn is a community organizer and political satirist focused on the impact of mass movements in American culture and politics. She is founder and Chief Agitation Officer of the Movement Vision Lab, bringing ideas to action and action to ideas (movementvision.org).

David A. Love is executive editor of BlackCommentator.com. He is a contributor to the *Huffington Post,* TheGrio.com, the Progressive Media Project, the McClatchy-Tribune News Service, *In These Times*, and the Philadelphia Independent Media Center. He also blogs at davidalove. com, NewsOne, DailyKos, and Open Salon.

Mike Madden is *Salon*'s Washington correspondent.

Stephanie Mencimer covers legal affairs and domestic policy in *Mother Jones*'s Washington bureau. She is the author of *Blocking the Courthouse Door: How the Republican Party and Its Corporate Allies Are Taking Away Your Right to Sue.*

Shannyn Moore is an Alaska-based blogger and host of *The Shannyn Moore Show* on 1080 KUDO.

Bob Moser, a *Nation* contributing writer, is editor of the *Texas Observer* and author of *Blue Dixie: Awakening the South's Democratic Majority*.

Scot Nakagawa is a consultant; he created the Fight the Right program of the National Gay and Lesbian Task Force and later served the task force as field director.

Suzanne Pharr is an author, organizer, and co-founder of Southerners on New Ground.

Katha Pollitt's new book of poems, *The Mind-Body Problem*, was published in June 2009 by Random House.

Sarah Posner, author of *God's Profits: Faith, Fraud, and the Republican Crusade for Values Voters*, is Religion Dispatches' associate editor and covers politics for the site. Her work has appeared in *The American Prospect*, *The Nation*, *Salon*, *The Washington Spectator*, the religion blogs at the *Washington Post* and the *Guardian*, and other publications.

Tarso Ramos is executive director of Political Research Associates.

Betsy Reed is the executive editor of *The Nation*. She and *Nation* senior editor Richard Kim co-edited the *New York Times* bestseller *Going Rouge: Sarah Palin—An American Nightmare* (OR Books, November 2009).

Steve Rendall is FAIR's senior analyst and is co-author of *The Way Things Aren't: Rush Limbaugh's Reign of Error* (The New Press, 1995).

Ruth Rosen is professor emerita of history at the University of California at Davis and the author of *The Lost Sisterhood: Prostitution in America* (1982) and *The World Split Open: How the Modern Women's Movement Changed America* (revised edition 2006)

Ken Silverstein is the Washington editor of *Harper's Magazine*.

Michael Tomasky is editor of *Democracy: A Journal of Ideas* and American editor-at-large for *The Guardian*.

Rebecca Traister is a senior writer at *Salon* and the author of *Big Girls Don't Cry: The Election that Changed Everything for American Women* (Free Press).

Eric Ward is the national field director of the Center for New Community.

Marcy Westerling is the founder of the Rural Organizing Project.

Tim Wise is the author of five books: *White Like Me: Reflections on Race from a Privileged Son; Affirmative Action: Racial Preference in Black and White; Speaking Treason Fluently: Anti-Racist Reflections from an Angry White Male; Between Barack and a Hard Place: Racism and White Denial in the Age of Obama,* and his latest, *Colorblind: The Rise of Post-Racial Politics and the Retreat from Racial Equity.*

Richard Wolff is professor of economics emeritus at the University of Massachusetts at Amherst and visiting professor in the Graduate Program of International Affairs, New School University, New York. His work appears regularly on many websites and publications. His website, www.rdwolff.com, provides free access to his writings as well as audio and video files of interviews, lectures, articles, and entire classes.

Kai Wright is the editorial director of *ColorLines.* He's an Alfred Knobler fellow of the Nation Institute; his investigative reporting and news analysis appear regularly in *The Nation, The Root,* and *The American Prospect,* among other publications. Kai is also author of *Drifting Toward Love: Black, Brown, Gay and Coming of Age on the Streets of New York,* as well as two books of African-American history.

JoAnn Wypijewski, a former senior editor of *The Nation,* is based in New York City. She has written for that magazine, as well as for *Harper's, CounterPunch, The New York Times Magazine,* the *Guardian,* and other publications. She is one of the founders and president of the Kopkind Colony, a summer project for radical journalists and organizers based in Guilford, Vermont, and dedicated to the memory of Andrew Kopkind.

Gary Younge, Alfred Knobler journalism fellow at the Nation Institute, is the New York correspondent for the *Guardian.*

Deanna Zandt is a media technologist, social media consultant, speaker, and trainer based in Brooklyn, New York. She is the author of *Share This! How You Will Change the World With Social Networking* (June 2010, Berrett-Koehler).

CREDITS

first appeared at OpenDemocracy.net on July 5, 2010. Reprinted with permission courtesy of Ruth Rosen.

Katha Pollitt's "Last Column about Sarah Palin—Ever" reprinted with permission from the November 24, 2009, issue of *The Nation* and TheNation.com.

Peter Hart and Steve Rendall's "At Last a Citizen Movement the Corporate Media Can Love" reprinted with permission from the May 2010 issue of *Extra!*

Glenn Greenwald's "Glenn Beck and Left-Right Confusion" first appeared in *Salon* on September 22, 2009, at www.salon.com. An online version remains in the *Salon* archives. Reprinted with permission.

Stephanie Mencimer's "Glenn Beck's Golden Fleece: The Right Wing's Paranoid Pitch for Overpriced Gold" reprinted with permission from the May 2010 issue of Mother Jones.

Veronica Cassidy's "Falling for the ACORN Hoax: The Strange 'Journalism' of James O'Keefe" reprinted with permission from the April 2010 issue of *Extra!*

Ken Silverstein's "Tea Party in the Sonora: For the Future of GOP Governance, Look to Arizona" appeared in the July 2010 issue of *Harper's Magazine*. Copyright © 2010 by Harper's Magazine. All rights reserved. Reproduced from the July issue by special permission.

Rebecca Traister's "Democrats: Remember the Ladies!" reprinted with permission from the September 29, 2010, issue of *The Nation* and TheNation.com.

Chris Hedges's "This Country Needs a Few Good Communists" first appeared at Truthdig.com on May 31, 2010. Reprinted with permission courtesy of Chris Hedges.

Max Blumenthal's "Obama, the Fallen Messiah" first appeared at Talking Points Memo on December 16, 2009. Reprinted with permission courtesy of Max Blumenthal.

Bill Fletcher Jr.'s "The U.S. Social Forum: The Anti-Tea Party Experience" reprinted with permission from the July 1, 2010, issue of *Black Commentator*.

Jim Hightower's "Populism Is Not about Mobs, Antigovernment Rants, or Opinion Polls: To Put the Progress Back in 'Progressive,' We Need a Real